The Open System

The Open System

*Redesigning Education and
Reigniting Democracy*

Landon Mascareñaz, EdLD
Doannie Tran, EdLD

HARVARD EDUCATION PRESS
CAMBRIDGE, MASSACHUSETTS

Paperback ISBN 978-1-68253-813-5

Library of Congress Cataloging-in-Publication Data is on file.

Published by Harvard Education Press,
an imprint of the Harvard Education Publishing Group

Harvard Education Press
8 Story Street
Cambridge, MA 02138

Cover Design: Endpaper Studio

The typefaces in this book are Sabon and Frutiger.

This book is dedicated to past, present,
and future leaders who seek to build a better
world, moving from closed to open in their
hearts and in the places they call home.

To Keara, Robyn, Bill, Lauryn, and Jackson:
I dedicate this book to you, to our
ancestors, and to our entire family, whose
inspiration shows me an open future is not
only possible, it is within our grasp.

To Holly, Elliot, and Louise:
You opened my heart to what is possible
and necessary for this world, and each day,
you give me the courage to see it through.

CONTENTS

Introduction to the Open System

Closed systems have no potential for life's adaptive capacity. They work like machines, passive travelers on the arrow of time, deteriorating and losing capacity, predetermined to waste away because of the Second Law of Thermodynamics—the trajectory of heat energy from useful to useless.

MARGARET WHEATLEY, *WHO DO WE CHOOSE TO BE*

Overhead ether flow, moment, colors run, Time so slow, slow I've never seen the arrow of time fly So low . . . and time flows on

TAME IMPALA, "THE BOLD ARROW OF TIME"

The redesign of institutions, from firms to governments, from educational establishments to social services, is the end to which survival-minded people must address themselves.

STAFFORD BEER, *DESIGNING FREEDOM*

FROM A BREAKING POINT TO A TURNING POINT

Schools in downtown Denver that avoid partnering with families across the street. A library in rural Georgia that doesn't work with its community to understand what books to put on the shelf. School curriculum and books which don't reflect the cultural context of a small town on the Navajo Nation. Community organizing groups that take orders from Washington, DC, instead of the states where they operate. A democracy increasingly isolated from its citizens with increasing barriers to entry and challenges to access the franchise.

These are the troubling manifestations of closed systems that make up our daily life. For years, it has been clear that our public institutions, including education, are too unresponsive to the communities and people they serve. For many of our American communities, especially those furthest from opportunity, institutional decline and relevance has reached a breaking point.

The Open System is a how-to guide and call to action for leaders and advocates to redesign education institutions, reenergize local communities, and reignite local democracy through civic participation. The weakness of our democratic institutions, including education, have prompted important and critical conversations about the limitations of our current systems. We must act.

If we are to act, then it is our belief that the most important choice we face in education is between *open* and *closed*. Closed systems have failed the communities they serve through distance and separation, calcifying decades of institutional avoidance into legacy school systems, reducing trust, and limiting democratic energy. In contrast, we seek open systems—those that are designed to co-create, co-produce, and redesign public education through the active participation of families and communities. Open systems foster a sense of responsiveness to and reciprocity with the communities in which they are embedded.

The origins of *open* and *closed* in organizational theory are rooted in whether an entity, say a school or a system of schools, can accept or adapt to information, stimuli, and provocation from its external environment. We believe that creating, building, and sustaining open systems in education is the key to solving some of the most intractable inequities in our education system. With an open systems lens, we can see that many of what we call the "~isms" (structural problems of racism, classism, colonialism, paternalism, and so many more) in education are structural features of institutions built years ago, created and sustained by the conscious and unconscious biases of the leaders and communities that built them and sustain them today, and reinforced by closed system behavior.

Closed systems do not prioritize connections to the communities they serve, and therefore are forced to make inferences about what communities value and need. They may accept the results of a survey—it just may not lead to any new actions or shifts, and if it does, those actions aren't co-created with the community. Closed system inferences are laced with the biases held by those in power, and they take the inequitable biases, beliefs, and assumptions of their designers and calcify them like amber in the structures of organizations and institutions. Good-intentioned technocrats that seek to remedy inequities through more closed system work fail to bring the voices of those they serve into the conversation and in turn take even more power away from those communities.

Education is at the center of this book, not only because it is at the center of our hearts, but because it is at the center of our democracy. We believe that as we watch our democracy struggle, we are watching education struggle. And inversely, when we see communities of education reimagine their way through our endemic crises with an open system approach, we are seeing democratic practice reignite and spread.

This provocation is at the heart of *The Open System*: that education is our greatest democracy-building endeavor, and by opening it up to the communities it serves and redesigning it, we can reinvigorate our democracy and build a more just society. In the 1930s, George Counts offered a challenge to reimagine American education that we still find compelling today:

> We have a haunting feeling that we were born for better things and that the nation itself is falling far short of its powers . . . the times are literally crying for a new vision of American destiny. . . . To refuse to face the task of creating a vision of a future America immeasurably more just and noble and more beautiful than the America of today is to evade the most crucial, difficult, and important educational task.[1]

Over and over again, we have seen a breakdown of local democratic capacity cause us to repeat cycles of oppression that result in institutional decline and consistent inequality. We have seen firsthand how opening the system and confronting the immoral contradictions in our local democracy can address institutional bias and injustices deeply entrenched in our legacy closed education systems. Co-creating with families and communities can reinvigorate local democratic capacity and allow districts and schools to confront real systemic biases with an action orientation. We believe these stories, and the approaches they have yielded, point a path forward for a field deadlocked by national debates and local fear of failure, emerging from the greatest challenges to public education in our lifetime.

The audience for *The Open System* is both school system leaders and community advocates who are ready to reimagine and redesign their education systems. This book is designed for leaders who hunger for a community renewal in their local public systems but lack the path to show them the way. As we've learned along the way, leaders inside and outside the system often lack common, accepted language and approaches for co-creation and are too often provoked to approach the work in a confrontational versus a cooperative posture.

We call leaders who seek community-driven change "openers," and throughout this book we will hear their voices and perspectives. Many of these leaders have been instrumental in co-creating and inspiring this book and the discipline contained within. Our first group of openers initially came together in 2019 in response to the realization that whether we were organizers, family engagement leaders, or system leaders, we lacked a shared language but had a common goal of community-driven change. By generating a shared discipline, principles, and practices across these diverse and rarely united groups, we are attempting to lay a common foundation for the education field to open systems in rural, urban, and suburban communities around our country.

This book is committed to rejecting previous tropes and stigmas of community-driven work, synthesizing old and new wisdom on family partnerships and public-sector change while elevating the stories of transformation. Our experience shows us that many leaders simply lack the language and structure to enact their ambitious community plans, which lead to fear of failure. To support leaders such as this, we offer no easy solutions and no easy choices, but principles and practices that we believe create the most opportunity for transformative shifts in systemic behaviors.

WHO WE ARE

We are two close friends and educators who have committed to working together to open systems and lift up open leaders around the country. Doannie lives in Georgia, with experience in education systems in California, Massachusetts, and across the South. Landon lives in Colorado; having begun his education journey in rural New Mexico, he now works across the Mountain West. We both have worked nationally across a variety of contexts, coalitions, and partners, witnessing the power of opening systems across contexts and time zones. In our own way, we have each strived to build a purpose-driven life around opening systems up to the communities they serve. While the book you are about to read is centered on narratives and examples from our journeys, leveraging our personal experiences, it also includes stories from many incredible leaders we've met along the way.

Over the past few years, we came together as friends and colleagues to formally launch the Open System Institute. More recently, we launched our Opener-in-Residence Initiative, bringing together diverse leaders from around the country to contribute to our shared understanding of open system change. Like any co-creation and adaptive process, much has changed since then as we have learned from our residents and extended network. From the very beginning we co-created with a broader community of openers. We sought to create a place that could turn our collective instincts into practices, which then saw practices evolve into principles, and they have now become an emergent discipline in your hands.

We honor all those involved along the way, and those we have not yet met, who have helped us keep the co-creative spirit alive in this project.

WHY NOW?

Our experience tells us that we are at an urgent crossroads where we can choose whether or not to open public education to the communities it serves. The COVID-19 pandemic and the public policy reactions to it have not only laid bare the deepest structural oppressions in our systems, but have also created cracks in the system that leaders can leverage for real change. The education field learned the hard lesson that decades of closed system behavior had left them without the most valuable asset of all—the trust of the communities they served. In an effort to seize this transformative moment, *The Open System* offers a potential path forward to rethink education alongside students, families, and communities instead of using the closed, top-down approaches of the past.

This work was emergent and growing in strength even before the cat-alytic and catastrophic events that shook public systems worldwide start-ing in March 2020. Since then, it has become clear to many who were involved in education and public systems that we were beyond a breaking point and had arrived at a turning point. The pandemic, the stress on our democratic institutions, and the social justice movements of this country prompted questions about what had been previously built and what we had assumed about the way we live our lives.

We found that in cities and towns across this country, there were schools, organizations, and systems across all sectors that somehow man-aged to adapt at this moment. They adeptly met the crisis and coura-geously faced reality to bring something new into existence. The rural school system that met with all of their families one-on-one during the summer, the district that set up navigators to meet with every student, the coalition of community organizations that banded together with an abun-dance mindset and forced change on an unwilling system—they often did not make the headlines given all the noise, cynicism, and failure narrative surrounding education. But across all of these sectors and topics they had one thing in common—they were opening previously closed systems.

In our experience, open system transformation cannot be an "all at once" endeavor. We are very clear from the examples and stories that each of them are incremental, specific, and discrete projects that have created opportunities for openness. Over the course of this book, you will hear us use the phrase "progress not perfection," borrowed from recovery literature, to show our understanding that openness requires breaking addictions from closed systems, building muscle over time, and most importantly, embracing the wins the community can achieve now so that more can be achieved later.[2]

In a world too often resigned to dooms and claims of institutional failure, we stand committed to telling a different story of institutions and systems who have made responsive changes that have created meaningful impact. These changes did not come without a cost, and they have cre-ated new challenges that leaders must manage. We all have professional scars and personal wounds from our mistakes and trials. Committing to opening systems is not committing to a panacea and is not about a particular destination or arrival point—but it is needed in our time more than ever.

OPEN SYSTEMS AND OTHER APPROACHES

The Open System describes an emerging discipline that includes a set of principles and practices that have been co-created to build the capacity of public education systems to share power and build common vision with the families and communities they serve.

Over the course of the book, we will explore many of these ideas, how they intersect or diverge from open system work, and how they build the shared understanding needed to redesign systems during this time. We will go into further detail about the definition of an open system in chapter 1, but as you look at these examples of open and closed systems, consider the extent to which each increases the flow of information across boundaries and enables co-creation and co-production.

- *Open:* When a teacher goes on a home visit, opening up their classroom to include parents' perspectives.
- *Closed*: When a teacher allows one ten-minute window on one day over the course of a full year to speak to a parent.
- *Open*: When a school creates an opportunity for parents to explore the academic standards all students must meet, opening up the learning environment for parent involvement.
- *Closed*: When a school hosts a back-to-school night with English-only materials and presentations, even though more than half of the parents speak another language.
- *Open*: When a school undergoes a community-driven turnaround process, opening up design and creation to parents and families.
- *Closed*: When a school loses enrollment, or experiences academic decline, and refuses to take feedback from families about why.
- *Open*: When a district or network decides to redesign their accountability system alongside students, families, and communities who help to design and build it.

- *Closed*: When a district or network decides to create internal data systems for accountability without sharing any of that information with families or communities.
- *Open*: When an advocacy group pushes on a system to transform their practices and the district responds in kind.
- *Closed*: When a district makes a major decision without any input from families, communities, or other stakeholders.

These examples are just the beginning of what it means to see and envision an open system in our education system. For too long, closed systems have represented too many of our legacy education districts and structures. In many cases, the best laid plans of governors, presidents, and educators have failed because they failed to build legitimacy with the very communities they sought to serve. Institutional distrust is a hallmark of our time not just because systems are old or inefficient, but because they have become unresponsive to the communities they serve. Once we take on this frame, we can see closed systems and open opportunities everywhere.

THE BOOK AHEAD

The Open System is organized into a set of six open principles that leaders and advocates can use to move their systems toward openness.

- Activate open leadership
- Know your community
- Design breakthrough spaces
- Model creative democracy
- Assemble abundance partnerships
- Expand openness

The chapters follow an important design arc to support the reader in going deeper into what it means to be an opener, beginning with a significant theoretical understanding of the work, and then moving into the three phases that provide a container for the six principles: *preparing* (activate open leadership and know your community), *provoking* (design breakthrough spaces and model creative democracy), and *propelling* (assemble abundance partnerships and expand openness). We intentionally use momentum and movement-based language to convey the gathering of energy and the impact that system change requires.

The Open System places these narratives in the inspiring and challenging local and national context of the early 2020s—a global pandemic, a racial awakening, democratic decline, and an increased urgency to build a more inclusive society. We cannot cover all the major problems facing public education, such as pandemic response, critical race theory, and gender identity in schools, to name some other common topics. But a key component of our proposition in *The Open System* is that through community-driven redesign, leaders and advocates can take on some of the most challenging issues in their communities. Therefore, our case studies run the gamut, including rural revitalization, urban school turnaround, school discipline redesign, reimagining accountability, locally generated family partnership strategies, internet connectivity in the COVID pandemic, and a variety of types of advocacy to challenge closed systems. All of these stories showcase the promises and perils of open system work, the breakthroughs that are possible, and the humility of what we still must learn together.

Each chapter is organized around keystone questions, practices, and concrete ideas for how to enact each principle in projects or opportunities that can create conditions for open transformation. Throughout the book, narratives and examples will help us share real-world examples of how different communities have approached this work. These narratives pull throughout each chapter, lifting the interconnectedness of the principles, the evolution of our experiences with open system work, and the iterations and struggles we've had along the way. Also in each chapter, you will see quotes from interviews, most of them conducted by our friend and partner Matt Klausmeier in 2022, to help you hear the perspective of open leaders throughout the country.

The Open System is intentionally populated with activities, reflection exercises, and sidebars throughout each chapter to create engaging moments to provoke the reader. As readers learn, these activities help them reflect and plan for how to apply these practices in their own context. This is extremely hard and perilous work, so we offer perspective to the reader along the way of how we and others have struggled, where we've failed, and how we've lifted ourselves back up to continue our mission to open up local democracies.

Critical to the understanding of open system redesign is the idea that we can liberate ourselves from the closed systems of the past through interrogation of ourselves, the organizations we work in, and our broader communities. In each open principle, we specifically call out what the important liberatory moves are in each section. We prefer this term to equity in this context because it more directly confronts racism, classism, sexism, colonialism, and the rest—all the ~isms that are structurally fused into our legacy systems. Readers are asked to reflect on these questions as they go on the journey of this book. The sections that follow outline the course for readers through the book.

Understanding How Open Systems Can Redesign Education and Reignite Democracy

This chapter dives into the theory and intellectual architecture of open systems. We start with cybernetics and organizational design, and explain that open systems are based on information flows. We embrace the fundamental definition of open and closed: whether or not the entity can accept or adapt to those information flows. Then we explore why the issue of who gets to see and design with these information flows matters, and we consider the elegant strategic triangle that serves as a core framework to understand co-creation and co-production. The chapter also makes the case for why education systems must be a priority target for open system work, with a particular focus on the obligations and challenges of building an inclusive democracy for all races, classes, and communities. It surveys the history of open and closed systems across education and positions the need for a major democracy-building initiative within our education system.

Open Principle 1: Activate Open Leadership

None of these insights, practices, or endeavors can come to pass unless we are led by open leaders, both inside and outside the system. What are the characteristics and practices of these leaders? How do they need to reconceptualize their roles from the way we typically think of education leaders? How do they sustain themselves given the immense challenges of co-creation and democratic leadership? To conceptualize the open leader, we must bring in ideas from democratic leadership across sectors to re-think the role of education leaders and transition them into being public leaders. Based on a case study of the Homegrown Talent Initiative in Colorado, we will show how leaders in rural communities co-created to build breakthrough community revitalization. In addition, open leaders must confront their own biases—not only about traditional system behaviors, but also about issues of race, class, and other ~isms that they hold. We will discuss how local democratic leadership may not be sufficient to solve all the deeper structural problems in every situation. Yet it is fundamentally necessary, given the core foundation of our education system and the failure of other structures (judicial, legislative, etc.) to address systemic inequity. In this chapter, we will also directly address the feelings of fear and resistance that many education leaders have for open system change. To address these concerns, we will help leaders build a scaffolded path forward where they can build open system muscle on clear opportunities that allow them to triangulate between actors within their systems, reducing fear and stress.

Open Principle 2: Know Your Community

Open system work is hyperlocal, and openers must always consider and analyze the broader community context that public education sits within. This chapter explores the practices of defining communities, naming the particular dynamic tensions in exploring communities, and diagnosing ecosystems through analyzing whether an ecosystem is open or closed. Readers will explore and identify their "open moment"—the window for co-creation and community redesign that exists in their unique context. In this chapter, the case study will be of community organizers provoking change in Denver, leading to the community-driven Year Zero turn-around project in the Denver Public Schools. We also include examples from community organizers in Memphis and New Orleans, showing both internal and external strategies so that the reader can fully consider the impact of community dynamics.

Open Principle 3: Design Breakthrough Spaces

After building awareness of your personal leadership capacity, mapping and designing the community and ecosystem, and identifying your "open moment," readers will next consider how to design a space and process to break through closed systems. This begins with radical clarity about the problem or opportunity at hand, recruiting in new and dynamic ways to bring voices to the table, intentionally creating momentum for the breakthrough, and building shared understanding of the liberatory shifts that are possible. Through learning about the Boulder Equity Council process, the reader will ideate and practice building an ideal breakthrough process, test potential pitfalls, and then create an action plan for next steps.

Open Principle 4: Model Creative Democracy

As openers cultivate and support spaces to open up systems, they must commit to exploring the possibilities for reinvigorating democratic activity in practice. In our experience, our communities and institutions have atrophied so fundamentally that even individuals who deeply value democracy and community have lost the ability to listen, hear, and act together. In exploring the Kentucky accountability redesign work, which included local communities across the state, openers understand that they must not only sustain spaces in a politically charged environment; they must also build shared understanding among all participants, commit to the work of reciprocal co-creation, repair the inevitable ruptures that occur, and generate consensus in fractured communities. We will also explore the Colorado Youth Congress, which brings creative democracy to life with civically minded students. If successful, openers may find a shared sense of *communitas*—a group experience of joy and possibility that can be a powerful incentive to encourage future opening.

Open Principle 5: Assemble Abundance Partnerships

After creating breaks and cracks in closed systems, openers must stay vigilant to resist the forces of scarcity and co-contamination that will emerge. Assembling abundant partnerships means employing a different set of practices, seeking clarity that enables openers to share power in the long term and to build even more opportunity for open system work across their local context. These partnerships can allow systems to build in more openness through enabling higher-order goals to be achieved that could never be done alone. In exploring case studies from New Mexico, Georgia, and Chicago, leaders can see the impact of cultivating partnerships to do more than any one organization can do alone. To do this work effectively requires managing co-contamination, a significant fear of partnership work, and sustaining the work in the face of the inevitable return of a scarcity mindset. The reader will be asked to reflect on current partnerships they are involved in, what abundance partnerships practices they may be able to start up, and what challenges may occur through building them out.

Open Principle 6: Expand Openness

The final open principle is about the long-term work that systems need to address to build the dynamic equilibrium to remain open. Leaders will be faced with an important challenge: as open system efforts move into long-term efforts or endeavors, how should leaders or communities sustain, expand, and integrate their openness? This means moving from co-creation toward co-production, the less exciting but more necessary work that enables long-term change. In this chapter, we will revisit the case studies from all the previous chapters to explore how they are continuing to see the work thrive and succeed. Openers must identify other slipstreams or opportunities for open system work that can intersect with their projects. They must also lift up others in the system, both inside and outside, who will commit to the work moving forward in their own ways. Throughout the chapter, the reader will reflect on their current open system work and process as it reaches the next stage of maturation, and they will plan a set of actions to build and amplify the co-creative spirit in their communities.

Conclusion: Building an Open Future

In the final chapter, we will conclude with ideas, musings, and recommendations for further open system work in terms of practice, policy, and political change. While the bulk of the book is designed for practitioners and system leaders who will be building change in their respective educational communities, there are enormous policy implications for leaders in other sectors. These potential policy opportunities include recommendations for higher education, teacher preparation, philanthropic investment, and partnership between organizations.

MOVING FORWARD

What does it mean to build a better world, one community at a time? This is the question that all of us wrestle with throughout our purpose-driven lives, and it pushes us to the frontiers of human understanding. *The Open System* is our answer to this question; this book is a guide to what we've learned.

We are both incredibly fortunate to be supported and sponsored in this work by our two organizations, the Colorado Education Initiative (CEI) and the Center for Innovation in Education (CIE). We are honored to work at organizations that are so committed to co-creation and systems change. We thank our teams for their trust and wisdom that helped make this book possible, and we are honored to feature much of their incredible work in each of the case studies across the chapters of the book. We want to share a bit more about our organizations.

CEI is a long-standing education intermediary operating across Colorado and the region, working in partnership with a significant number of districts and schools, and charged with igniting the power of public education. CEI is currently leading consequential system change work blurring the lines between K–12 and higher education, developing social-emotional ecosystems to promote whole child success, supporting community-driven equity work, and enabling local conversations about community visions for the future.

CIE supports equity-seeking systems change by co-creating new systems and policies with communities, particularly in the areas of education assessment and accountability. CIE brings a collection of tools, resources, and examples of co-creation at the local, state, and federal levels. Their support allows us to cultivate projects in Vermont, Kentucky, and Georgia that serve as critical proof points for this new approach to cultivating deeper accountability between schools and communities.

We have focused this work on projects we personally have experience and relationships with, in order to bring their stories to life with the depth of knowledge they deserve. But we must also acknowledge that there are many projects and partners, known and unknown, that didn't make it into the book. We are hopeful that future interest in this work will allow even more exploration of their (and your!) stories.

We are grateful for the time and thoughts of all those who were interviewed and who spent time with our team to make this book possible. We want to take a special moment at the start of the book to thank Matt Klausmeier, who led the opener interview process and supported the overall project for us. Matt's insight, analysis, and commitment to exploring the narratives of the openers and honoring that community continually inspired us.

To write this book is an incredible honor and privilege, but it contains an enormous irony: open system work is by nature differentiated, adaptive, hyperlocal. We know that as soon as we write this book, new learnings, new leaders, and new experiences will push us to new manifestations of the open principles. We are grateful for readers now and later as we continue to build community openers who will speak their truth and bring people together in their communities, and who will build an ever-growing network that we are proud to call family. Each era and community will have new opportunities for openness, and our hope is that future leaders will find ways to innovate and show us new ways to handle the challenging topics of their day.

Let us now move to the theory and the history of open systems—grounding us in an understanding of how together we can redesign education and reignite democracy.

CHAPTER 1

How Open Systems Can Redesign Education and Reignite Democracy

We hone our skills naming and analyzing the crises.
I learned in schools how to deconstruct—but how do we move beyond
our beautiful deconstruction?
Who teaches us to reconstruct?

ADRIENNE MAREE BROWN, *EMERGENT STRATEGY*

That a system is open means not simply that it engages in interchanges
with the environment, but that this interchange is an essential factor
underlying the system's viability.

WALTER F. BUCKLEY, *SOCIETY: A COMPLEX ADAPTIVE SYSTEM*

To look closely at the structure of organization, the entailments of one
thing by another, the complexity of problems in relation to available
analytic power . . . may offer a degree of sanity in handling practical
affairs, and even a mode of spiritual realization . . . How aggressive
such humility can be!

STAFFORD BEER, *DESIGNING FREEDOM*

What compels a system to gravitate away from the community it serves?
Why do public systems draw hard, brutal boundaries that may serve
some, but end up serving few in the long run? How does closed system
behavior degrade democracy and institutional trust? How has the history
of education shown patterns of closed and open systems? These are the

big questions we will explore in this chapter to prepare readers and leaders for the work of open system building.

BIG IDEAS IN THIS CHAPTER

- Building trust across boundaries
- Defining features of open systems
- Open and closed systems across education history

BUILDING TRUST ACROSS BOUNDARIES

In a democracy, we must understand the real and problematic outcomes of closed system behavior not only on system performance but on trust building across institutions and civil society.

Open systems are fundamentally grounded in the idea that through co-creation, communities, schools, and other public systems can overcome distrust and build legitimacy. Seeking trust demands more open systems. In education, the failure to build trust has had enormous consequences for generations of system change work. In Katherine Schultz's book *Distrust and Educational Change*, she rightly identifies the failure of education efforts to build trust across society.

> Across the United States and throughout much of the world, there is a general feeling of dissatisfaction with the educational opportunities available to children and youth, particularly those living in high-poverty urban and rural areas . . . Beneath the discussion of possible solutions lies persistent and somewhat intractable feelings of distrust . . . Education policies are often based on blame and distrust and in turn, all too frequently perpetuate more distrust.[1]

We identify this dilemma as a problem of closed systems. To fully understand the implications for education, we will first begin broadly with civil society at large to clarify the dire need we have to address the dramatic trust deficit in our society.

Figures from across the political spectrum have rightly identified institutional decline and trust as linked together in our modern era. The Edelman Trust Barometer, a survey of perceptions of trust in society, organizations, and government that has been conducted annually for over two decades, found recently that we've lost a significant amount of trust in government to solve the most pressing problems facing our society.[2] They found globally that "Nearly 6 in 10 say their default tendency is to distrust something until they see evidence it is trustworthy. Another 64% say it's now to a point where people are incapable of having constructive and civil debates about issues they disagree on. When distrust is the default—we lack the ability to debate or collaborate."[3] This is an alarming and troubling finding that has major implications for our future as a society.

Another serious finding is that "In many of the democracies studied, institutions are trusted by less than half of their people, including only . . . 43[%] in the U.S. Moreover, no developed countries believe their families and self will be better off in five years' time."[4] At the core of this book and concept is the belief that open system work creates the conditions for trust building through participation and engagement. Research suggests this is an important link. In the World Bank's 2020 report *Building Trust in Government Through Citizen Engagement*, they suggest that:

> Citizen engagement offers a way to (re)build and enhance trust, according to several scholars of social capital theory . . . This notion was also reflected in an OECD civil society organization survey which found "with respect to the benefits of open and inclusive policy making with regard to citizens, close to half of the respondents saw it as 'important' or 'very important' in increasing citizens' trust (43 percent)." The origin of the study of the causal relationship between citizen engagement and trust in government can be traced to the first half of the 19th century when Alexis de Tocqueville wrote that to align people with diverse interests toward the common good, they had to participate in democratic decision making.[5]

But even movements to increase public participation in decision-making face significant headwinds that can undermine trust. Powerful interests can co-opt structures that are designed to increase the voice of citizens, a process that researchers call "regulatory capture" or elite capture.[6] Powerful groups and individuals can seize processes that were originally meant to amplify the voices and concerns of marginalized groups and interrupt projects that would benefit many, such as increasing housing density. In the words of journalist Jerusalem Demsas, who writes frequently about this kind of co-opting of democratic systems:

> You have structural issues with the fact that people who are willing to engage in these kinds of local politics are systematically older, systematically whiter, and systematically they're more likely to be homeowners and have a preference towards stability rather than growth and change.[7]

We are also compelled by the work of Hélène Landemore, who in her book *Open Democracy* presents a strikingly aligned understanding of how reimagining democratic governance could build a better future:

> Openness is an umbrella concept for general accessibility of power to ordinary citizens . . . an open system guarantees that citizens can make their voices generally heard at any point in time and initiate laws when they are not satisfied with the agenda set by representative authorities. Openness prevents closure and entrenchment of the divide between the represented and representatives that inevitably accompany representation.[8]

It would be hard to find public leaders in a democracy who do not profess to want to build trust with the communities they serve, even with these significant issues in the way. A fire department seeks to earn trust as they quench fires. A new mayor wants to earn the trust of the city so that they will approve new improvement initiatives (or at most self-serving, the mayor's reelection). In practice, there are often two distinct approaches in public system leadership and management on how to build trust. One is a closed system approach to trust building, focused on effective outcomes over process conditions. The other is an open system approach to build a stronger democracy and achieve outcomes through co-creation and co-production. In the reflection question below, take a moment to consider your experience with trust and public systems.

 Can you build trust with closed system approaches? In civil society, this is the technocratic "build X super well and trust will come" approach to public education leadership. It's possible, but fraught with

---

Institutional Trust Reflection

- What have been your experiences with trust in public institutions?
- How have you seen closed systems degrade trust and democratic capacity?

---

enormous political peril and likely to invite backlash. Public systems built with closed system approaches can often inspire and move people forward, yet fail to build the real, long-term institutional trust necessary to build a future we all see ourselves in. An open system approach would invite well-implemented citizen engagement to build a shared vision. In the World Bank research, they draw on analysis across countries, including the United States, to help make the claim that citizen engagement and participation is essential for effective governance.

> [T]rust in government and citizen engagement form a mutually re-inforcing, interdependent dynamic in the policy arena that is affected by common attributes and affects development outcomes and effectiveness. Inclusive citizen engagement is an approach for state-citizen interactions in a policy arena to provide citizens a stake in decision making. When citizen engagement is designed and implemented well, it provides government an opportunity to foster "process-based" trust in public deliberation and service delivery.[9]

A key term in the research is "implemented well"—a challenge and charge that led us to generate the principles and practices detailed in this book. In our experience, much of the discourse around community participation is that it must be slow, messy, and imprecise. We reject this stereotype of open system work and so in this book put forth principles of strategically aligned, high-impact trust-building work through open system approaches.

Open system leaders understand that by utilizing all components of public leadership, building real legitimacy and support from the broader community can not only build a much more stable and steady long-term trust spiral, but can also illuminate blind spots that any leader or

Landon's Narrative

The following is a story Landon has often related to groups of openers and partners to understand the human impact in our society of closed systems.

I believe we must build open systems because of my grandmother. This story begins in 1920s Mexico in the state of Zacatecas. My grandmother's parents were living in the turmoil that followed after the Mexican Civil War. My great-grandfather, who had lost many of his children to starvation, found himself wrongly accused of stealing.

A noose was put around his neck for his punishment. At the very last minute, providence intervened, and another local man ran up and told everyone that my great-grandfather wasn't the thief; the crime was committed by a recently apprehended criminal. After that, my great-grandfather decided to flee Mexico and move his family to Boulder, Colorado.

Not long after, my grandmother was born in the US and attended school in Boulder. Her family strived to enter the American middle class, and my great-grandparents tried to provide a stable environment and education. My grandmother entered the American education system in a land that, not long before, had been almost a part of Mexico. Yet she was teased incessantly for bringing tortillas to class instead of bread. And at the end of one year, her teacher decided to hold her back. The reason? She didn't speak English.

The shame, the pain, and the bewilderment of this experience has tortured her for the rest of her life. When she was married and had her own children, she couldn't bear to have them experience anything like that. So she decided that her children would never learn Spanish.

And just like that, the closed system ripped our language from my family. My father never learned Spanish and therefore was never able to teach me. What would life for my family have been if the school system had been open to our language, our culture, our life?

institution has. Trust building is directly connected to the rebuilding of a democratic capacity for action. The work of co-creation and co-production that we will spend a great deal of time on later in the book are information-opening channels that, if managed appropriately, can convert static systems into dynamic ones and increase the possibility of trust in competent public systems.

DEFINING FEATURES OF OPEN SYSTEMS

In pursuit of a system that cultivates and sustains trust, we propose a definition of an open system that builds on the rich tradition of open systems theory, captures the key elements of educational systems that we have seen create transformative and sustainable results, and provides leaders with tools to achieve this result. We want to acknowledge that the definition of an open system is complex and multidimensional. The convergence of factors and circumstances, structures and behaviors that encompass openness can seem impossible to attain. And yet, we see that when organizations make progress on these dimensions, they catalyze trust that supports greater equity and liberation throughout their systems. We propose that open systems accelerate trust and expand impact through the ways that they:

- *Increase the flow of information across boundaries.* Open systems accelerate the flow of information throughout the system and with the surrounding environment.
- *Design for high variety.* Open systems acknowledge that they cannot create a playbook for every eventuality, but instead must build capacity to be responsive at every level of the system.[10]
- *Incorporate strategic co-creation and co-production.* Open systems unlock operational capacity, legitimacy, and support through the processes of co-creation and co-production.[11]

While it is true that many of our institutions could technically be considered "open," given that they conduct surveys, respond to urgent matters, and the like, we would offer that the transformation we seek requires a fundamental rethinking of the mental model of public system leadership to fully embrace the power of openness. It is not enough to technically be an open system, as you will learn throughout the book. The opener must commit to the co-creation and trust building necessary if they are to redesign and reinvent with the community they serve.

Increasing the Flow of Information Across Boundaries

To fully build open systems, leaders and advocates must understand the dynamics of open versus closed organizations and institutions, high-variety systems, and how to leverage the strategic triangle to analyze and manifest openness.

In the twenty-first century, we live in a world abundant in organizations and institutions. Particularly in the United States, we exist within an institutionally dense, diverse civil society full of actors and entities. Yet, surprisingly, this is a recent shift, though centuries in the making. When we look back on history, we see a world with informal organizations transformed into an ecosystem of formal systems—a tremendous revolution in how humans operate. As Charles E. Lindblom describes in W. Richard Scott's *Organizations and Organizing*, the twentieth-century proliferation of institutions, community organizations, bureaucracies, and large corporate systems is a seismic shift.

> Never much agitated, never even much resisted, a revolution for which no flags were raised, it transformed our lives during those very decades in which, unmindful of what was happening, Americans and Europeans debated instead such issues as socialism, populism, free silver, clericalism, chartism, and colonialism. *It now stands as a monument to the discrepancy between what men think they are designing and the world they are in fact building* [emphasis added].[12]

In the years following World War II, western understanding of organizations and institutions began to evolve rapidly. The study of organizations and institutions has many facets for exploring their structures, markets, organizational designs, governance structures, and missions. Yet they all have one essential, original thing in common: the boundary between themselves and their outside environment. Whether a food delivery nonprofit or a federal Medicare provider, all organizations and institutions operate with an internal structure, work within a broader community, exist within a larger ecosystem or society, and must make continuous choices and decisions about how to interact with that external environment across that boundary.

There are many elements that move across this boundary that can be broadly categorized as "information." The information that passes (or is restricted from passing) through the boundary of that organization represents a potentially infinite number of new paths, ideas, learnings, or opportunities. For institutions and public systems, this information can be generated by citizens, taxpayers, advocacy groups, vendors, or others—at the basic level, this is the information that organizations make choices around how to adapt or ignore. Fundamentally, organizations are faced with an ever-present choice in an era of increasing data and information: do they see themselves as fully separate entities, apart and closed from their environment, or as responsive, open systems that are designed to adapt?

While this may seem an obvious answer to readers or sympathetic community-minded individuals, the truth is that too many of our modern public systems see themselves as separate from the communities they serve, though assuredly across a spectrum of closed behavior. This closed, technocratic thinking has roots in the early stages of organizational and institutional academic theory where diagnosis and analysis centered on these entities as being separate and distinct from broader environments. The "rational system" approach saw organizations as islands unto themselves. Historically, this is when many of our legacy public systems were initially designed and built. Over time this approach began to shift to accommodate a changing world and changing science, and open system theory was born.

> The open system perspective emerged as a part of the intellectual ferment following World War 2, although its roots are much older. This general movement created new areas of study, such as cybernetics and information theory; stimulated new applications, such as systems engineering and operations research; transformed existing disciplines, including the study of organizations; and proposed closer linkages among scientific disciplines.[13]

An open system line of analysis sought to explain a world of inter-connected global capitalism, environmental ecosystems, information computing, and the construction of the modern welfare state, chang-ing the understanding of how organizations operated. Open systems, acknowledging their broader environment, respond to external stimuli and information. Whether it is a plant, animal, or machine, or a school, hospital, or community center, open systems are in dynamic interchange with the information they receive from the outside world. Open systems are obsessed with their external environment because they know that the exchange of information between the internal and external is the critical lifeblood of how to make the system relevant and dynamic.

> Some analysts have mistakenly characterized an open system as hav-ing the capacity for self-maintenance despite the presence of throughput from the environment. Their assumption is that because organizations are open, they must defend themselves against the assaults of the envi-ronment. This view is misguided and misleading, since interaction with the environment is essential for open system functioning.[14]

Closed systems analysis and design draws hard lines and barriers. They are designed to limit the throughput and absorption of information. The choice between open and closed comes down to how an organization operationalizes, interacts, and sees itself within that broader world. The open system analysis therefore asks us to examine the interconnectedness of all systems, people, cultures, and environments even across areas of study or sectors—perhaps acknowledging that there are actually no truly closed systems!

In her book *Who Do You Choose To Be?*, Margaret Wheatley chal-lenges the readers to begin to see this distinction between closed or in-organic systems and open or organic systems. Closed systems eventually fail, becoming isolated from those they serve.

> The arrow of time applies to all closed systems in the known universe, but the new sciences reveal this is not the predetermined fate of living systems. A living system has permeable boundaries and sense-making capabilities. It is an open system, capable of exchanging energy with its environment instead of using up a finite amount.[15]

Information. Energy. Viability. These are the hallmarks of open systems that have the potential to change, shift, and co-produce via dynamic interaction with the environment. Dennis Sherwood, in *Seeing the Forest for the Trees,* explains open systems as self-organizing systems that:

> all have a flow of energy passing through them, a flow of energy that connects any given system with its appropriate environment . . . Once again, it is the connectedness of the component parts of the system with each other, and of the system as a whole with its environment, that is the central reason for order being maintained, and indeed created . . . and so fall into a class referred to as "open" systems.[16]

If we can understand the evolution of closed to open system analysis, the question then becomes, how do we build a design for openness? What does it mean to build these self-sustaining and open systems through our institutions and organizations? How do we understand what it looks like in practice and how we build it in public systems?

Designing for High Variety

In his seminal work *Designing Freedom*, Stafford Beer discussed how systems and structures in our society adapt and adjust to new information. Beer posits that there are two ways organizations or systems engage external systems. Beer suggests that either a system plans for every single interaction ("low variety") or designs themselves for the opportunity to adapt based on circumstance ("high variety"). These high-variety systems can be exposed to a significant amount of information and respond

---

Imagining an Open System Reflection

- Identify two or three examples of closed or low-variety system behavior you've participated in as a leader or advocate in the system.
- What could be possible in your community if the education system was open to the broader environment it is situated within?
- What are the issues and topics most needing an open system approach?

not with an ever-expanding list of rules and regulations, but with human relationship and openness to the external stimuli.[17] We see these concepts as related to open versus closed system redesign, and both are critical for leaders to break previously held schema around closed systems.

This is not an abstract technical idea; it is a foundation to the idea of open systems and therefore our endeavor: Do we build organizations that attempt to plan for every interaction possible with its external environment? Or do we build organizations that are designed to adapt to their external environment, regardless of circumstance? Low-variety systems are inclined to force complex situations into the limited number of cases they are designed to handle. When we design for open systems, we design for the opposite: building high-variety conditions that are specifically intended for dynamic responsiveness and partnership with their environment.

This design element is of significant societal import. Choosing to not build high-variety or open systems ensures that eventually our systems and institutions will gravitate away from their external environment— the communities they serve. By resisting this dynamic interchange, school districts and other public institutions will eventually become unmoored leviathans. Designing for high-variety systems leads us to a rethinking of boundaries: what is outside and inside, who and what crosses that boundary, and how systems can be designed to make this possible. Beer argues that these closed systems should not be seen as random aberrations but rather intentional choices that have enormous ramifications.

> Thus is freedom lost; not by accident, but as the output of a system designed to curb liberty. My message is that we must redesign that system, to produce freedom as an output. If we are inefficient about that, on the grounds that scientific efficiency threatens liberty, then the institutional machinery that acts in our name will fail to prevent the spread of tyranny, war, torture, and oppression. We speak of the growth of prosperity; but the growth of those four things throughout the world today is yet more real.[18]

Beer's statement that low-variety, closed systems are anti-liberators is tremendously important for the book ahead, with two very important

Doannie's Narrative

The experience of Doannie's family illustrates what getting rail-roaded by a low-variety system can feel like.

My family came to the United States after the fall of Saigon and the end of the Vietnam War. I was not yet born, my sisters were very young, but my mother's youngest brother was high school–aged. He enrolled in the same high school my sisters would attend years later in Richmond, Virginia; the same high school where my grandfather found a job as a janitor. Richmond is a place where, until very recently, Confederate soldiers were memorialized with huge statues along one of the city's most central streets, a clear signal of whose traditions and values were most prized.

My uncle did his best to fit in, adopting the hair and the fashion of his peers. But it was a lonely time for him and for my whole family, as they were flummoxed by the language, customs, and processes of their new home. As often as we encountered someone who welcomed us, we also encountered someone who would mock and ridicule us for our foreignness. Even as more and more Vietnamese immigrants like my uncle were settling in the community and entering its schools, the system never took a hard look at its culture, systems, and processes to wonder how they might change them to make a way for their newest members.

I imagine that in the mind of many educators in my uncle's life, the job of the school was to provide a specific set of content in a specific way by a specific date. It was not the job of the school to create community, cultivate belonging, contribute to community prosperity, or truly respond to the young people in front of them. In the face of new circumstances, the system was not dynamic enough to reimagine its role and function for a situation for which it had never planned but was now facing.

implications. First, systems are infused with the biases and perspectives of those who designed them, and are explicitly designed to constrain freedom—what we call closed system behavior. Secondly, Beer points out that low-variety systems intentionally cannot respond to changes, systemic oppressions, or other challenges. In our experience, even the best leaders who care about system change will sometimes attempt to create highly functional, well-intended, low-variety systems that don't address the root issues of the closed system structures they lead. We've also learned that even the best designed low-variety systems can be crushed in a crisis or resort to their preferences even when their community seeks another path.

Our argument throughout this book is that it is precisely because of Beer's charge that we must resist the anti-liberatory trajectory of closed and low-variety systems. Through understanding open system design, we see another truth—that the structures at the heart of our democracy and public systems contain the very levers for change that can create opportunities for liberatory redesign.

Incorporating Strategic Co-creation and Co-production

In graduate school, we both had the incredible opportunity to learn from Dr. Mark Moore, who pioneered and designed the strategic triangle, a concept fundamental to the understanding of public institutions and organizations. Professor Moore has worked in the federal government and was a founding member of the Harvard Kennedy School of Government, bringing significant insights to the field of public sector change.

The strategic triangle is a core concept for navigating the boundaries of public systems, showing who gets to name and generate public value, and explaining what it means to build dynamic public endeavors.[19] In our view, it is an essential concept for mapping and analyzing public systems and breaking apart closed system structures. Our work in the field has also taught us, year after year, that the simplicity and design of the triangle appeals to leaders both inside and outside of public systems. We see Moore's strategic triangle as *the* critical tool for leaders to strategically interrupt closed systems, build high-variety open systems, and create strategies for communities and systems to co-create and co-produce. We must first begin to understand the most fundamental components that we have synthesized and redefined based on his work. Figure 1.1 shows how the strategic triangle operationalizes the power of public system design.

- *Public Value.* The articulated rationale and benefits to the community of the initiative, department, or, in our cases, a school or school district.
  Example: A charter school's public value proposition is that it guarantees that all students will attend college.
- *Organizational Capacity.* The systems, structures, and components of the organization that realize the public value proposition.
  Example: A district has a superintendent, a chief of schools, and a significant human resources department investment to ensure it can recruit the talent and leadership it needs to achieve its public value.
- *Legitimacy and Support.* Exceptionally important in the public sphere and divergent from the private sector, public organizations and enterprises must constantly be building credibility and authorization from the broader community, whether those with the formal power to approve or push back against the endeavor, or those with informal power who can reduce the credibility of the effort. This is truly the work of aligning values and actions with broad stakeholders, whether they are named or not. This includes the concept of the "authorizing environment."

Figure 1.1 Moore's Strategic Triangle: public value, operational capacity, legitimacy and support

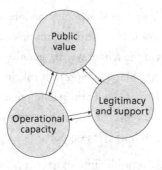

Source: Adapted from Mark Moore's Strategic Triangle.

Strategic Triangle Reflection

Map a current project or potential project against the strategic triangle.

- What is the public value proposition you are currently building?
- How are you building legitimacy and support for the public value?
- How is the operational capacity aligned?
- Are you moving across (i.e., rounding) the entire triangle to ensure alignment across all the elements?

– *Authorizing Environment.* An essential element in the work of building legitimacy and support is understanding who is in your authorizing environment. Building legitimacy and support from broad stakeholders is good, but unless you build legitimacy and support from those most critically invested in your work (your "core co-creators") then your project will likely struggle to represent those you serve.

Example: A district has a board of directors, who are elected from the community. They also work with the local city or municipality to build schools and with a set of community organizations for feedback on key initiatives.

Professor Moore and former Baltimore City superintendent Andrés Alonso connect the strategic triangle with embracing the "public" in public systems in their article "Creating Public Value."

Consequently, insofar as Public School Superintendents use their positions to participate in or lead those public discussions they end up acting not only as managers of the school system, but also as political and community leaders . . . they play an important role in calling a public into existence that can deliberate about the public values that they would like to see achieved by, and reflected in, the operations of the public school system that citizens and taxpayers support.[20]

How can leaders call a public into existence? We advocate for the concepts of co-creation and co-production as essential terms for leaders inside and outside the system to embrace. It is the work "to do *with*" rather than "to do *for*" or "to do *to*," and it is integral to open system design. In our experience, it's the most impactful way to build the high-variety systems that Beer talks about. The concepts, if sharply applied and not used too loosely, can create enormous strategic targeting of specific ways to build the capacity of families and communities to negotiate across the boundary, creating open systems. In their article "A Systematic Review of Co-creation and Co-production," William Voorberg and colleagues conclude with a striking thought on the relevance of co-creation and co-production in social change.

> Policy makers and politicians consider co-creation/co-production with citizens as a necessary condition to create innovative public services that actually meet the needs of citizens, given a number of societal challenges . . . Hence, co-creation/co-production seems to be considered as a cornerstone for social innovation in the public sector.[21]

The strategic triangle offers us a powerful tool to understand, diagnose, and facilitate co-creation—*with* rather than *on behalf of* or *to* communities. By identifying strategic opportunities for co-creation and co-production within systems, leaders can create dynamic open systems, generate natural attenuation to the information variation Beer proposes, and manage dynamic exchanges between systems and the broader ecosystem. This allows the system to gain new insights and perspectives as well as the capability to manage crises, deal with unforeseen dilemmas, crack open biases, and create liberatory shifts.

Since co-production and co-creation are often used interchangeably, we see this as an opportunity to be more discrete and sharper with language. In fact, in their survey of hundreds of articles, Voorberg and his cowriters concluded that the terms were used too interchangeably.[22] They conclude that sharper definitions ought to be used for the sake of clarity and consistency. Therefore, for clear open system work, we propose the following definitions to help build alignment and focus:

Co-creation: In the genesis of assembling a public value proposition, members of the authorizing environment are given the ability to shape the design and final product, producing what they believe is needed.

Example: A community design team is formed to guide a turnaround process. This design team gets to name the school and the type of program involved, and they build the blueprint with the school leader.

Co-production: In the ongoing work of producing public value, members of the authorizing environment help and are involved in the organization directly. This can range from being deeply involved in directly running the operation to simply having oversight and steering responsibilities. *Example: The school district appoints a citizen oversight council that helps place new schools, guides the chartering of new options, and advises the board and superintendent on critical issues.*

Figure 1.2 shows some of the relationships involved in managing co-production.

OPEN AND CLOSED SYSTEMS ACROSS EDUCATION HISTORY

Openers need to situate "open versus closed" within the longer arc of education redesign to challenge dominant historical narratives, explain why previous reform efforts have failed, and understand why open system work is needed now more than ever.

We must begin with a simple, clear, and powerful sentiment: any design is a product of its time. Each generation's aspirations for American school systems are anchored in the (often problematic in retrospect) optimism of that era. In any subsequent era, each of these designs has to be reimagined to break up their ill-conceived notions of progress or their inevitable failure to achieve the goals the designers sought.

Figure 1.2 Strategic co-creation (left) and co-production (right)

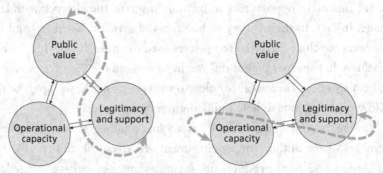

Source: Adapted from Mark Moore's Strategic Triangle.

Co-creation and Co-production Reflection

- Have you attempted either? Which is easier for you? Which is most challenging?
- In your community, reflect on previous processes that have attempted to utilize these concepts.
- By effectively understanding the distinction—co-creation as a genesis activity and co-production as an ongoing process—we can then move into seeing this pattern across education history.

We believe this perspective can help challenge the traditional analysis of the history of American education and help us understand the dynamics we find ourselves in here in the 2020s. We see this push and pull across the eras of American education: that the various approaches to changing that system, whether it be in the design (the "one best system") or in who gets to attend (segregation, busing, market reform), clashed later with community demands to reimagine it for a new moment. We believe this pattern is especially present in the American education system given our radically localized and democratized education system, giving us a front-row seat to the closed and open tidal forces throughout the history of our system. Our modern story becomes crystalized in the progressive era, laying the foundation for our current structures.

> Led by an elite composed of "good government" reformers, foundations, business elites, university presidents, and professors of education, the movement had considerable success in creating the system of organized schooling that still prevails . . . The reformers sought to concentrate administrative power in the superintendent . . . and oversight power in a small, ostensibly nonpolitical school board, largely composed of themselves or men of a similar class background.[23]

This closed technocratic model is the basic foundation for our system, and was unchallenged for the most part until society began to transform in the aftermath of the second World War. After World War II, the great battles of education in the twentieth century turned more toward access, integration, and the emergence of democratic policy levers in school change efforts. Efforts for school integration were clearly efforts to address deeply held closed system structures of racism and classism in the American education system. Here we begin to see the challenges and failures of community building in the face of structural closed system oppression, legacies that linger in our systems today.

Efforts for community inclusion persisted in other arenas. To fight the War on Poverty, policy makers and regulators promulgated a wave of federal laws and regulations requiring advice, consent, and notification. Head Start, Title 1 family engagement rules and funding set asides, home visiting programs, and a variety of other initiatives ought to be called our first wave of modern open systems transformation in education, demanding limited co-creation and co-production with communities. Yet it is important to note that during this time, advocacy work around education was limited compared to other issues. Mark Warren shares, in "Communities and Schools," how the focus was on other battles. This is an important observation that we will return to shortly as we notice the broader ecosystem of actors and players that our education system operates alongside in the 2020s.

> Years ago, one would have been hard pressed to find a community-based organization that was actively working on education issues. The young community-development and organizing groups that had arisen in the wake of the 1960s typically focused their efforts on housing, safety, and economic development initiatives . . . For the last half of the twentieth century, educators and community developers have operated in a separate sphere, both institutionally and professionally.[24]

As the twentieth century advanced, and amid a growing reactionary consensus that the War on Poverty had failed, the Reagan Revolution of the 1980s stripped many of these requirements out of the Great Society legislation. While some requirements remained, districts and states had more latitude to operate without family involvement. What we often call the modern education reform coalition emerged in the wake of the *A Nation at Risk* report of the 1980s, empowering state governors around the country to take control of education systems that were deemed unresponsive and in decline. The irony of these new leaders attempting to wrestle top-down responsiveness from a system that had just lost its ability for bottom-up power building is an important observation for those wishing to work toward open systems.

In the 1990s, there was a new wave of school redesign energy that we might consider "open system adjacent." Not quite the standards or assessment push of the late 1980s or early 1990s, it instead was a progressive effort to rethink school pedagogical models, including some powerful efforts like the Coalition for Essential Schools. At the same time, charter schools were beginning to emerge, first out of the union-supported enclave of Minnesota as a way to give teachers a space to explore learning strategies, and then, sponsored by the Clinton administration, emerging as a community-anchored co-creation challenge to the closed monopolies of districts. In some ways, these approaches created structural conditions for even more openness to emerge even though they were educator driven and not necessarily community driven. Many would argue that these efforts would later get co-opted by major philanthropists and corporate interests who sought accountability and new efforts to transform the system. In their book *Gardens of Democracy*, Eric Liu and Nick Hanauer make special note of the challenges that emerged along an open-closed spectrum in the dawning of our current era.

> Somewhere between the one-room schoolhouse of the 19th century and the assembly-line high school of the 20th, Americans came to accept the tacit notion that the walls of the school are to keep kids in and others out. As public education has become more bureaucratized and rule-bound, and the actual work of teaching more test-driven, it's become easier for parents to drop their children off and check out of the process of education. At the same time, it's become harder for parents—or for that matter, neighbors, or grandparents, or mentors—to enter the classroom and become a truly integrated part of the schooling experience, let alone improve the actual quality of the school.[25]

We argue that this pattern is an essential component of the closed system structures that have calcified over decades even through all the transformation and reform energy of the twentieth century.

In these first two decades of the twenty-first century we have seen the promotion and escalation of reform initiatives, culminating in portfolio school systems in large metropolitan districts and significant policy levers at the state and federal levels. At the beginning, this nascent group of reformers (originally a broad-based group of civil rights leaders, district leaders, governors, and philanthropists) began to speak with an incredible urgency and focus to introduce measurement, accountability, and market mechanisms into what they perceived as an unresponsive, closed system.

This era of education reform had emerged from an alliance between progressive groups, who believed that standardized tests shone a critical spotlight on equity issues, and conservative groups, who believed the same tests could be used as political leverage to accelerate choice (and in some cases naked privatization) in public education. This alliance doubled down on a closed system fallacy—the belief that an abstract set of aims created by external experts should trump the priorities and aspirations of communities.

They argued that the current public "one size fits all" system was a monopoly and that, like any monopoly, it had become unresponsive and undynamic, and therefore outside pressures were needed to open it up. The bipartisan No Child Left Behind Act of 2001 included powerful levers for parental notification and choice for failing schools. Charters and then innovation schools emerged to give educators and communities more opportunities to envision alternative infrastructure in education.

Summarizing much of the reform progress and strategy, David Osborne, in *Reinventing America's Schools*, claims that this "new formula—school autonomy, accountability for performance, diversity of school designs, parental choice, and the competition between schools—is simply more effective than the centralized, bureaucratic approach we inherited."[26] While this remains a much debated proposition, as open system advocates we appreciate the work to crack open the closed monopolistic systems that were holding too many kids back from their full human potential—in particular those furthest from opportunity. Unlike many books or advocates in the education space, we believe there is space for schools of all governance types (district, charter, innovation/pilot, etc.)—as long as they seek to be open systems. We propose that all of these innovations in governance and school design are proxies for the core demand of open systems: the need to design for greater responsiveness to communities and to the young people in schools every day.

While important open system breakthroughs remain and have objectively created opportunities for children, the reformers' overall coalition and efforts had lost momentum by the end of the 2010s. Often, they failed to challenge the actual adaptive dilemma of system-level responsiveness through co-creation with communities and families. From efforts as disparate as blended learning, teacher evaluation, assessment and accountability, and teacher pipeline development, they pushed policies and practices through a closed system technocracy. In too many cases, processes of co-creation were overly focused on creation and too short-lived or limited in scope to provide for co-production.

For all their potential progress and innovation, these reformers could rarely escape the closed behavior that would later put entire projects in peril. This failure cannot be overstated. Reformers wanted to open the closed system, but they believed they already had the solution. And therefore, as they perpetuated closed system mechanisms, their affinity patterns replicated the dominant race, class, and gender patterns of American society and ended up generating substantial opposition to their efforts from the very communities they sought to serve.

During this era, many education leaders across the country were inspired by Albuquerque's Native American Community Academy (NACA). Born from an authentic community-driven process to create a space of belonging and relevance for the Native community of New Mexico, NACA became a pilgrimage for many educators frustrated with closed system approaches. Kara Bobroff, founder of NACA, speaks to the importance of the school and the lessons indigenous leaders can teach us:

> Indigenous communities have always existed, lived, and thrived together grounded by universal core cultural values related to nature and ceremony. The US education system and the US government destroyed our ways of living, being, and thriving for their personal gain. We came together and lead with our strengths to serve our children and families in the restoration and sustaining of our life ways, culture, and identities. In 2005, the NACA community did just that—we created a school through

our community's vision for the possible and thus led the movement of Indigenous education and opportunity.[27]

This school and space was a key part of many journeys, including the authors', as they explored an emerging space for co-creation.

Community Engagement Partners, in their October 2019 report *From Tokenism to Partnership*, identifies this challenge as it calls for a new paradigm, stating that "grasstops reformers of this period made some significant errors . . . a group of predominantly elite education leaders and philanthropists designed and led reform efforts in communities of color with little attempt to meaningfully partner or engage with those most impacted by their decisions."[28] This left the reform movement exposed and tied to the real critique of replicating systemic oppression and ignoring the voices of stakeholders. In the box below, reflect on how you consider and understand the history of open versus closed across education.

An important development occurred in the early 2010s, as reformers and other education leaders across the country began to privately and publicly admit either real shame or simply clear-eyed realism as the backlash gathered against their efforts. After losses and public challenges to their authority in the early 2010s, reformers began to adjust course and speak with a new urgency about working with communities and families who had lost trust in education efforts. The convergence of interest in these efforts represented a broad spectrum across left, right, reform, and antireform agendas.

The newer tactics covered a spectrum of family engagement strategies, mobilizations, and community organization techniques that became critical infrastructure in education spaces. In 2017, the Carnegie Founda-

---

Open and Closed Systems Across Education History Reflection
- How have you seen closed and open systems in education and community work in your context?
- How did you react to this history of education systems through an open system lens?
- What other public sector initiatives ought to be analyzed through an open-closed perspective?

tion published a national survey and analysis of philanthropic investment in family engagement. They stated that "funders recognized the importance of this area, especially as they reflect on how past education reform efforts have been stymied." They calculated that there was "a combined investment to be [about] $230 million annually . . . concentrated among 10 foundations that direct [about] 75% of the dollars in the field."[29] This is a significant national investment based on the idea of increased partnership between systems and stakeholders to impact change.

To aid this growth, philanthropy and practitioners continued to look for ways to work and guide the field. In the *50CAN Guide to Building Advocacy Campaigns*, Dr. Marc Porter Magee shared strategies for education coalitions to come together and confront systemic problems. These efforts showcase the renewed education investment in advocacy in the 2010s. Magee defines this advocacy as "the natural and necessary process within a democracy of responding to problems with concrete solutions (organized into campaigns) to achieve a clear goal in a specific amount of time."[30]

This boom in the field led to an increased recognition of the diversity of strategies. In *From Tokenism to Partnership*, Community Engagement Partners offers an important graphic (see figure 1.3) to showcase the variety of typologies of work that was funded and grew during this time.

Organizations such as Nuestra Voz, Memphis Lift, and many others named and unnamed in this book all emerged in this wave, while many others, such as Padres y Jóvenes Unidos, have been around for decades. With this changing environment, the rising generation of education leaders continues to challenge the reform orthodoxy and to ask bigger questions about the systemic injustices occurring in education systems, indicting both reformers and reactionaries.

In the final years of the 2010s, this emergent and fractured ecosystem was full of those organizing families, charging ahead with district family engagement departments and considering what it meant to really include community in a process. Language of co-creation and co-production began to slip into regular discourse. It was at this moment that we hosted our first open system conference, in 2019, entitled "Beyond

Figure 1.3 Typology of unique family and community strategies

EFFECTIVE COMMUNITY ENGAGEMENT AND EMPOWERMENT STRATEGIES[6]	PARENT AND FAMILY EDUCATIONAL JUSTICE ORGANIZING	MULTI-ISSUE ORGANIZING	MULTI-STAKEHOLDER EDUCATION COALITIONS	NEW SCHOOL EXPANSION ORGANIZING	FAMILY & COMMUNITY ACADEMIC PARTNERSHIPS
OVERVIEW	Parents and families of color and low-income parents and families organize to explicitly address the root causes of education inequity and transform their public education system	Grassroots stakeholders organize using a school, district, and/or charter network as a mediating institution to address a range of issues impacting families and students within a community	A community organization is created to align and organize grassroots and grassroots leaders to advocate for local education change	Parents/families, educators, and community leaders in existing schools or within a community organize to create new high-quality schools	District/CMO/School intentionally partner with families & parents to enhance their involvement in their child's schooling and classroom, leading to stronger academic outcomes for students
ENGAGEMENT OR EMPOWERMENT	Empowerment	Empowerment	Both	Empowerment	Engagement
INTENDED IMPACT	• Builds a permanent grassroots organization led by and creating action for educational justice • Builds a base of parent and family political power • Explicitly addresses systemic racism and classism that lead to educational inequity • Develops strong grassroots relationships and networks across school communities	• Builds a permanent grassroots organization • Builds a base of political power (voter reg and mobilization) • Broad enough to tackle non-education issues • Develops strong grassroots relationships and networks • Opportunity to impact system-level change and build a movement	• Builds coalitions with power and legitimacy to address an array of local education issues • Family and educator leadership development and organizing • Policy research, analysis, and education • Opportunity to create a c4 to influence electoral politics	• Builds grassroots stakeholder power • Creates new high-quality schools aligned to the values and needs of communities • Places pressure on decision makers to address struggling schools • Opportunity for leaders to give input to the school design process	• Builds strong relationships between schools/districts/ networks and community • Trainings covers root cause analysis and uncovering • Opportunity to improve academic outcomes
CHALLENGES	• Traditional education reform funders have yet to make significant investments in this organizing • Education must allow for an adaptable and flexible set of outcomes	• May or may not address struggling schools • Requires funder comfort with supporting issues outside of education • Evaluation must allow for an adaptable and flexible set of outcomes	• Balancing multiple stakeholder needs and voices • Strategy may be difficult to measure due to the intersection of multiple workstreams and stakeholders	• May not lead to the creation of a lasting grassroots-led organization • Somewhat-scripted campaigns • Few examples and currently limited to charter school expansion	• May not change underlying school quality • May not lead to broader systemic-level change • Requires an effective committed school leader
PROOF-POINT EXAMPLES	RISE Colorado	United Parents and Students	GO Public Schools	Innovate Public Schools	Flamboyan Foundation

6. Created with support from Mark Fraley and adapted from his School Organizing Framework

Source: Charles McDonald, From Tokenism to Partnership, Education Cities, 2018, ERIC Database (ED586954), https://files.eric.ed.gov/full text/ED586954.pdf.

Equity: Liberation & The Open System." Our hope was to bring together a group in fellowship and community, building new language for the system change efforts we were all leading. This is where our first set of co-created open principles was developed. We came to envision a new way and left with hope in our shared efforts.

Only a few months later, the global COVID-19 pandemic unleashed massive disruption across education. And only a few months after that, a global movement for racial justice helped so many in this country see what was so obvious—that the foundational design of our public systems, whether education or policing, was encased in the closed legacy cement that our collective feet were stuck in.

As we've seen across the eras of closed and open dynamics in education, in 2020 our modern closed education systems buckled under decades of institutional distrust and decline. The pandemic created a turning point that allowed many of these educators, organizers, and system leaders to make real and concrete efforts to open up the systems they led. Systems began to experiment with new listening, learning, and co-creation methods that yielded both technical and adaptive benefits. Others leapt forward with bold new initiatives to give power to families, new ways of designing learning, and bringing partnerships together to build better visions of what is possible. Sometimes, these initially tokenistic efforts gave way to openings that mattered, leading to questioning of the systemic structures overall and green shoots of liberation. In their powerful report for the Carnegie Foundation, Dr. Karen Mapp and Dr. Eyal Bergman state the current challenge and opportunity for "liberatory family engagement" at this moment, a call to arms that very much resonates with our diagnosis of the field.

> Such power dynamics have persisted because our sector has never prioritized authentic, solidarity-driven engagement . . . we have an education sector where many cannot imagine a world in which their work is inextricably tied to authentic partnerships with families. Models for effective family engagement have not been baked into our educational system.[31]

We agree and believe that we have arrived at this question of consequence for education and our democracy—to open or close the system?

CONCLUSION: IMAGINING THE OPEN SYSTEM

Openers should begin to see a new world emerging in front of us, where their leadership can redesign systems with the communities they serve, reigniting the potential for democratic revival.

Now visualize a new system, one that recognizes that times change, that consensus builds trust, and that agency of students and families is critical. In the classrooms of this system, all students are seen, heard, and honored as co-creators of their learning journey. At the school level, when a school falls short of an aspiration, it is not a moment for blame, but a moment for shared learning. Leaders embody the democratic spirit, share vulnerable information with families and students, and engage them in shared inquiry and problem solving. Leaders and communities lean into the vitality and energy of individuals and groups to collectively open their perspectives, their hearts, and the possibilities for the future.

Education's proximity to local communities, its centrality to the aspirations of all Americans, and its place as a touchstone of local democracy make it the most dramatic revitalization opportunity of our time. We are asking not just for a technical change but for a deeper adaptive shift and transformation for redesign. One that sees every stakeholder opening up information to create more of a living education system that inspires future generations to expand the power of our democracy. We are asking leaders to leverage co-creation and co-production to ignite the spark of trust and democracy in our local communities. John Dewey, one of the great thinkers of democracy and education, saw this evolving nature of democracy and education as critical for the functioning of society. In 1937, celebrating the one hundredth anniversary of Horace Mann becoming secretary of the Massachusetts Board of Education, he wrote of this challenge.

> Just as democracy in order to live must move and move forward, so schools in a democracy cannot stand still, cannot be satisfied and complacent with what has been accomplished, but must be willing to undertake whatever reorganization of studies, of methods of teaching, of administration, including that larger organization which concerns the relation of pupils and teachers to each other, and to the life of the com-

munity. Failing in this, the school cannot give democracy the intelligent direction of its forces which it needs to continue in existence.[32]

Educators often argue that democratic society requires an education system to produce civic leaders responsible for its maintenance. If our democracy is sputtering nationally, ought we not look in the mirror? As educators, shouldn't we look around and see institutional decline, mistrust, and democratic degradation in society as a direct outgrowth of our inability to practice democratic, inclusive, and open systems in our schools?

At the first open system convening in 2019, Drew Schutz, the former principal of Valverde Elementary in Denver, Colorado, shared a powerful insight with us: "This isn't my school. This is the community's school. My expertise is to help build and actualize that vision."[33] We should all consider the broader democratic implications of that statement.

In public education, the forge of our society, we are too often content with a system that almost never seeks to ask important questions of our families and communities. Building a future in education where we harness this shared responsibility for community-driven redesign to emerge from this crisis is to design a renewed society that would astound and honor our ancestors. This new foundation could reinvigorate not only our public systems but potentially reignite the American dream, helping us to bind together our imperfect union.

We need open leaders who will get serious with redesign and democracy building as core aspects of our education system—beginning with activating you, the open leader.

CHAPTER 2

Open Principle 1

Activate Open Leadership

The human heart is the first home of democracy. It is where we
embrace our questions. Can we be equitable? Can we be generous?
Can we listen with our whole beings, not just our minds, and offer our
attention rather than our opinion? And do we have enough resolve in
our hearts to act courageously, relentlessly, without giving up—ever—
trusting our fellow citizens to join with us in our determined pursuit
of a living democracy?

TERRY TEMPEST WILLIAMS

The first duty imposed on those who now direct society is to educate
democracy; to put, if possible, new life into its beliefs; to purify its
mores; to control its actions . . . to adapt government to the needs of
time and place; to modify it as . . . circumstances require.

ALEXIS DE TOCQUEVILLE

Audaces fortuna iuvat.
Fortune favors the bold.

VIRGIL

BIG IDEAS IN THIS CHAPTER
- Energizing purpose, passion, and place
- Democratic leadership
- Open hearts, open minds, open paths

Figure 2.1

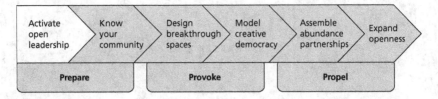

ACTIVATE OPEN LEADERSHIP

Not long after our very first convening in 2019, it was clear that open leadership was a critical factor that needed to be named and cultivated. All of us in that room, whether we were in family engagement, organizing, or working toward state-level policy change, understood that not every leader led for openness, and that too often our education leaders, both inside and outside of systems, were instead leading for closed system behavior. We knew then and still see more evidence all the time that a leader who is willing to open up to the community is imperative for open system work.

We consider these first two open principles to be part of the *preparing* phase of an open system process, because it is here that the conditions are set for future success. Both activating open leadership and knowing your community help leaders and communities align, build readiness, and ask the right questions for the open system moments that they seek.

We have seen open leaders across the country, in every potential context you could imagine, and with a range of personality types. There is no one type of open leader, but open leadership does have some important commonalities that we will explore and identify. Open leaders must model the openness for the systems they lead and seek to open. No community facilitation in the world can be successful at shifting systems if leaders aren't grounded in their purpose and ready to open their hearts and minds to their community. None of the principles, practices, or breakthroughs in this book can come to pass unless we are led by activated open leaders, both inside and outside the system.

Open Vignette: Homegrown Talent
Initiative in Rural Colorado

In the spring of 2019, an idea and project started evolving between multiple organizations, funders, and community leaders across Colorado. Nationally and locally, momentum had been growing for career-connected learning (such as internships, pathways, or concurrent enrollment) and for blurring the lines between high school and higher education. While this work had been making significant progress in cities and suburbs in Colorado, there was a growing desire to see this work brought to rural communities across the state. As many know, the story of education and economic investment over the past two decades has been one of monomaniacal focus on urban cities. Over time, the concept became branded the Homegrown Talent Initiative, jointly launched and supported by the Colorado Education Initiative (CEI) and Colorado Succeeds (CS).

These two organizations came from different approaches and backgrounds in the education space. CEI is an established district redesign intermediary with deep reservoirs of trust and respect in the education community, long valued for expertise with significant systems change initiatives. CS, an advocacy organization led by the business community and committed to agility principles, had been a go-to resource for out-of-the-box education leaders.

In the initial design work, the idea and concepts of supporting rural communities across Colorado to build a local "educonomy" that would blend economic development and education infrastructure began to manifest. Both organizations were inspired by two communities in particular that had achieved breakthrough results in vastly different contexts. St. Vrain School District, an i3 (Investing in Innovation federal grant) winner in the Denver metro area, had built exceptional workforce partnerships and community investment across the K–12 system to national acclaim. In Cañon City, a small rural community nestled near the Royal Gorge in central Colorado, the community had banded together to launch the country's first rural P-TECH (career apprenticeship) model, where students are provided internships and opportunities to obtain college credit while in high school.

Rebecca Holmes, the chief executive for CEI, described this emerging vision for change. "We started seeing the best leaders in Colorado embracing community leadership with economic development. They understand that the school system they're building is a talent development engine for their community. In both Cañon City and St. Vrain, they saw themselves as doing something for the community rather than solely requesting something from it. It's a significant mindset shift that called us to spread and sustain the practice."[1]

Launched in the fall of 2019, communities were recruited in a unique way, with leaders being asked to bring a coalition of businesses, board members, community leaders, and educators to the table from the very beginning of the process. Eventually eight communities were selected and began their journey through a community-driven redesign of their educonomy in the fall of 2019. In the Homegrown Talent Initiative (HTI), rural communities began their process by establishing a community design team to work together to build a graduate profile. Amy Spicer, senior director at CEI, led the graduate profile design process for the HTI communities.

A graduate profile is a document that visualizes the competencies that communities want for their graduates. Graduate profiles typically include academic skills, but they break beyond that to include things like problem-solving skills, adaptability, and empathy. To create a graduate profile, we have system leaders ask their communities what hopes and dreams they have for their students. The responses are always inspiring and humbling, and we make sure that the final product reflects the community values and priorities that they have unearthed through the process.

Through this process of co-creation, communities established a community north star to focus all of their efforts. While many organizations build and have provided graduate profiles for communities, from the beginning the vision for HTI was to produce explicitly community-driven profiles that truly embodied the spirit of the town and the essence of their place. The map in figure 2.2 shows the truly statewide and diverse effort of the initiative.

Figure 2.2 Map of HTI communities

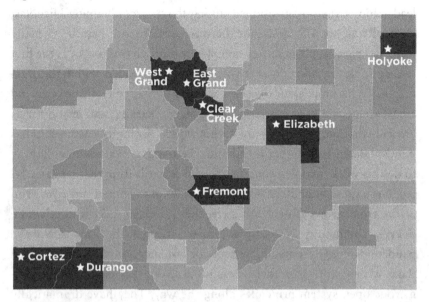

Source: Homegrown Talent Initiative, www.homegrowntalentco.org.

As the community-driven work unfolded, HTI gave the organizations an up-close look at leaders from 2019 through 2022—essentially before, during, and well into the pandemic. They had the chance to see leaders engage with and stay committed to partnering with their communities throughout the entire process as they worked to redesign their systems. The HTI leaders encountered enormous challenges and obstacles to implementing effective career-connected learning, through the turbulence of the pandemic, school closures, and numerous political battles.

In each of these eight communities, over the course of three years, we saw numerous examples of opportunities for them to back down, retreat from open system work, and go back to business as usual in a closed system process with their communities. Like schools and districts across the globe, HTI communities saw a frustrating number of pandemic resets, local community conflicts, and political controversies emerge over the 2019–2022 school years. In some cases, the challenges directly resulted from leaders offering up community co-creation of a new vision of the future, stirring the pot for change.

The open system work occurred both in the communities and in the leadership of the organizations running the project. Shannon Nicholas, chief of staff for CS, describes the transformation in herself: "I really think my paradigm has shifted completely through this work . . . the first thing I think we had to do as an organization and leaders within the organization is be a model for the communities. We had to really be open and transparent, and that was kind of the bigger learning and lesson for us around what our intentions are in this work. Our larger partnership has only validated for me that the abundance mindset is absolutely the way to do this work, and you continue to reap rewards from that mindset."

In the summer of 2022, at the conclusion of the initial three-year run of the Homegrown Talent Initiative, there is much success to celebrate in every community. Not only have they arrived at the other side of the pandemic (fingers crossed), these school systems have completely shifted the way they work with their communities, and they have leveraged numerous open system principles along the way. They have dramatically increased concurrent enrollment and internships in their local businesses, and many of the districts passed bonds or mills for the first time in decades in their communities, creating new public investment. In their stories of perseverance and openness, we can learn deeply from these activated open leaders and their journeys to reignite the educational, economic, and democratic systems in their communities. The overall outcomes show enormous progress:

- All eight communities developed or expanded internship programs
- Three hundred students participated in an internship during the 22–23 school year
- All eight communities increased concurrent enrollment and certification opportunities
- Over five hundred business partners were engaged across the cohort
- All eight communities leveraged aligned funding, programs, and policies[2]

How did these leaders activate open leadership during the greatest crisis facing public education in our lifetime and not only survive, but thrive while building vibrant rural innovation breakthroughs?

ENERGIZING PURPOSE, PASSION, AND PLACE

Open leaders generate sustained open systems when they build energy between *their professional* purpose *and their* passion, *in a* place *they deeply care about.*

In the last chapter you learned about the foundational framework for co-creation and co-production, the strategic triangle. As we've worked with leaders from across the country on this concept, we talk about "rounding the triangle"—that is, moving between all three elements to foster dynamic, open public systems. Not long into working with leaders on this concept, they began to ask: What does it mean to have the energy to sustain that level of change? We offer that we've seen something inside the triangle: the passion, purpose, and place-centeredness of activated open leaders, which allow them to adeptly maneuver across the challenges of building capacity, authentically engaging stakeholders, and reimagining public value. Figures 2.3 and 2.4 show how we see purpose, passion, and place as central to providing the human energy to sustain this tough work.

Over the course of our experience, we've seen a fascinating alignment across many of these leaders. Some are new to open systems or public leadership, others have been in it for decades, but all have a sense of

Figure 2.3 Activating open leadership through Purpose, Passion, Place

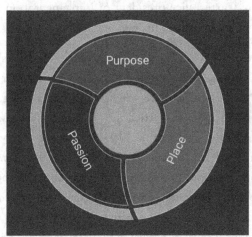

Figure 2.4 Purpose, passion, and place at the center of the strategic triangle

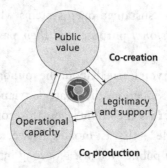

purpose for why they are in it and why they are there. They find passion and energy in their unique roles within their jobs and organizations. And while the grittiness of the work is at times exhausting, and may stifle others, these leaders tackle challenges with an energy and flow that can turn hours into moments. And perhaps most consequently for community-driven work, they are connected to their place, with their geographic impact based on a sense of respect, admiration, or curiosity. They leverage all three of these facets together to energize them, creating a flywheel effect that starts to move first the leaders and then the systems they seek to open toward action. Many educators and community leaders are full of fear, self-doubt, loneliness, and uncertainty that must be overcome. The shift to becoming an opener is enormous, and the transformation profound. Alex Carter, vice president of implementation at CEI (and a former superintendent) shares his perspective:

> We have seen leaders who have decided to become openers completely change the way they show up as leaders—sometimes after decades in that role! Previously, they were weighed down by a belief that as the chief executive, they alone carried the "burden of the change agent." They had to be the source of the ideas for and the energy behind all of the change efforts they wanted to lead in their districts. Once they began to open themselves and their systems, however, they came to understand that by partnering with their community to co-create the public value, their authorizers eagerly shared the burden of building the organizational capacity needed to fulfill the purpose. Therefore, the

democratization of their system made change more effective, efficient, and sustainable.

In this section, we will learn through the example of Summer Kreider, who was the HTI coordinator in Holyoke, Colorado. Holyoke is a small town of about twenty-two hundred people on the northeastern plains of Colorado, near Nebraska. A mom, a former counselor, a school board member, and the HTI coordinator in her community, we watched Summer activate her leadership to open enormous possibilities in her community. "It's empowering to think that we have the ability to help shape not only new ways to educate our kids . . . so I think that's a really empowering part for me . . . that it's not just finding small opportunities for kids. It's really changing how our whole community works together." The Holyoke graduate profile, shown in figure 2.5, stands as a testament to significant movement toward a clear vision for a community moving forward, and Summer was at the center of that effort.

Purpose

We find that open leaders are very clear about what they are there to do, to achieve, and to build. Another way to consider this is that open leaders understand the question or problem they are interested in solving. If you are afraid of community work or have self-doubt, then uncertainty about your purpose—your why—can be enormously challenging. Openers are clear that the goal is to work and live with a purpose to build a better community, not just a school system. Rebecca Holmes often refers to this change in mental model as "think like a mayor"—to fully live in the community and public role required. This shift in approach and tactics allows open leaders to be charged with purpose, full of the clarity and energy required to take on the daunting task of community-driven system change.

The HTI created a vehicle through which these leaders could drive that sense of purpose with all of the leaders in the various community design committees and processes they enabled. Summer Kreider speaks to this purpose-driven calling: "Sometimes we just don't understand the power that we do have as an individual, and I guess that's where I've always tried to tell kids like you that one person can change. Don't settle for small things like you have the power to change."

Figure 2.5 Holyoke graduate profile poster

Source: Used with permission from Homegrown Talent Initiative.

Openers share a deep sense of purpose of why and how they need to facilitate community-driven change, to move systems from closed to open. They see their current roles as opportunities to make a significant impact in the communities they serve. This is a personal mission, a critical task and endeavor in their lives, giving them the strength and courage to face down the likely challenges from others in their communities.

Passion

If purpose is the deeper understanding of why you are called to serve, then passion is the excitement you feel about the specific domains you choose to impact and the joy you feel about how the work is done.

Purpose Reflection
- What are the important choices you've made in your life?
- How are you able to actualize your purpose in your current, past, and potentially future roles?
- What are the throughlines that have brought you to seek to open systems?

Passion is a feature that we see in many openers, striking us as similar to the ancient Stoic maxim *Amor fati,* or love of fate, "not simply to bear what happens, but to love it." The openers we work with do not seem to overly despair at the ever-changing environments in which they work, the ebbing and flowing of policy opportunities, the adaptation required to open systems to changing communities. Many of the events and challenges that come the way of the opener—such as a challenging caregiver or a questioning newspaper—ought not to be seen as challenges, but as great ways to move the community forward.

Many would read these sentences and say, "That's not me—I am so burdened by these challenges, I am barely able to accept what the world gives me, let alone love it!" This is very natural and important. To these openers, we would ask you to explore the connections between passion, purpose, and place. In our experience, most of the time when we find openers lacking passion, we find it is a symptom of their current purpose and place being misaligned. Passion is the fuel for the flywheel, but it needs an engine (purpose) and a location (place) to center us on the journey.

During the launch of the HTI, we saw that many communities were faced with numerous challenges and problems during the COVID crisis and subsequent pandemic. These massive disruptions created enormous opportunities, but also a never-ending series of challenges and dilemmas that leaders had to face on the ground on a daily basis. Yet throughout it all, these leaders embraced their passion to create breakthrough partnerships and system designs that transformed the energy of change into energy for opportunity. Summer Kreider speaks to this activated energy and connection: "My role now is just really to be constantly talking about school and opportunities for kids. No matter where we go. No longer do

---

Passion Reflection

- What aspects of your current life and work give you flow and energy?
- What currently depletes or exhausts you?
- Does your passion live in another place or purpose? What could that be?

I feel like I'm just the middleman—this is just what we should be doing all the time. I think it's my job to learn about our industries and how that's going to help our kids."

Summer embraced her passion for community and for open system transformation to manage the inevitable daily and weekly challenges. There was no playbook or guidebook for leaders to design and lead for community co-creation during a pandemic in rural America, arguably the hardest years in education history—except their passion for supporting their communities.

Place

Community-driven work requires a community. It could be a neighborhood, a city, a village, or even an entire state. Opening up a system to a community requires leaders who are centered and connected to the places they serve.

One of the first mistakes we make in community-driven work is to assume that there is only one type of connection to place, often the one requiring a leader to be born and raised in the community, or at minimum a resident for a significant amount of time. While this situation can create powerful connections that can undoubtedly be critical levers for opening work, we have also seen these deep connections mask blind

---

Place Reflection

- What are you continually curious about in your community?
- What keeps you grounded in your place?
- What are the things you really admire about your community?

---

spots and assumptions. When we talk about being grounded in a place, we see activated open leaders who are admiring of and curious about the community (or communities) they serve. The fear or concern leaders face can be significantly mitigated by standing in a place of certainty that this is the place where you are called to do your work.

When you hear Summer Kreider speak about Holyoke, you can just hear the admiration, curiosity, and groundedness:

> I've always thought that Holyoke is unique. I just think of all the little towns out here. I think it's just that it's thriving, and there's lots of opportunities. I obviously am committed to Holyoke just because of my past here, and I think it's a great place to raise kids. I love the diversity of Holyoke and it's one thing I've always said as my kids started growing up. They didn't even realize they were growing up in such diversity. It's just what they know, and so I think that shapes them into good human beings.

In Summer's case, her place is Holyoke, the small town in which she lives. What about an even larger scale? Landon sees his place in the mountain west, Doannie all across Georgia. Can openers see themselves in larger places? Other openers we know operate nationally, grounded in a continental consciousness. The key is to know it, to name it, and to honor it in the context in which you operate. When this clarity for place intersects with purpose and passion, openers can activate all three aspects for transformation in their lives and communities.

Purpose, Passion, Place Reflection

Readers should reflect if they are not finding the energy for sustained effort within themselves. Where is the breakdown occurring? Purpose, passion, or place? Through examining which area is in tension or challenge, openers will ask new questions of themselves and learn how to realign to sustain their impact.

- How does it feel when you are energized or at full power in your role working with communities?
- Where are you not energized or in alignment?
- Where do you need to change or adjust your current path?

Liberatory Open Leadership Activation

As leaders engage in the work of purpose, passion, and place, it offers an opportunity for them to navigate with a liberatory open system lens. Here are key questions leaders must ask themselves to maximize the liberatory impact:

- *Purpose.* How is my purpose connected to the needs of those furthest from opportunity in this community? How do I see them in the manifestation of my purpose?
- *Passion.* When I am at my most passionate about my work, am I creating opportunities for those in my community furthest from power? Or am I replicating the closed system? Who is helping me notice these patterns? How do I de-center myself as the most important component and examine my own privilege and power?
- *Place.* Am I grounded in understanding the role of historical oppression in my place? Am I curious about the patterns that exist? Am I admiring those who have come before and are working now to liberate us from the closed systems of the past?

DEMOCRATIC LEADERSHIP

Open leaders resist traditional authoritarian leadership practices and build an inclusive, pragmatic sense of possibility through their work.

Openers embrace public and democratic leadership. Whether you're a district superintendent entrusted with a billion-dollar enterprise, a school leader leading a community design process, an advocate pushing to build a better system, or an educator working to break down walls between your classroom and community, you can ensure that democratic leadership and open systems go hand in hand.

We cannot tell you how many superintendents, school leaders, and advocates shy away from public leadership and tell us they hate politics or local board issues. Leaders trained in the traditional closed education system approach are often taught to be technocrats reluctantly embracing democracy to cover their tracks. Open system work flips the script. Activated openers confront and embrace the fact that our school systems are grounded in democratic structures and in local or state politics, and they leverage this truth to maximize system change.

To avoid the study and discipline of democracy, politics, and public leadership in education is akin to avoiding biology when studying genetics —you will miss the entire point of the endeavor! Leaders must understand that politics is not something that is normatively good or bad, and in avoiding local politics or local democracy, you are in fact short-circuiting the very foundation and design of the education system, reducing trust in the long term.

As we've stated throughout the book and will continue to make clear, this avoidance, elitism, and detachment contributes to institutional decline and irrelevance, and it has larger implications for the functioning of our broader democracy. Rebecca Holmes, of CEI, agrees, and she makes the case for a dramatic shift in how we see the role of a democratic leader.

> The education field has made significant strides in understanding the role of a district superintendent as an instructional leader and as an organizational leader, akin to a CEO. But our public systems are far more complex than private businesses because of their public nature, and open system leaders have to acknowledge that complexity. You must marry your internal focus—on components like talent, resources, and outcomes—with an external focus that allows you to interrogate how your school system mirrors, leads, and partners with its community. This requires getting honest about and paying attention to where the system has upheld promises to that community and where it has broken them.

Professor Brian Danoff, in his books *Educating Democracy* and *Why Moralize on It?*, asks important questions aimed at integrating democratic leadership and its educational role more robustly. Danoff describes democratic leaders as "moral artists" who work with communities and citizens to educate them about what the future could hold.[3] He suggests, for both elected and informal leaders, that educating the public "is the most important task of the democratic leader."[4]

Over the course of the book, Danoff articulates his concepts for democratic leadership, which we synthesize into three major orientations for openers: catalyzing community leadership, building shared direction, and moving toward the democratic ideal.

In this section, we feature Amelia Joe-Chandler, the former tribal outreach coordinator for the Cortez-Montezuma School District in the Four Corners region of Colorado. A member of the Navajo Nation, or Diné, Amelia has a long history of advocacy and relationship building across her communities. She became involved in HTI to ensure that the district built authentic partnerships with tribal communities. Through her activated open leadership, the graduate profiles were translated into Navajo and Ute through conversation with elders, something that had never been done for a major district initiative. As Amelia says, "You can't get any more closed system than the reservation school system. I've been trying to break down walls for years." The Cortez graduate profile, shown here, illustrates her balance and perspective.

Catalyzing Community Leadership

Democratic leadership requires a belief that you cannot go it alone. Danoff argues that "democratic leaders try to foster political freedom by helping their followers become visible political actors with an equal voice."[5] We call this democratic leadership practice "catalyzing community leadership." In all open system processes, we must begin with leaders who see among them other emergent political leaders, then create and sustain open mechanisms for these leaders to activate and become empowered, whether it is in a high-stakes equity conversation or inside of a classroom. This is not a deficit-based orientation around what is possible, but rather a guiding belief in the potential of the entire community to come together to transform. Amelia Joe-Chandler shares how she thinks about this work:

> When you're working with multiple cultures you have to study it. You got to understand it. You got to learn to speak the language, and blend in and not be so vocal or don't put yourself higher up so that people have to look up to you and see that you think you're that type of a person. You got to stay level-headed, you got to stay right where the people are,

Figure 2.6 M-CHS graduate profile poster

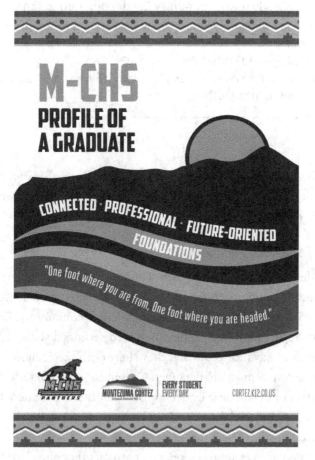

Source: Used with permission from Homegrown Talent Initiative.

and be a part of the people and not above the people. Don't go so low that you get trampled on either. You've got to figure out where you are on that. Listening to the board say one thing, and then going to the Ute Mountain Tribe and listening to the Council say another thing, and not saying anything about either side. Just listening and understanding.

This belief in the potential of every community makes open system initiatives fundamentally different when a leader or a group of leaders come together to design. They create systems and structures—sometimes permanent and sometimes transitory, such as standing governance

---

Catalyzing Community Leadership Reflection

- Have you ever catalyzed community leadership for open system change?
- What happened? What did you learn?
- If not, why not? What scares you about it? What support would you need to lift up others?

---

councils or task forces—to catalyze the political leadership of the broader community, finding a place for all the other community members to activate their open leadership as well.

Building Shared Direction

One of the great challenges of democratic leadership is the challenge of balancing the opinions, perspectives, and expertise of the leader alongside the wisdom and potential of the democratic community. Danoff argues that "rather than pursue their own predetermined goals, democratic leaders seek to advance goals that they share with their fellow citizens."[6] This is one of the most challenging and mindset-breaking aspects of an open system or democratic leadership. We call this orientation "the willingness to build shared direction," and it is at odds with the decades-long belief in authoritative, top-down leadership.

Education leaders are too often taught to "set the course" or "steer the ship" and rarely embed with any deeper understanding of what it means to surrender their own goals to build shared goals. The open leader sees themselves as the conduit and connector between the emergent goals of the community, connecting the disparate aspects of the vision and then creating the potential for it to happen.

Yet, it is important to understand that this does not mean their leadership goes away! In too many instances, we find the "just listen to the community" crowd rejecting leadership in community-driven work. We find this to be a self-defeating notion that ends up reducing trust in systems. The work is not to wish for the elimination of leaders but, through modeling, guiding, and facilitating, to adapt and transform the concept

---

Building Shared Direction Reflection
- Where have you prioritized building shared direction?
- How is it challenging to balance your individual beliefs with the community perspective?
- Where have you seen this work or fail?

---

of leadership away from the dominant authoritarian idea to a new vision that shows that local democracy can flourish through leadership.

In Cortez, the community organizations and businesses were yearning for a common path and direction. HTI supported this endeavor, but Amelia Joe-Chandler was essential in building that shared direction among all the leaders, through participating in the design team, graduate profile, and ongoing partnership work, creating high-variety interactions across her community.

Moving Toward the Democratic Ideal

A consequential component for open leadership, and essential to enacting the liberatory promise of open system work, is the ability to be honest about the challenges of the system while also making a compelling case that things can get better.

Danoff suggests that democratic leaders return to the founding optimism and lessons of the American story and therefore "uphold and further realize in practice the principle of equality which undergirds democracy."[7] Lifting up from Danoff, we call this "moving toward the democratic ideal." In his deep historical and philosophical grounding in the original sins of America, he is directing democratic leaders to confront the moral conundrums at the heart of their public endeavors. Yet they should not stop there—they must educate and persuade the community to move closer to the founding idealistic principles of America. In education, this resonates deeply with the activated openers we've seen leading breakthrough work. They are not avoiding the difficult conversations about racism, classism, sexism, and colonialism in their education spaces, yet they are also not perpetually perseverating in these conversations and are eager to move toward action.

This is another place where open system work diverges significantly from the "doom chatter" that infuses much of the equity and justice work in public education. In too many conversations we have heard others willing to engage in the easy part of the conversation (discussing the original sins of America) but avoid the hard part (actually building a stronger and liberatory democracy). By only engaging in one side of the issue—the problem—and refusing to push for progress in redesigning systems through a calling to our founding ideal, they are undercutting the best leverage we have to build a more perfect union—our democracy. Here, we recall the maxim, "progress, not perfection," which we believe is central to moving open system work forward. We need openers to understand that, as Danoff suggests (through connecting to Ralph Ellison's *Invisible Man*), "the best democratic leaders can fashion 'a raft of hope' to help the citizenry move further toward 'the democratic ideal.'"[8]

Every community has a past that must be reckoned with and confronted to move forward. In Cortez, Colorado, the legacy of colonization and confrontation looms large in any community work. The failures and tragedies of the past have, not surprisingly, left many community leaders and members with the belief that the system is closed, and will stay closed, and that this pattern is destined to repeat itself. Amelia Joe-Chandler, in her effort to bring the community together in pursuit of shared vision, discussed how she approaches this tension:

> I acknowledge the past. I acknowledge the animosity that some people had against Navajo tribal people, and I assured them that I was not there to hurt in any way, that I was there to help their children manage their way through K–12 and with their help I think we can get there. I introduce myself as a person that is going to help children first and parents along the way. We must create that trust by acknowledging the past and acknowledging how the relationship was. And so, once I stated who I am and where I'm going, and what my objectives are, then I saw them come down and say, "Okay."

While the challenges faced in Cortez are unique to their community and the Four Corners, this issue presents itself in every community. Closed systems have failed communities, sometimes intentionally and sometimes unintentionally, for decades. The legacy of ~isms and structural oppression haunt the ability to move forward, and for many community members and advocates, getting stuck in this truth is a common and real dilemma. Activated open leaders must call upon the potential for a better future by acknowledging the past, holding within their leadership the ability to move a community forward together.

Our firm belief is that our experience and the expertise of the activated openers throughout this chapter and book prove it can be done. It doesn't mean that we, like the generations that come before us, won't fail to meet that bigger vision of what is possible. We have seen the progress and know that it has meant real and sustained difference in the lives of students and families. We can open the system—if leaders can call upon our communities to move toward the democratic ideal.

Democratic leadership does not come without other burdens. It must come with hard choices and trade-offs. It doesn't always mean leaders agree with where the community is going or where it wants to go. Open leadership cannot be about democracy only when our side is winning or when our argument is more righteous.

Open leadership gets even more complicated because it begins with a belief that local institutions and democratic structures can adapt and get better. In our time of decreased faith in institutions, this can be a hotly debated topic with real disagreement. There are plenty of books, advocates, and thought leaders who may disagree and say we need to completely avoid the legacy structures and systems that we've inherited.

Moving Toward the Democratic Ideal Reflection

What are the unique challenges and barriers that you need to name as a leader in your community?

- How have you struggled with naming the problems in society while rallying others to solve the problem? How is this different from others who seek alternatives to building an open system?
- What would happen if your community got stuck in the failures of the past?

> ### Democratic Leadership Reflection
> - How will you have to shift your leadership practice in discrete ways to include more democratic practices?
> - Which of these practices do you feel the strongest or weakest in?
> - What support structures do you need to build your leadership skill in this area?

We wish those leaders and thinkers well, but we have an entirely different mission as openers—to address the students, communities, and resources present in closed systems. Ironically even those who would build entirely new systems often fail to do it in an open system way, recreating closed system patterns. And most importantly, they fail to address the tens of millions of students inside closed systems. Openers suggest a different path.

Danoff discusses how critical this path is in the context of our time:

> In our current age of extreme polarization, the danger of a fanaticism which refuses to see any validity to opposing views is quite great; at the same time, the political dysfunctions caused by this polarization may leave some citizens in a state of apathy or even paralysis. Achieving the ability to judge and to act "in the convulsion of the world" such that one avoids both paralysis and fanaticism is thus no small achievement, and it is this form of action which may be particularly needed in our own age.[9]

If we run away from democracy in education to preserve our vision for education, we've already lost. Democratic leadership is essential to rebuilding the community and the education system's capacity to foster a new birth of democracy and community building in our era.

OPEN HEARTS, OPEN MINDS, OPEN PATHS

If open leaders are to truly live in the spirit of the work, they must be prepared to open the deepest parts of themselves—their hearts, their minds, and their paths in order to press themselves and others to maintain openness to challenging narratives and ideas.

In pursuit of democratic leadership toward improvement, leaders can inadvertently narrow the scope of their ambition by only listening to people and ideas that align with what they think is possible. Open leaders press themselves and others to maintain openness to challenging narratives and ideas. They keep themselves and their systems open to paths they may not have predicted or thought possible. We have watched as leaders who were creating powerful co-creation or co-production were showcasing a different type of leadership in public spaces. Openers who see themselves as public leaders are the first step. We often casually remarked that "openers need open hearts and open minds" as we worked with leaders across the country.

Imagine our surprise, after we launched the institute, when we were introduced to Otto Scharmer's *Theory U* which explicitly makes the connection between "open hearts, open minds, open wills" and the leadership capacity to lead the community to a new future.[10] Scharmer writes, "the primary leadership challenge today is the fact that our economic reality is shaped by globally interdependent eco-systems, while institutional leaders, by and large, operate with an organizational ego-system awareness."[11] To overcome this challenge, we must help leaders move past a focus on themselves and their organizations to hold a dynamic future for a whole community. As we dove in, we were exposed to a review of emergent literature by Peter Senge and colleagues in their incredible piece, "The Dawn of System Leadership," which summarized the concepts:

> In their book *Leading from the Emerging Future*, Otto Scharmer and Katrin Kaufer describe three "openings" needed to transform systems: opening the mind (to challenge our assumptions), opening the heart (to be vulnerable and to truly hear one another), and opening the will (to let go of pre-set goals and agendas and see what is really needed and possible). These three openings match the blind spots of most change efforts, which are often based on rigid assumptions and agendas and fail to see that transforming systems is ultimately about transforming relationships among people who shape those systems. Many otherwise well-intentioned change efforts fail because their leaders are unable or unwilling to embrace this simple truth.[12]

Fundamentally, Scharmer and his cowriters examine how leaders hold and shape space for an emerging future to form through these openings.

They see this work as directly tied to the ability to fight the "triple tyranny of 'One Truth, One Us, One Will' . . . as fundamentalism" that sadly permeates too much of our leadership discourse.[13] We are excited to bring their powerful and aligned concepts to bear directly on education and democracy-building leadership specifically.

In this section, we are going to feature an important leader in HTI—Karen Quanbeck and her community in Clear Creek County, Colorado. Karen was appointed superintendent and lead learner of schools in Clear Creek County in the summer of 2019. The county encompasses nearly four hundred square miles and includes the first set of rural former mining towns that tourists drive through on their way up from Denver to the ski resorts. Affectionately known as Q by her friends, staff, and community, she enthusiastically jumped into the chance to partner with her new community, leveraging the career-connected open systems work through HTI. "When HTI started, I was trying to figure out how to fit into this overall community, cause I'm really just one cog in this larger wheel—the community itself is rich and vibrant." The Clear Creek graduate profile is shown in figure 2.7.

Open hearts is the idea of empathy and compassion. Co-creation and co-production can be technical pursuits and structures deployed by the system, but we don't need the cold technocracy to deploy co-productions left and right. We need leaders who deeply care and build relationships with all stakeholders. This is a challenge in public leaders that often requires an intervention. Built into the ideas of open system work are structures that force leaders to meet individuals like students or families to begin the process of open heart work. And even then, sometimes the amount of avoidance is incredible. People are resigned to a cold, technical distance—especially when we are discussing the ~isms. Yet, if an open heart is maintained, the transformation can be remarkable.

As we've shared, we find that fear is a serious barrier to so much open system work. Fear of failure, fear of the community, fear of losing control. We believe that to truly activate openers, we must name that overcoming this fear must begin in the heart of the opener. When given the opportunity to build real and deep relationships across differences, leaders begin

Figure 2.7 Clear Creek graduate profile poster

Source: Used with permission from Homegrown Talent Initiative.

to ask different questions. They start to see in their hearts, through real empathy, the people around them that both keep the system as it is and those who have the potential to manifest what it can be. Parker Palmer, in his book *Healing the Heart of Democracy,* calls into account the connection between the human heart and democracy building.

> For those of us who want to see democracy survive and thrive—and we are legion—the heart is where everything begins: that grounded place in

each of us where we can overcome fear, rediscover that we are members of one another, and embrace the conflicts that threaten democracy as openings to new life for us and for our nation.[14]

As openers dig more into cracking open systems and energizing the self and others, they must remain vigilant to patterns of thought and behavior and remain committed to liberating themselves and others from the same static thinking. Now, an open mind also means being able to see a group making a decision as a positive thing, not inherently a negative thing. Openers know that all groups have the right to share similar thinking. Openers, as key leaders bringing a new reality into existence, and as public leaders standing in the gap between closed pasts and open futures, have a special obligation to hold that open mind and perspective.

Activated open leaders see themselves as the conduit and connector between the emergent goals of the community, connecting the disparate aspects of the vision and then creating the potential for it to happen. Q speaks powerfully of holding her heart open to her community:

> When I think about the community itself, the people who are here are what ground me. It's probably the most challenging job I have ever had in all my years of education, and yet it's the people who I interact with that keep me going on a regular basis. Who again, I feel very account-able to, whether they're educators, or kids, or family members, or non-profits, or government or business leaders, and, as you know, from our work, that's really been core as we've built out the partnerships.

An open will is the work of understanding that open systems require knowing that processes may not end up the way you want. This is one of the most fundamental barriers to beginning open system work. We already know what we want to do, the leader says, so why ask? If you could put a finger on a problematic statement that lies at the heart of democratic decline, this is it right here. We saw leaders go in entirely different directions in HTI, showing how leaders both inside and outside the systems held open perspectives about the future paths they would take. Q, from Clear Creek, speaks to the need to hold an open path: "We have to understand that it's the beginning. I get really excited about the system change in one year, three years, five years. We ask, 'How will our system look

> **Open Hearts, Open Minds, Open Paths Reflection**
> - How do open leaders serve as conduits for the expression of community will, even those that may be deeply challenging?
> - How do leaders ask themselves, "Am I really here for everyone or just those I want to work with?"
> - How do open leaders sustain political courage to co-create when so much closed system schema exists?

different in ways that we can't even imagine right now?' Then we get really boxed into our time and our schedules, and how we're thinking about the course work because that's what we know. If we were to fast forward through, or five years out, what might be true that we can't yet identify?"

Openers know that the process is just as important as the outcome. They know that smart leaders can create real and effective processes. They understand that the possibilities have to be held open in order to invite everyone into the process. They know that if they are really serious about opening the system, the process can provoke serious and new opportunities. They also know that they aren't the holders of all wisdom; they have blind spots and are willing to be surprised by the creativity and new perspectives of co-creation and co-production.

CONCLUSION

In this chapter, we've explored the frameworks and context for open leaders to become activated and begin their journey. Open leaders uniquely understand and hold the liberatory opportunities to push back against the calcified and entrenched ~isms in the closed systems. All together, these concepts push openers into deeper reflection about their wisdom and expertise, and what is required of them to truly maximize the impact for change.

From here, the leader can start to identify the right co-created community questions to marshal the collective will of the community. This includes important readiness analysis and ecosystem analysis. But the first step is for the activated open leader to explore the nuances and unique opportunities—knowing their community in a much more fundamental way.

CHAPTER 3

Open Principle 2

Know Your Community

Building community is to the collective what spiritual practice is to the individual.

GRACE LEE BOGGS

There is no power for change greater than a community discovering what it cares about.

MARGARET WHEATLEY, *TURNING TO ONE ANOTHER*

Life was always about waiting for the right moment to act.

PAULO COELHO

BIG IDEAS IN THIS CHAPTER

- Redefining community
- Mapping open and closed ecosystems
- Identifying your open moment

KNOW YOUR COMMUNITY

Now that we've explored how open leaders can create the conditions for open systems through the power of their leadership and their ability to provoke local democracy into action, we need to move to the next stage of the *preparing* phase: know your community.

To help us understand the power of knowing your community, we will be examining two different sets of case studies that help us understand

Figure 3.1

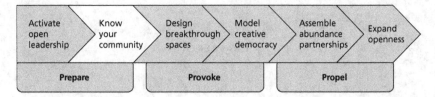

the methods and practices required to ground oneself in the community from both an inside and outside approach to open system change. First, the Year Zero project in Denver Public Schools, a community-driven school turnaround effort, showcases how a large institutional system can open up to communities when responding to community pressure from advocacy groups. To further explore the role of outside openers, we will lift up examples of communities forcing systems to open up to their needs through community organizing in New Orleans and Tennessee.

Pulling from these case studies, leaders will prepare for open system work through redefining community, understanding their ecosystem, and identifying their open moment. Too many leaders jump from their personal work into the pivotal phase of cracking open systems without a deep foundational understanding of where they are working and the dynamics that are at play, and without confirmation that co-creation is feasible in the moment. Leaders must hold space for the possibilities of openness, but only through seeking understanding of their community can they answer this question: which system to open, and with whom?

Open Vignette: Community Advocacy and Year Zero Turnaround in Denver Public Schools

In 2014, a constellation of Denver advocacy groups came together to launch the ¡Ya Basta! report. These groups were unusual allies, including A+ Colorado, Democrats for Education Reform, Latinos for Education Reform, Padres y Jóvenes Unidos, Stand for Children, and Together Colorado. Some of these organizations were considered reform advocacy groups, and others were longtime community-based organizations with a deep tradition of social justice organizing. Yet they all shared one piece of knowledge about their community—too many kids in southwest Denver were going to schools that were not serving their needs. The diverse branding and partners are shown in figures 3.2 and 3.3, both graphics from the report.

The report issued a call for action to the Denver Public Schools (DPS):

> Now is the time for parents to demand renewed attention to Southwest Denver so that every family has the option to send their child or children to an excellent school . . . If parents do not demand better schools, nothing will change.[1]

The report generated enormous political momentum. At a community meeting in the fall of 2014, following publication of the report, leading officials from DPS told the media that things would change: "Susana Cordova, the district's chief schools officer, said she and other DPS staff had already been in conversations with community members in the neighborhood. She said the district was taking a different approach to school improvement in the southwest than it had in northeast Denver, where dramatic changes and turnaround efforts led to some pushback from community members."[2]

Figure 3.2 Graphics from the ¡Ya Basta! Report

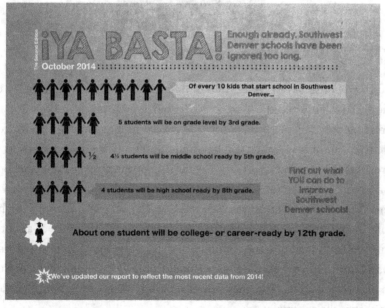

Source: Used with permission from APlus.

Figure 3.3 Graphics from the ¡Ya Basta! Report

Source: Used with permission from APlus.

In response to ¡Ya Basta! and amid greater system recognition to do more, DPS launched the Year Zero Turnaround project, in hopes of addressing some of the persistently low performing schools in southwest Denver and across the city. After undergoing a review and analysis of previous turnaround efforts, the leadership of the Denver Public Schools was prepared to reimagine turnaround through a community-driven lens. Borrowing from charter schools, which had a full design year before their actual launch (often named "year zero"), the district adopted this model to facilitate the community-driven redesign of schools at risk. Ivan Duran, former assistant superintendent in DPS, oversaw the project in his previous role. Now the current superintendent at Highline Schools, he shares the rationale:

The reality was that our previous turnaround efforts saw mixed results. I've always been an advocate to look at the data and best practice. When you look at the national models and research, the truth is that most of the time when districts were doing school turnaround, it was usually something being done to communities, not with them. Most of the time, communities and families had no voice in the process. While sometimes that led to success, most of the time the impact wasn't there. The Year Zero work flipped the model completely. We wanted to get the community, business leaders, families, educators involved in the process from the very beginning. Critical to that was hiring principals with proven results and giving them a significant time to build their plan with all the stakeholders. The community work was hard at the beginning but eventually, through collaborative efforts, it led to a clear vision and plan that everyone in a school community could sign onto and buy in.[3]

The four schools chosen for the effort were Valverde Elementary, Schmitt Elementary, Goldrick Elementary, and Harrington Elementary. A+ Colorado described the Year Zero core strategies in their 2019 report on school improvement in DPS:

- Hire a "Year 0" principal to spend one school year planning and implementing a redesigned model the following year.
- Hire and place an interim school leader to oversee the school during Year 0 while the "Year 0" leader led a school design process rooted in community partnership.
- Invest in comprehensive supports and professional development for the Year 0 principal, including an instructional superintendent focused on developing turnaround competencies, a dedicated project manager to support school design work, dedicated Family and Community Engagement staff members, and trips to visit high-performing schools nationwide.[4]

Van Schoales, of A+ Colorado, remembers the politics of the advocacy and the response from the district. "This was an enormously difficult yet exciting interaction between community and district leadership. It's an emotional and practical paradox to both trust and hold healthy skepticism with your partners. We did it through regular honest communications, checking assumptions, and returning to our shared goals."[5] Advocacy groups were rightfully cautious about the district response, and not always on the same page given the immense diversity of the community organizations at the table. The district and partners had to commit to regular conversation with these organizations, such as inviting them to the launch events for the new leaders and to individual meetings at the schools. Over the course of the process, advocates remained concerned whether the district would follow through with the spirit of ¡Ya Basta!

The Year Zero project intentionally focused on knowing your community: building relationships with each school's respective community by empowering school leaders with support and resources. The very first activity that the group embarked on was walking and knocking on doors across the entire neighborhood of their new school community. On a hot summer day in 2015 each leader walked alongside senior district leaders and the family and community engagement team, spending the entire day introducing themselves and connecting with families in their communities. This simple yet critical act shifted the mental model of leaders right out of the gate. Joe Amundsen was a lead for the project at DPS, and spoke to the decision at that moment in time: "In DPS, for example, there are certain communities that highly mistrust the school district. Highly suspicious. You know the structures that are in place because of things that have been done to communities. Before we could even start the conversation with the community, we had to address the harm and the pain and the change in the things that have been done to a community by the institution that's trying to engage the community."

Over the course of Year Zero (2015–16), the leaders of each of the four schools dedicated time to monthly meetings with community members, co-creating a community-driven plan and vision for the school. Advocacy groups continued to push over the course of the project, insisting on high-quality designs. At the end of Year Zero, dozens of parents, educators, and community groups crowded the board room in DPS to advocate for their new visions and plans. To achieve their plans, many of the schools also sought innovation status, a Colorado law and DPS waiver policy that supported even more flexibility and autonomy in their strategies.

Over the course of the next few years, progress manifested at each of these schools in meaningful and tangible ways. At the time of A+ Colorado's school turnaround report in 2019, every school had made measurable academic gains on all indicators and had rebuilt significant trust with their communities. Figure 3.4 showcases the progress that each of the schools made over the course of the project:

In DPS, like many other school systems, the Year Zero Turnaround process could have easily been another long, tortured example of why large school systems continually fail the members of their communities furthest from opportunity. Brittany Erikson, another lead for the project in DPS, shared this perspective: "Humility is key. The reality is that taking a school from chronically and persistently low performing on any number of dimensions and changing its trajectory entirely is very rare. Given that reality, all of us must have the humility to say that I alone can't figure this out. This task demands that we be in community with each other, and that we leverage our collective strengths every single time." The story of Year Zero is the story of systems and leaders humbling themselves to know their community—seeking both community and student success.

Figure 3.4 Improvements in Year Zero turnaround schools' DPS SPR ratings

SCHOOL NAME	2013	2014	2015	2016	2017	2018
				Interim Leader and School Design Process by YO Leader	1st Year with YO Leader and Redesign in Place	
Goldrick Elementary	Accredited on Watch	Accredited on Priority Watch		Meets Expectations	Meets Expectations	Meets Expectations
International Academy of Denver at Harrington	Accredited on Watch	Accredited on Probation	No SPF	Accredited on Probation	Meets Expectations	Accredited on Watch
Schmitt Elementary	Accredited on Watch	Accredited on Probation		Accredited on Priority Watch	Meets Expectations	Meets Expectations
Valverde Elementary	Accredited on Priority Watch	Accredited on Probation		Accredited on Probation	Accredited on Watch	Accredited on Watch

Improved DPS SPF Ratings in "Year Zero" Turnaround Schools

*Valverde was not given an interim principal.

Source: Used with permission from A+ Colorado.

REDEFINING COMMUNITY

Openers must embrace the dynamism and complexity of communities to build adaptive, responsive open systems.

Knowing your community requires sharper tools than many expect. Openers must challenge their own and others' assumptions through real community dialogue and analysis. It requires creative solutions and outside-the-box thinking—especially because the system is used to the same-old-same-old engagement. Openers need to constantly ask important questions about themselves in relation to the community they serve.

In this section, we will learn from the leader of Schmitt Elementary during the Year Zero process, Jesse Tang. Jesse explains the situation around community when he started at Schmitt: "The sense of community had been completely fractured at Schmitt. I was the eighth principal to be introduced in four years at Schmitt, and so there was a sense of distrust and willingness to wait for me to be replaced. I had to ask 'How do I rebuild this relationship that exists in our community?'"

Too often when openers are told to talk to the community, systems and leaders are actually reinforcing biases by assuming that all people in certain areas hang out together, speak with one voice, and act in concert. Whether it comes from a good place (to listen and learn), or a not-so-great place (to inform or justify without feedback loops), it often reinforces these systemic biases. Jesse shared his mindset as he approached this question: "I always tried to think about it as, 'How open am I? Do they know who I am? Do they know what my intentions are, and how am I reinforcing the right messages about those things through my interactions with them?'" Leaders like Jesse, who start with a more dynamic definition and an acknowledgement of these tensions, will have a head start in opening the system.

In our experiences there are many challenges with the way we use the term *community*. Similar to *equity* or *engagement*, community is a word that means a hundred different things to a hundred different people. We often hear the term wielded to increase otherization—usually through people describing other groups of people they don't personally identify with as "a community." This approach perpetuates implicit and explicit bias, creating mental models for communities that may or may not be rooted in reality. Often leaders in education who unconsciously or consciously use this approach end up leading to misunderstanding or challenge. In addition, we find that people often have ahistorical or ~ism-laced ideas of a community that are not backed by real data or information. To avoid this marginalization and truly know their communities, openers need to challenge themselves with a new definition and frame.

For the past seven years, we've used the definition below, provided by Mark Warren and Karen Mapp, to support leaders in fully exploring the complexities of community. Just as the Year Zero leaders took on their work to shift some of the unspoken and spoken myths of their community, redefining community is an important step forward. When groups begin to take on this activity, whether it's a group of senior district leaders or education advocates, it is always very rewarding to see leaders who

---

Liberatory Knowledge of Your Community

As openers seek to understand how to make liberatory moves as they get to know their communities, they need to ask themselves some important questions in the definitional stage. These questions can help address some of the underlying structural inequities and challenges at play.

- Who typically is defining or redefining community in your context?
- If you were going to redefine community, who would you bring into that conversation that is furthest from power? Who would you bring to the table, and how would you seek the tables not yet accessed, build new tables for connection, or directly confront problematic tables?
- What would you need to address language or cultural barriers to ensure all voices are included in that redefinition?
- What elders or young voices would need to be at the table to ensure generational perspectives on the path of liberation from closed systems?

have never defined a community, yet deeply believe in its importance, begin to unpack their own internal pretzel logic around the concept and debate it point by point with other folks in the education sector.

> [Community is] . . . a group of interconnected people who share a common history, a set of values, and a sense of belonging—in short a culture or identity . . . Implicitly, if not explicitly, however, most define community by local geography, typically the neighborhood . . . While local ties are important, however, they do not always present the most salient form of identity . . . People can be members of several communities . . . Communities can have different degrees of shared values, and individual people can have different levels of attachment to those values . . . What binds a community together can be contested and subject to change . . . Community implies some level of consensus, but healthy communities are dynamic . . . In the end, we understand community as a historically shaped and emergent phenomenon, not a static one.[6]

To further stimulate discussion and knowing, we are compelled by the provocative exploration of community in the book *Politics for People* by Dave Mathews. Mathews makes the case that for us to build a new citizen politics, we need to wrestle with the negative challenges of community building alongside the opportunities. We argue that openers must consider this definition as they pursue this work, and they must also consider the negative and challenging aspects of community building:

> The community is the little town in which some grew up—and couldn't wait to leave. Or the community is the rather hypocritical force that intrudes on personal liberty. The community may refer to people who are all alike—and unlike me—and who behave accordingly. Community may connote the narrow and the parochial . . . Certain senses of community are not very constructive in politics. Some communities get their sense of unity from opposing outsiders . . . Community can mean me and mine banded together to protect ourselves from you and yours.[7]

Openers must explicitly reflect on these broader and deeper reflections of community to expand their perspectives on the places and communities they work. By exploring both the Warren-Mapp definition and

---

Redefining Community Reflection

- What were the key words that jumped out to you from the Warren-Mapp definition of community?
- How does the dynamic definition of community challenge your traditional notion?
- How did the content from the Mathews conception of community resonate with you?
- How will you call together others to reflect on these definitions as you consider your opportunity for open system work?

---

the Mathews provocation, those leading or supporting open system ideas or work can truly begin to know their own held biases and beliefs about community, leading to more profound and important reflections about their role.

MAPPING OPEN AND CLOSED ECOSYSTEMS

Open leaders must analyze the closed or open structures within and outside their institutions or organizations.

Experience tells us openness may vary across a school, a district, a network, or a group or set of feeder schools. In any community there is a significant amount of interaction or noninteraction between public education (sometimes multiple actors) and the broader ecosystem. Openers need to map the broader ecosystem so they can understand the dynamics they are operating with along an open/closed spectrum. Once you begin this analysis, you can understand the system that you seek to open and how it operates within the broader ecosystem.

Let us come back to the strategic triangle. As you recall, the authorizing environment is the set of formal and informal actors in the broader community that have the ability to validate or challenge the public value proposition you are working toward. Openers in education know that the external environment is the source of all power to adjust the system dynamically and build real trust, and therefore to conduct co-creative redesign. This manifests in how you show up to create the conditions for openness. In figure 3.5, we can see formal and informal authorization patterns.

Figure 3.5 Understanding your authorizing environment

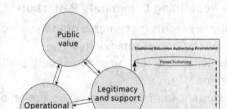

Example: In some school systems, families have tremendous formal power in where they choose to attend school. They also have informal power to protest and resist certain initiatives. Others (such as nonprofits or community groups) also have informal power that can weigh in and push their agenda, but they may not have the same levers of authority as a formal authorizer.

In the open system framework, all informal and formal authorizers are potential co-creators and co-producers. As in the previous scenario, a nonprofit might not have the power to approve your school application or new initiative, but they are ripe for co-creation in the design process.

Example: A new initiative is launched by a network of schools to mobilize parents and family around the next vision of the network. Families of various backgrounds are sought to co-create the scope of the project, the timeline, and how to bring other families in. As the project continues, families are interested in creating a steering body to assist the network and ensure family perspective. They also request that some local community groups, while not needed in the creation process, should provide oversight and additional capacity to implement the vision.

As the Year Zero case explicitly showcases, some of the most exciting and interesting open system work emerges from a dynamic interchange between internal and external openers. In our experience, the experience of open system change requires *both* internal leadership and external provocation or partnership.

Understanding the environment and the broader ecosystem is essential in order to engage in the complex inside-outside three-dimensional chess game that is required to open a system up. This allows partners on both sides of the discussion to have a shared understanding and language. Openers understand this and cultivate foils, allies, and counterpressure forces in their communities to sustain change.

Open Vignette: Nuestra Voz, Memphis Lift, and Nashville Propel

Community organizing has a long tradition and history in the United States and globally, of building community power to confront injustice. Through our work, we've had the opportunity to work with and learn from a variety of leaders of dynamic and inspiring community organizing groups. Two leaders, however, have really inspired us in their approach to knowing their community, Mary Moran of Nuestra Voz and John Little III of both Memphis Lift and Nashville Propel. Both leaders used a deep knowledge of community to create open organizations, which in turn leveraged their power to engage with closed school systems.

Nuestra Voz was founded in New Orleans, Louisiana, to be the voice for the Latino community. Mary Moran came to lead Nuestra Voz in order to realize that vision. Mary spent her first year listening to and learning from the voices in the community, and it became clear that *Latino* was not a resonant term for her people. The reality was that most of these families were Indigenous migrants from Central America who, upon arrival in America, felt forced to relinquish their Indigenous identity and become Hispanic or Latino. Nuestra Voz began to organize on two fronts: first, to support empowerment among the Indigenous communities in New Orleans and, second, to build solidarity between these newer communities and the African American community. In both cases it involved significant one-to-one meetings, listening and examining the difference between what folks in power described as a community and what was actually manifesting within the community. The result? Mary and Nuestra Voz were able to use a dynamic understanding of the open and closed systems around them to achieve a number of wins, including the first living wage campaign in the south, leading to a pay rate of $15 an hour for cafeteria workers in Orleans Parish; state policy shifts in parental notification around school improvement; and much more. Each time, she had to map the current configuration of the ecosystem, understanding where openings and closings were occurring and what the political reality made possible. For Mary, the work is personal and dynamic. "The very kind of energetic, spiritual piece of organizing, which is, you're building leaders. You're also attracting them to the hope and light that we're trying to create through either cultural organizing, or political organizing, or even something as simple as an education awareness campaign."

In Memphis and Nashville, John Little III was working with a variety of leaders and community members to build real parent power to address the long-standing inequities in the school systems. A veteran of numerous political campaigns, John realized that too many organizing efforts were top-down or "grasstops," failing to mobilize families without their authentic voice at the forefront.

> As I started to work in Tennessee, I realized that people didn't really work to build parent leadership, and so we created a model in education that had the objective to empower parents around the real issues and how the school system is currently engaging them in the process with actual decision makers. It's one thing to talk about it in the community and another thing to empower parents to take things to decision makers—until you do that, you're just talking. Parents needed to feel like they were good enough, smart enough, capable enough to lead their own movements.

Over time the Memphis Lift and Nashville Propel scored a number of important victories. They got schools to implement a parent dashboard to monitor academic achievement, drove the board to transform the enrollment process, and trained over three hundred parents to become advocates for their children and other families in the school system.

As these examples show, openers need to cultivate an ecosystem of open system actors and pressures. They help us show that open system work is not inherently just inside the system, but requires outside actors as well. These two openers, in very different political contexts, were routinely opening up systems from the outside by leveraging knowledge of the community to redefine community, map their ecosystem, and identify their open moment.

Open System Infrastructure Analysis

Openers must begin their analysis by understanding the current open system and human infrastructure for open system work. Understanding each of these components is necessary to understand the full capacity of an institution to break down the wall between itself and the community and become open. Before we begin the infrastructure analysis, readers should map their system across a closed-open spectrum using figure 3.6.

Too often, school and system leaders see family engagement or partnership strategies as discrete, nice-to-have elements that are helpful but not consequential. In an open system frame, we reject this notion entirely. We ask system leaders and community members to see family engagement as a conduit that carries energy from outside to inside the system and increases the permeability of the boundary between systems and the communities they serve, managing the movement of information. The best system leaders deploy these as high-variety design opportunities to expand the impact of larger open system redesign moments, creating significantly more trust and impact with families and communities along the way.

In pursuit of understanding the best practices around family and community partnership strategy and impact, we highly encourage any opener who is interested in exploring more high-impact family engagement and

Figure 3.6 Mapping your system across a closed–open spectrum

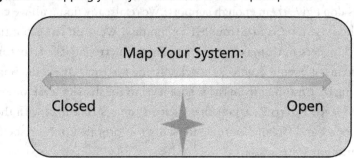

partnership strategies to read *Beyond the Bake Sale,* the indispensable guide by Anne Henderson, Karen Mapp, and colleagues. We are compelled by one of their macro frameworks to understand the position of schools vis-à-vis their communities that aligns directly to open system flows:

- Partnership school
- Open-door school
- Come-if-we-call school
- Fortress school[8]

Educators and advocates should consider the variation across schools inside of a system to begin to understand where schools are on this spectrum, which is very much aligned to open system thinking. At the top of the list, partnership schools are driven by the mantra that "families and communities have something great to offer—we do whatever it takes to work closely together to make sure every single student succeeds."[9] Henderson and her cowriters also describe how these schools share power, enumerating the moves that partnership schools make:

- Parents and teachers research issues such as prejudice and tracking
- Parent group is focused on improving student achievement
- Families are involved in all major decisions
- Parents can use the school's phone, copier, fax, and computers
- Staff work with local organizers to improve the school and neighborhood[10]

This is in direct contrast to the mantra of the fortress school: "Parents belong at home, not at school. If students don't do well, it's because their families don't give them enough support. We're already doing all we can. Our school is an oasis in a troubled community. We want to keep it that way."[11] Openers must make special efforts to interrogate the structures and systems of openness across the schools and systems. One could imagine taking that framing from the school level to the district level, or even the state level. Patterns suggest that closed system structures, with their deficit views and isolated norms, are sadly too prevalent in our society and education system.

Now that we have oriented to the macro framing of types of schools and systems related to families and communities, we will turn to Mapp's "dual capacity-building framework," reproduced in figure 3.7, which shows how educators and families should consider what it means to build systemic shifts for family engagement.

We see that these are the critical mindsets that must be embedded within any high-functioning open system organization. To narrow the focus for our purposes, she identifies four outcomes for educators and for families that we think are critical to help openers identify the current infrastructure at play inside their systems.

Educators are empowered to:

- Connect family engagement to learning and development
- Engage families as co-creators
- Honor family funds of knowledge
- Create welcoming cultures
- Families engage in diverse roles:
- Co-creators

Figure 3.7 Understanding the dual-capacity framework

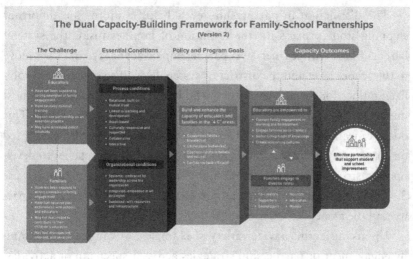

Source: Anne T. Henderson et al., *Beyond the Bake Sale: The Essential Guide to Family-School Partnerships* (New York: The New Press, 2007).

- Supporters
- Encouragers
- Monitors
- Advocates
- Models

Openers both inside and outside the system should take special care and consideration to analyze the current infrastructure within their institutions for these outcomes. We also believe it's important to consider the level of impact for the potential outcome or infrastructure.

An important shift in considering partnership or open system infrastructure came from work inside the Denver Public Schools that focused on understanding levels of partnership. There emerged the concept of three distinct levels of partnership within the school system—learner, school, and district or system—that create the opportunity for a more strategic approach to an open infrastructure analysis. Each level requires a different question and structural focus inside the system. We find that systems rarely consider this distinction, leading to confusion over which level of partnership a given strategy is employing. This focus allows openers to sharpen their understanding of what each level signifies for a different set of opportunities for partnership, engagement, and co-creation.

The distinction in partnership levels helps reinforce an important stepping-stone process for the evolution of families inside the system. Parents begin with learner-level partnership or advocacy, and then move to the school level and the district or system level. It's very hard to mobilize families for district-level work who haven't yet been asked the most important question: "How can we partner to support your child?" This doesn't mean that advocates or openers can't choose a specific level based on community need, but it does encourage strategic approaches to developing a stronger base for action higher up the system structure. Figure 3.8 shows the need to understand the various levels of partnership capacity and the associated relationships.

Upon considering a wide variety of examples, we can see various family engagement or partnership strategies across a spectrum of activities. The Flamboyan Foundation, based in Washington, DC, rightly prioritizes learner-centered partnership strategies, like home visits, that educa-

Figure 3.8 Partnership capacity levels and their associated relationships

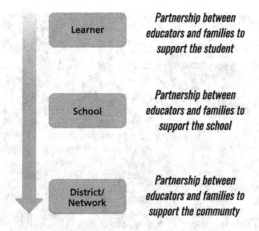

Learner — *Partnership between educators and families to support the student*

School — *Partnership between educators and families to support the school*

District/Network — *Partnership between educators and families to support the community*

tors must employ to maximize the potential of open activities. Organizers like the Memphis Lift and Nuestra Voz often target district or system-level activities for community action.

In figure 3.9, we have mapped a variety of high-impact family and community partnership activities to this level framework to help openers understand the ways in which certain programs can have more strategic impact. In the Year Zero case study, each school prioritized home visits as a critical learner-level strategy to launch the stepping-stone effect and maximize the potential social capital and partnership opportunity for parents. Through leveraging this open system infrastructure for the turn-around project, leaders were able to expand their impact. At Valverde Elementary, this took the form of a parent-teacher leadership team. This team was composed of teachers and parents from each grade level that came together once a month for an active discussion about the future of the school. Drew Schutz, former principal at Valverde, described what it looked like:

> They would all be in the room every morning, right down the hall from the office, and I was always popping in and chatting with them, and sometimes doing a little temperature check on this or that, and that was wonderful. We had a required cadence around when we would do data reports because we were a turnaround school, and so we were commit-ted. One of the things that the community asked for when I got there

Figure 3.9 Partnership capacity levels and their associated activities

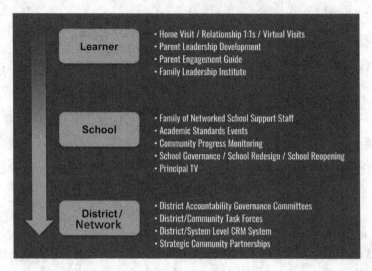

was, "We want to know how the school's doing. We never know until the report card comes out over the summer. We want to have an ongoing conversation about the school." So, we got into this group where we would share our periodic outcomes with families, and say, here's how we're doing. Here's where we're leading and some successes and celebrations. We ended up having this really rich conversation about school performance that was ongoing monthly. We would invite community members to share, and then we would always bring in some sort of outside resource or someone to connect with our families, and that included Padres y Jóvenes Unidos who came to us to do certain presentations, or sometimes the city of Denver.

Drew's example from Valverde shows the power of developing deeper school-level partnership to expand the potential for impact between families and schools. He knew that by expanding family engagement as a reciprocal conduit of energy and information between families and the school, the opportunity for trust building was dramatically increased. Openers must take time to analyze the family and community partnership infrastructure inside systems, how the levels interact, and how they must take a larger view and observe to what extent organizations are operating within the broader ecosystem.

Infrastructure Analysis Reflection

- What is the current status of family and community partnership?
- Which level is currently an opportunity for co-creation or partnership in your system?
- Are there ways to reconsider your level to maximize the stepping-stone effect?
- Are there currently outside actors targeting opportunities that can be leveraged for inside opening?

Ecosystem Analysis

Openers must spend time understanding the relationship between institutional action, like the family and community partnership strategies outlined above, and its relationship with outside organizations. The interplay between both is critical for the development of social capital and for deeper understanding of ecosystem dynamics. Mark Warren, in his article "Communities and Schools," calls out these consequential interrelationships:

> The relationship between the school and other community institutions can also be understood in terms of social capital and social closure . . . We can ask to what extent institutions in a community collaborate with each other and work together for the development of families and children. Institutions serve as sites for building social capital as they bring networks of people and resources to bear on achieving collective ends. Interpersonal relationships between individuals across institutions provide the glue for these collaborations, so the personal and institutional levels interrelate. We should be interested, therefore, both in the ways schools and community organizations form collaborations, and in how these partnerships strengthen relationships within school communities.[12]

As we shared earlier in the Year Zero project vignette, the partnership dynamics between DPS and advocacy organizations were essential in provoking ecosystem shifts toward openness. Knowing your current context helps openers diagnose and consider implications, confronting the historical, present, and future dynamics in the community you work in.

Openers need to understand what is currently being built in their community. Another method and strategy for building shared direction and vision among systems and stakeholders is called the "collective impact" approach. As defined by Strive Together, a leading organization in collective impact work, their theory of action includes: shared community vision, evidence-based decision-making, collaborative action, and investment and sustainability.[13] In communities, collective impact approaches are powerful ways to provoke open system change, and it is a key strategy for leaders across sectors to work together toward shared goals. We encourage readers to learn more about these approaches and whether they are occurring in your community. These are often expansive and comprehensive efforts, requiring significant time and energy—full co-production—which is critically important for openers as they strategically consider ecosystem dynamics or partnerships for their open moment.

Openers should map the organizations in relationship to schools and to the potential open moment that is materializing. The Colorado Education Initiative has often deployed a mapping activity (shown in figure 3.10, below) to help leaders see the connections across their community aligned to an aspiration. It's important to leverage each of the four categories: higher education, business, K–12, and civic. In our experience, leaders in education are really good at the K–12 community mapping but lack either the insight or the commitment to successfully map the other three necessary quadrants. This expansive vision for mapping is also a critical strategy for mitigating elite capture, where those with immense resources take over community processes, and is critical to ensuring that certain voices don't manipulate the democratic system.

By placing the co-creative moment or public value proposition at the center, and then naming and identifying all the stakeholders in relation to the co-creative vision or aspiration, openers can start to identify and map all the potential stakeholders in their community. This rejects traditional "power mapping," and converts a conflict-based approach into a cooperative, shared vision opportunity.

We also strongly recommend that openers spend time understanding the racial, class, gender, and other dynamics of the current community organizations, especially those that have the most power and proximity

Figure 3.10 Colorado Education Initiative mapping activity

Community Mapping

Source: Used with permission from CEI.

to the institutions. Who is the system most keen on partnering with? What are the patterns of affinity at play in the deployment of open system infrastructure inside the system and outside? For example, are organizations committed to open sharing of power and co-creation as they facilitate their agendas? Are partner organizations helping districts understand how to co-create and engage parents and families? Beyond these organizations, are parents and families in communities setting the agenda for the district and for local organizations? If the district is leveraging open system infrastructure to engage parents across the system, are other organizations or organizers working to further the leadership of these families? These are critical questions openers must examine.

Infrastructure and Ecosystem Analysis

Using a closed and open analysis, we propose that there are four types of ecosystems to consider. Table 3.1, along with the explanations below,

Table 3.1 Mapping open and closed ecosystem dynamics

		Institution or System (district, school, or organization)	
		Open	Closed
Ecosystem (community, partners, advocacy groups)	Open	Open-Open	Open-Closed
	Closed	Closed-Open	Closed-Closed

helps openers begin to unpack and understand their context by analyzing open versus closed in both institutional and external contexts.

Closed-Closed

The direst scenario is sadly too common in our educational system. In these cases, both the school systems that serve our communities and the surrounding community organizations are operating in a closed position. A closed ecosystem occurs when both the district or school is closed to engagement, and the actors surrounding the system are closed to partnership. Actors demonstrate a closed position by being unwilling to engage in processes or by refusing to engage productively. Unproductive engagement can grow out of an understandable lack of trust. It can manifest as low energy or low trust across actors. They perpetuate suspicion, mistrust, failed partnerships, and a continual state of friction.

> *Example: The school district releases its school quality system with no community feedback, including no feedback on the design of the report, and it fails to translate the documents into multiple languages. Community organizations don't even know it has been released, and nearly all parents have no idea the district published the material. Advocacy groups either don't engage or don't exist.*

Open-Closed

In this scenario, a district is not committed to building the open system, but ecosystem actors partner and work collaboratively. Often in this scenario, government agencies, nonprofits, and other entities spin around the district's orbit, trying to crack open pieces for partnership or changed outcomes. This often leads to massive conflict, isolated work, and resistance to openness and partnership. But, through breakthrough leadership in both external and internal roles, the possibility of moving to open-open exists.

> *Example: A local advocacy organization builds a coalition around an important issue that parents and families are concerned about. They present their findings to board members and district officials with some interest but no urgency. Eventually, the parents and community organizations take their concerns to the media, who publish a report highlighting the frustration and holding the district to account. The district is faced with a decision—to open or to remain closed?*

The Memphis Lift often found itself in this position, seeking to provoke the local school district into action on issues of justice and inequity. John Little shares:

> You know I'm a rabble-rouser. I have to show them that I'm not afraid to challenge the status quo. I want you (the parents) to watch me, because I want them to watch me because I'm going to ask you to do the same thing to learn how to challenge, to learn how to then forge and build relationships when you challenge somebody. The first thing they're going to ask for is a meeting, great. When you get into this meeting you have to narrate, "This is how you conduct the meeting, you're respectful, you listen but you make your demands upfront," and I tell you they're going to be very nice to you. They're going to offer you coffee because that's what people do. But stick to your guns, and you don't shy away.

Closed-Open

In this ecosystem, the district or system is attempting or committed to openness, but the actors surrounding the system are resistant to partnership. Maybe there is precedent that has disappointed or burned families or community partners in the past. Or perhaps there is organizational resistance based on a personality conflict. In many cases, people often doubt (with good reason) the sincerity of the open system's attempt to build a culture of engagement. So even if the system is attempting or generating openness, the actors are resistant to fully partnering in openness.

Example A: The district is seeking to build a new community advisory panel to help them understand how to expand to a new neighborhood. After years of pushback, mindsets have shifted inside the organization and the leadership is deeply committed to giving power to others to shape the course of a network. However, given the history of nonengagement and previous interactions with other closed systems, families and advocates are unwilling to partner. They say, "It'll just be another stupid committee that doesn't follow through."

Example B: A charter school is launching a new initiative and fails to build any community buy-in or participation to guide the work. Advocacy groups and parents are used to this and become disengaged, so whatever proposal comes out is met with suspicion and/or resistance.

As many readers can attest, too many efforts in our communities fall into closed activities or mindsets. History of oppression and institutional discrimination create patterns where both sides fail to build the openness that would take them to the next level. Due to these factors, a closed ecosystem prevails.

Open-Open

In this setting, systems work hand in hand (sometimes cooperatively and sometimes antagonistically, maybe both in different ways through public and private dialogue) in a spirit of push and pull with organizations and groups who are also committed to community co-creation. These temporary alliances emerge like tidal forces where the give and take generates tremendous amounts of open energy between all actors. The community and civic organizations will connect schools to the entire fabric of civic life and provide a vital feedback loop.

In this open-open model, the building of a circle of exchange between system-level efforts to open up schools to communities and families is consciously matched with a partnership orientation toward community and civic organizations. In *The Gardens of Democracy*, the authors describe the opportunity that results from this amount of feedback and partnership and state that "modern governments should seek also to create hurricane-like storms of pro-social activity."[14] Open-open ecosystems generate these storms intentionally.

In these systems, the openness of the education system and schools produce partnerships and new potential in other organizations. This is the ideal goal that we aspire to as we seek to build open systems in communities. It is not a paradise or a gauzy cooperation, but rather dynamic tension between actors inside and outside the system who understand that open moments must be seized and leveraged. Openers in these situations are not immune from outside critique, but actually seek the pressure from outside actors to further the impact and political leverage inside the system.

Example A: A school district is working to build a home visit system that trains educators to go out and spend time building relationships and partnerships with families. At pilot schools, the district partners with local parent organizing groups. The parent organizers work with the leadership of the schools to take the newly activated parents from the home visitations and form parent leadership teams to work on community and local issues. The parents, along with community organizations, present back to the Board of Education to advocate for a change in discipline policy.

Example B: An advocacy group creates a media campaign suggesting that a charter network doesn't promote the leadership of its parents. In response, the charter network creates a family leadership institute to develop parents as advocates, partnering with the advocacy group directly. The network works with a local network that includes civil rights groups so that parents in the leadership institute can work with organizations across issue areas. These civil rights groups build a new coalition with the parents to help them understand community needs, and together they propose new initiatives to be responsive to community concerns.

Understanding the institution and ecosystem behavior along a closed-open spectrum allows openers to fully map and understand the current state of interaction in their environment. We saw this work manifest in the Year Zero schools, where each of the leaders was committed to the co-creation and ongoing partnership with their families and other local organizations, while at the same time the district overall leveraged the pressure from outside groups to ensure political sustainability for change.

Ecosystem Reflection

- How would you diagnose your ecosystem?
- Is the ecosystem around the district or schools helping the system become more open?
- What other actors are operating in your ecosystem and supporting either closed or open behavior?

As we shared earlier, over time the increase in institutional trust and partnership led to increased academic and social outcomes. This powerful reparative work increased parent involvement and trust, creating conditions to show communities that their voice and power in local democracy could matter. As openers move into the next section, on identifying your open moment, it is critical to start from a reasoned and sharp analysis of the current state of opening in your community.

IDENTIFYING YOUR OPEN MOMENT

Open leaders identify opportunities for cracking open the system when the leadership, governance, and community align in their aims and capacity.

We cannot assume that co-creation or co-production is always possible just because we, as openers, believe it is, or because others we trust tell us it is the right thing to do. To provoke or push a system to co-creation, in particular the American education system, without fully acknowledging the political and practical realities and dynamics of representative democracy is a mission to lose trust and credibility within a community.

This is a challenge for many openers and community-minded leaders. The first natural and often admirable instinct of many leaders who seek transformational redesign is to "do what the community wants!" We understand that after years of top-down "reform" this orientation can feel very attractive. Identifying the right strategic opportunity for internal and external co-creation is a central precept of open system work—this is your *open moment*.

Leaders at every part of the education system often find themselves pinched between multiple levels of authorization and accountability.

School leaders sit between communities and the district. District leaders sit between communities, schools, and the state. State education leaders get pinched between districts, state government, and the federal infrastructure. Sitting between these multiple authorizers as an open leader in any role can lead to paralysis—the inability to act, even as the political pressure mounts. Serving as an open leader in this context requires identifying an open moment that does not go beyond what a leader is authorized to do, but also does not avoid the issues that are at the forefront for the community.

For example, if in the Year Zero work each of the leaders had led on their own, without a broader commitment to the full investment of their governance structure (DPS school board), leadership (the superintendent), or community, each of the Year Zero schools would have failed in either the early phases, when it became clear there wasn't deep investment for the work (either operationally or from resources), or in the later phases when the work would have required governance sign off from the school board. The end result would have been an overall degradation of trust in the capacity of the system and real blowback from the community. Imagine if after all of that political pressure from the ¡Ya Basta! coalition, the district had decided to focus on middle schools in southeast Denver instead. It would have completely missed its open moment, perpetuating mistrust and closed system structures.

In the Memphis Lift and Nuestra Voz examples, each of the organizing efforts began from an understanding of whether or not there was board or leadership support to be able to deliver the win. In cases where that didn't exist, or where the additional pressure from outside the system wouldn't materialize the support, the result would either be a failure or a loss for the community. Organizers and mobilizers know this work intuitively. They must take care and effort to identify the possible constellations of system alignment or misalignment so that a push will provoke real openness. If they constantly launch provocations that are misaligned to the moment, they will lose the trust of their members, and therefore their power to provoke change.

This open moment is the strategic alignment of executive sponsorship, governance support, and community energy around a particular strategy or goal. The work of the opener is to identify—through a deep understanding of their community, their broader ecosystem, and their own leadership—the moment when and the place where the maximum impact can be leveraged.

What is the specific co-creation question and opportunity you are intending to pursue? Is this redesigning a school? A statewide initiative? A school discipline system? An afterschool program? Whatever the first answer, get even more specific—the sharper the question, the deeper the open moment becomes. In the following chapters, you will learn of more open moments—at the district level in Boulder, the state level in Kentucky and New Mexico, and the city level in Chicago. Each example helps us understand the strategic choices leaders create to facilitate openness in their communities. But for now, begin to name what it might be for you.

Your Open Moment, Version One

Use this space to sketch out your first thoughts on your open moment . . . what are you called to co-create?

Diagnosing the Moment

Let's dig into the open moment you just identified. Where does it stand inside the system, with community partners, and with the governance of the system itself? We offer an open opportunity matrix (see table 3.2) for you to map out a current initiative for which you are thinking about leading co-creative work. The matrix is designed with the assumption that external actors (such as organizers or community groups) are aligned for the open moment. This is a critical first step that is necessary for open moment seeking. To move into your open moment, you must know the ecosystem is called to the topic . . . even if it is emergent and not fully formed!

This matrix helps open leaders inside the system find the strategic sweet spot where they can find the commitment to the co-creative work from both the governance (legitimacy and support) and leadership (operational capacity) partners. Without these two critical democratic actors in play, the co-creation will be ground down in the political jaws of a struggling board or disappear into the bureaucratic dust of resisters.

No-No: Opener as Listener. If both commitments are a No, then the work of the opener is to listen. In this case, they are misaligned with both of their key constituencies and routes for opening. It is a moment for humble reflection on the co-creative task and question at hand. It may mean rethinking the open opportunity and reflecting on whether or not you are particularly attuned to the moment. In many cases, it may mean pivoting to another issue where you can find co-creative alignment. Remember, this is about long-term systems change and building the capacity to move from closed to open. Just because the current issue isn't ready, doesn't mean it won't be ready in the future, and it may mean that another topic is ripe for co-creation.

Table 3.2 Open opportunity window matrix (assuming the community is aligned)

		Governance commitment to co-creative work	
		No	Yes
Leadership commitment to co-creative work	Yes	Learn	Lead
	No	Listen	Learn

No-Yes: Opener as Learner. When either the governance or the leadership says No on a specific co-creation proposal and the other says Yes, the work of the opener must turn to a learner posture. The opener must pivot toward a deeper understanding of what is possible, asking important and tough questions about what is on and off the table. This may mean political compromise and shifting the question itself around.

Yes-Yes: Opener as Leader. If both the leadership and governance commitments are aligned as Yes on the opportunity for co-creation, even if they are not 100 percent aligned on what it means, it creates the potential for openness. In the Year Zero process, the superintendent and senior district staff were committed to the project, and the board was invested in the potential for the transformation. In Memphis and New Orleans, the opportunities for the biggest changes came from when the Memphis Lift or Nuestra Voz understood where the governance structure was and where the leadership was, creating the politically catalytic moment to provoke them to action. Sometimes, these actors need to be

---

Considering Shifting Alignment

It's important to remember that these positions and contexts are variable and movable based on the politics and changing contours of narratives at play in your community. This is why we are using frames such as *listen* and *learn* when the misalignment is occurring for co-creation, pushing you and your partners to understand how you might shift to facilitate the alignment of the opportunity and political moment. What is aligned in October may not be in January, hence much of the cadence work we will discuss in the next chapter.

This is where the examples of Year Zero and the community organizing groups we've identified are so important for this chapter. In one case we have a system that wants to open up based on their learnings and leadership, having aligned all the relevant actors to produce an open moment. In the other cases, we have community organizations who are in the business of pushing systems to move toward alignment.

Identifying Your Open Moment Reflection

- Where do your current thoughts and ideas about co-creation align on the opportunity matrix?
- If you are in listener mode, why do you think that is?
- If you are in learner mode, what do you still need to learn and explore?
- If you are in leader mode, what other questions do you need to ask or answer to fully ensure that this is correct?

---

pushed or pulled into full Yes mode, but the key here is understanding alignment.

To redesign education and reignite democracy requires a strategic opportunity that aligns with the current context and political situation of an institution or organization. If openers are not directly attuned to the realities of this on the ground and to these ever-changing dynamics, they can inadvertently create a situation that actually pushes a system toward closed behavior out of fear or distrust, or that reduces the belief that the system has the ability to change. Open system work requires educational and community leaders and members to consistently assess and maximize the constellation of opportunities for co-creation and co-production.

CONCLUSION

Throughout this chapter we have explored how to think differently about community, how to get specific and sharp about the co-creative moment in your particular community, and how to map out the current ecosystem you are operating within. We must begin with community, understanding it and cultivating ecosystem awareness if we are to begin any open system work. The fundamental nature of open system work means we must be students of our communities, in learner postures and collaborating alongside others to make it happen.

After *preparing* for the past two chapters, we now move into action to transform systems from closed to open. In the next chapter, we will move into the *provoking* phase, beginning with constructing the vehicle for breaking through closed systems with your co-creative work—designing breakthrough spaces that move a system from closed to open.

CHAPTER 4

Open Principle 3

Design Breakthrough Spaces

We need to create spaces to understand how people see education . . . knowing that the community is broad and encompasses people of different roles, backgrounds and interests . . . All of these things are important to consider so that when you reach a decision under these conditions, you can be accountable for the results of the space you've created.

Dr. Antwan Jefferson

The promise of community is not a pledge of easy intimacy or innocent harmony.

Philip Selznik, *The Moral Commonwealth*

He that will not apply new remedies must expect new evils; for time is the greatest innovator.

Sir Francis Bacon, quoted in *The Crisis of the Old Order*

BIG IDEAS IN THIS CHAPTER

- Radical clarity
- Inclusive democracy
- Cadence for maximum impact
- Breaking the addiction to closed systems

Figure 4.1

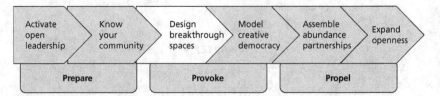

DESIGN BREAKTHROUGH SPACES

Starting a community-driven process can sometimes feel like watching a train wreck happen. Many times, when we have supported or watched a group launch a large- or small-scale public process, the question of who got to be involved in the process and how the process was built felt like a trap leading directly into the closed system. Countless hours were lost in the quest to get it right and ensure a stakeholder process that had the right people involved. Inevitably, community members were frustrated and angry. We often were too.

It is always very disappointing when, even in the most exciting or generative project, we are left with a sense that the closed system prevailed. It sometimes feels as if time and the closed system are meeting secretly to work against us. Over time, through open system analysis, repeated failures, and honest conversation about our traditional methods of building spaces we have determined that they require an innovative design to break through closed systems.

The last two chapters have been about the *preparing* phases for open system work—activating open leadership and knowing your community—each creating the potential conditions for change. These aspects ground openers in the personal and professional conditions of open system work so they can sustain themselves personally and arrive with a deep understanding of their community in the open moment that they are called to act upon. We now turn to what we call the *provoking* phases of the work—designing and holding space to break through closed systems, and then modeling the creative democracy necessary to inspire an open system.

Here, in the provoking phase, we will challenge the closed system directly and build new ways of opening up. Leaders often find it easy to commit to co-creation, bringing along communities who are inspired and ready to take on big questions, yet lose their will when designing and modeling the path forward.

Provoking this change means we need to hold spaces prepared for the incredible resistance and challenges they will meet. Failure happens when leaders or systems are blurry about the target for change, recreating patterns of bias and affinity through co-creating and co-producing with the same people who had a hand in creating the legacy closed system, and failing to build real momentum for the change. In most processes, this means that the possibilities and potential for open system work never truly crack open the system completely.

Through the case study of Boulder Valley [Colorado] School District, we will explore how the system came together to design a breakthrough space to address one of the most closed systems that all communities struggle with—school discipline—and ended up creating an innovative, community-owned solution.

In this chapter, you will be exposed to real and concrete strategies for designing these spaces. These strategies—radical clarity, democratic inclusion, maximizing cadence, and liberating from addiction to closed systems—can collectively provoke numerous opportunities to open the system up. Since we believe there are many variations on the ideas included in this chapter, we encourage you to go out and explore and innovate yourself. Openers must heed the lessons and warnings to ensure the spaces they create can hold the power of the community change they seek. From our experience, these strategies are essential not only to ensure a successful process but also to reach the larger goal—provoking the system to open up.

Open Vignette: Boulder Equity Council

In Boulder, Colorado, in the aftermath of the George Floyd murder in June 2020, the local NAACP passed a resolution requesting the removal of School Resource Officers (SROs). In many school districts around the country, SROs act as extensions of local police departments operating in schools, sometimes hired by the district directly and sometimes outsourced to the police department. Over and over across the country, both educators and advocates have called attention to the disturbing and structural disparities in discipline that often lead to what some call the "school-to-prison pipeline."

While some leaders may have either ignored or attempted knee-jerk responses to the community push, Boulder superintendent Rob Anderson, his board, and his senior leadership team decided to commit to deeper community co-creation in the process. They reached out to the Colorado Education Initiative (CEI) to support a community process to look at the issue. After initial discussion, it became clear that by establishing an equity council that represented the most impacted stakeholders, Boulder could get important recommendations for the question at hand and build up long-term infrastructure in the district for equity-related community decision-making.

As the superintendent established the council tasked with this important question, he created even stronger conditions for modeling and setting up democratic leadership in his system. In partnering with his board for this co-creation, he was also able to model the power of coordination and cooperation. Richard Garcia, a Boulder Valley School Board member and longtime community activist, explained why they approached the issue: "The school board had a pretty lengthy conversation on removing school resource officers from our schools. Based on research, we understood that the school-to-prison pipeline is a real challenge. We started understanding the disproportionality of discipline between kids of color and the white students. So we charged the superintendent to think of ways that he might be able to be inclusive in getting people together to talk about school resource officers."[1]

Open leaders like Rob Anderson understand the need and urgency of this open approach, while also acknowledging and incorporating the inevitable realities. Superintendent Anderson shared his thoughts on the issue:

> The stakes in the conversation and decision are really high. This was right on the heels on the murder of George Floyd. I knew that it would be important to not make this in isolation, but together with our community, because these decisions have lasting impacts for decades. We felt

like it was really important not to go too fast, to take the right amount of time to make a decision that we could move forward with confidence. It shouldn't be a decision that just boards or superintendents make in isolation, because we come and go—it was absolutely the responsible thing to deepen the community engagement to get it right.

This was a politically fraught endeavor, involving multiple police departments and pressure from the left and the right, along with divisions on the board. Yet Anderson challenged himself and his community to a community-driven process, not only with the new equity council but with a district accountability committee to ensure that different groups had a voice in the process.

From the beginning, Boulder was committed to creating a different approach to co-creation to ensure maximum impact for the recommendations of the equity council. Boulder has experienced pain and challenges in recruitment for task forces and committees before, including low turnout and the "same ol' recruits" problem. To innovate in this important conversation, Boulder approached the work with a different lens, building the potential for democratic inclusion. To form the council, the district employed three recruitment strategies with support from CEI, ultimately gathering a group that dynamically reflected the district.

Going through the process, the Boulder equity council committed to spending time listening and learning about the current challenges in the system surrounding student discipline and the exploring the realities of the current system. Leaders from the district had to confront painful and honest truths about the challenges of the SRO process. This included uneven requirements for the role, different expectations in different schools, and real-life consequences for Black and Brown students' experiences with SROs. The equity council also committed to urgent action and momentum, driving toward a decision within six weeks to secure board votes on any recommendations. There was vigorous discussion in the space around the real safety implications of the potential decisions and no clear preference in the group for a path forward.

At the end of the process, the recommendations that came through the group showed that clear consensus existed around ending the current configuration of the SROs, transforming and redesigning the role, moving forward with students and communities, and partnering inside the system to address further systemic issues.

Over two years later, the new Student Safety Advocates are living examples of a co-creation resulting from a breakthrough space that created maximum political capital for leadership to push a system forward. 2022 Data from BVSD shows substantial shifts in the system:

- Overall reductions
  - 390 fewer suspensions
  - 108 fewer referrals to law enforcement
- Overall increases
  - 935 more restorative interventions
  - 60 more alternative suspensions
  - 89 fewer Latino students were suspended or expelled than in 2018–19[2]

While issues of disproportionality and efforts are still needed to address systemic injustices in the Boulder system, these significant improvements show the power of the community-driven approach to solving one of the most pernicious issues in education. How did this space get designed? How did it represent the community? How did the space withstand the political pressure? These are the questions and discussions ahead.

RADICAL CLARITY

To fully break open closed systems, leaders must be exceptionally clear about the parameters of the space they are seeking to hold.

The closed system conspires to blur, confuse, and obfuscate leaders. When addressing the natural and real complexity of communities that we've discussed in the previous chapters, closed systems fail to get entirely clear about the purpose and task ahead. Closed systems prey upon the anxiety of leaders who fear "the community" or the strain of a long, protracted political process. There are so many issues to talk to a community about, so many potential questions—so why choose?

Why is there this belief that during community processes, our most important democratic ventures in education, clarity can be shortcut?

Why are we stuck in the same pattern of ineffective community building? The phrase "building the plane while flying it," flippantly yet seriously uttered too often in community work, is a recipe for disaster. Designing breakthrough spaces should commit us to intentionally seeking clarity to ensure that open moments lead to lasting change.

Leaders must be sharp and clear about what the space will or won't hold, and they must be particularly clear on the timeline and the opportunity that it entails. Does that mean a process for open system work must be narrow? Not necessarily. We've seen strong processes that include multiple questions for discussion or recommendation. But they are always trickier than others and more complicated. They require significantly more maneuvering, and the potential for the space that is created during the process to do more than boil over—even rip apart—is tremendous.

In Boulder, Rob Anderson was very clear on what was on the table—recommendations about SROs moving forward. Within that, he was willing to embrace the depth of complexity in SRO roles—where they were located, their job descriptions, how they partnered with the system, and the like. Inevitably, when smart people get together in a co-creative space like the equity council, people illuminate other issues that invariably touch on related issues. But the tight framing and clarity of focus was able to ensure that we were able to refocus the group when the context was challenging. At multiple points in the Boulder process, the group wanted to expand and extend the scope of the questions the board and superintendent had requested. What about school discipline systems? What about recruiting teachers of color? How about afterschool opportunities for students who are more likely to suffer in a challenging discipline system? While all these issues relate and are interconnected with school discipline and the SRO role, they had to be off the table in order for the district and community to achieve anything in the process. Superintendent Anderson shared the need for radical clarity:

> You see it all the time: a loosely defined process, people with agendas they want to push, bad outcomes, and then we wonder why it doesn't go well. We knew people would be passionate on both sides of the issue. This will always be the case if you're trying to open things up. The

Why Call It a "Space"?

We design these spaces using technical and adaptive strategies for calling a community into existence and action, whether it's the parents of your classroom or a new district task force. This isn't just your regular school task force or district initiative—designing breakthrough spaces is directed toward provoking disruption in closed systems. That is a concept that goes beyond a simple committee meeting, and we have to see it as a space that holds the energy and potential for hopes, fears, healing, and more to be explored and pursued.

We are particularly compelled by the metaphors and images conjured by Otto Scharmer in *Theory U* about social emergence, adrienne maree brown's concepts of "holding fractal change," and Ron Heifetz's work around holding environments. It has been helpful for us to conceptualize these events, processes, and projects as "spaces" that we are holding alongside communities. In her book *Holding Change*, adrienne maree brown states it beautifully as she learned from a teacher:

> When we are in proximity to each other . . . we are literally sitting in each other's fields, co-creating a vibration unique to us. As often as you can, move people into proximity with each other, into direct conversation and mutual exchange of energy. Allow relationships in the room to grow at the scale of reality—initially one to one.[3]

We have seen how intense these spaces can get, especially when issues of liberation and transformation get discussed. Within these spaces people begin to see the "other" as connected to them, confronting long-held assumptions about themselves as well. Creating these opportunities requires the channeling, holding, and sustaining of enormous potential energy. In turn, holding these spaces allows openers to reimagine their role as beyond a simple task force facilitator or convener. As Valeria Martinez, manager of implementation and partnership at CEI, reminds us often, "We are in the business of holding spaces for people to dream and build, to process their trauma, to see each other as humans."

Understanding these opportunities as spaces allows us also to accept that they can take many forms and manifestations. You could be designing an event, a multiday discussion, or a long-term committee. In the provoking phase—this chapter and the next—we get very technical about our experiences with how these spaces get strong enough to sustain the powerful forces of closed systems.

difference is getting to a solution that we can move forward on together. A lot of good intentions and smart people lead to scope creep that changes the task into everything everyone cares about. It feels counterintuitive, but you have to go narrow and sharpen the focus. The idea of radical clarity helps us understand that there is a relationship between time and intensity to get you there. How can you be radically clear if you're working forever on something?

Let's think about potential versus kinetic energy. If the space designed is not sharp, clear, and designed to hold the energy that the community and political system is prepared to wield, then it will likely overload or be underwhelmed. If we imagine radical clarity as our first attempt to wire the system up for transformation, then we cannot be sloppy about the electrification system required.

That's why we often say "clarity is a gift you give to yourself and other people" at the outset of a process. At the beginning of designing a space, openers and the system leaders they partner with spend extra time asking more questions at the front end, exposing potential contradictions in processes or structures, and consolidating tasks whenever possible. By confronting these process vagaries with clarity questions, openers can begin to sharpen their open moment into a clearer sense of how the space can be built, energized, and defined. The questions in table 4.1 help you explore potential vagaries and how to push clarifying moments.

Liberatory Breakthrough Spaces

In this provoking phase of open system work, we are constructing vehicles and mechanisms for the disruption and shifting of systems from closed to open. Here are some important questions to ask as you are designing a breakthrough space:

- *Radical Clarity.* Who are the voices building clarity for the project? How can you ensure the voices furthest from power are also shaping the articulation of clarity?
- *Inclusive Democracy.* How are you rigorously ensuring the participation of the broadest range of races, classes, ages, backgrounds, languages, and identities in the process? How are you challenging the tendency for systems to say that re-cruiting these voices is too difficult?
- *Cadence for Maximum Impact.* As you are moving and ac-celerating for maximum impact and effectiveness, are you creating one-to-one and small-group opportunities to check in with those furthest from power in the process? How are you adjusting or augmenting based on their feedback?
- *Breaking the Addiction to Closed Systems.* As you are no-ticing addictions to closed systems, are you checking your thinking with others in the community or inside the system to confirm or pressure-test your assumptions?

With radical clarity, we can see how the absurdity of "building the plane while flying it" ensures most open system or partnership processes fail, reinforcing closed system behavior instead of opening it up like they ought to. Nothing reinforces a closed system more than a big political disaster spurred by an attempt to open up to their community.

Openers need clarity for another reason: it helps ensure accountabil-ity when opening goes off track. As we've discussed before, opening is no easy task. Whether it is an effort to open a classroom or a district enroll-ment system, once multiple perspectives and stakeholders enter the equa-tion, we are working under pressure. Openers need clarity so that they

Table 4.1 Seeking radical clarity

Process Vagaries	Clarity Questions
Too many ideas of what the space needs to take on	What is the work at the center we are trying to get to in this process? Are there other processes that could reduce this burden? How can you find more depth in the sharpness of the question vs breadth in too many issues?
Different concepts of the open moment	Have you asked a variety of partners if they see the opportunity or question for co-creation? What is on and off the table?
Unclear roles of staff supporting the process	Who will lead the staff side? Who will be responsible for ensuring the work keeps moving? Is there an outside partner that can help?
Not sure how the space is functioning within the current system	Is the task force reporting back to the board? To the superintendent?
Another process starts and complicates the mission of the process	Can we narrow the work of this process and ask the other group to take on some of this work? Can we pause the other process?

can know their role and hold others accountable for not meeting the moment the process requires. The history of public education is replete with leaders who act big at the start of the process and then disappear when it gets hot. Clarity ensures they stay close to the fire like they promised.

INCLUSIVE DEMOCRACY

To achieve significant breakthroughs, openers must build responsive democratic spaces that include and represent community voices.

The democratic promise of a breakthrough space relies on the thoughtful composition of who is involved. As Mark Moore taught us, the ability to gather legitimacy and support from the authorizing environment is critical to public system design and to the ability to generate co-creation. In our education system, the inability to build legitimacy and support erodes trust in the institution and the ability for decisions to lead to breakthroughs. Process after process fails because it doesn't meet the democratic opportunity that co-creation requires—that is, not having the right people at the table. In *The Moral Commonwealth*, Philip Selznick poses a line of communitarian inquiry critical to co-creation: "The

---

Radical Clarity Reflection

- Where are leaders or partners trying to widen the scope for breadth vs building capacity for depth?
- How are you staying close to the fire when the process challenges you and others?
- Have you named what you are concerned about and worried about to others? Do they share the same concern?

---

political community is led to ask: 'What kind of a people do we believe we are?'"[4] This is the central question in designing a breakthrough space, ensuring the space represents and is a democratic exemplar of the community it belongs to.

The practice of inclusive democracy ensures not just that the process is stronger but that the democratic potential grows in a community. This section highlights our first attempts to create this in action through the Boulder equity council, now replicated across many projects.

Over time, we've been forced to unpack this addiction to closed system and antidemocratic mental models in education task forces or committee design. We believe it stems from the intersection of lack of creativity, incomplete analysis of the problem, and inadequate capacity to address the issue. District and school leaders are so busy that often to be creative with their approaches runs up against real time constraints. Many people just go forward with committees or structures without understanding the relevance to legitimacy or democracy building. Leaders fear the results of innovation, deciding against manifesting their exciting ideas for how to build open, dynamic spaces.

During our writing and research, we were exposed to the exceptional book *Open Democracy* by Hélène Landemore. The central premise of the book is to explore the nature of an open democracy that can manifest the full power of participatory democracy beyond current structures of representation. We were inspired to see how her writing and analysis reinforced what you are about to read, including how leveraging random selection of parents and students could be a form of open democracy. She describes her concept:

[It] aims to change minds, develop intuitions, and expand our imagina-
tions by introducing into our conceptual toolbox a new paradigm of
democracy and a new metaphor: open democracy. Open democracy is
the ideal of a regime in which actual exercise of power is accessible to
ordinary citizens via novel forms of democratic representation.[5]

In our previous experience with districts or schools, we often would
use one application process to construct a democratic space. Applications would open, and then the battle would begin to construct a group
that satisfied all stakeholder groups; usually, this battle for the future
of the committee was being fought behind closed doors. In her book,
Landemere calls this "enclosure of power"—the restriction of democratic
processes.[6] Inevitably, the trade-offs and challenges create real strain on
internal and external relationships. Internal advocates jockey for those
they believe would be strongest. External advocates are always skeptical
about who gets selected and why. The legitimacy of those at the table is
called into question, trust is degraded, and the circle begins again. Rob
Anderson explains the pattern we are trying to break and the work to
address it.

Some people view the committee as the solution. We know the solution
was never to put together a committee. If leaders invest in a committee
and then, when it fails to build momentum, the community says it didn't
work, the committee becomes a joke, which degrades the trust in committees to do the work, and good people don't want to serve. Depending
on the problem, if the committee fails and falters, the response back to
the board is that "Oh well, the community couldn't figure it out." This is
why the practice shifts matter to build a more representative community
space. You need to form a team that is a reflection of the complexity of
the issue. If you seek that out on the front end, then you'll have more
confidence on the back end that it represents the issue and to speak for
the community.

Failure to build a space that represents the community is a reminder of
how closed systems fail communities in this essential task. Openers must
see their work as creating inclusively democratic spaces to lead a community through its open moment. Many of the communities furthest from

power and opportunity have been repeatedly burned by community processes, so they are afraid of ever participating again. For them, poor facilitation and even poorer outcomes have taught them to steer clear of such potential open moments. They have seen the elite and powerful co-opt processes for their own benefit. In other cases, the system itself is terrified of what it would mean to put a diverse group together. But here we must come back to Selznick's question. Whether in Boulder; Chicago; Burlington, Vermont; or Raton, New Mexico, democratic inclusion requires us to build a space that represents what kind of people we see ourselves as, in particular as related to the question and open moment at hand.

Over time and with practice, we began to understand and apply potential solutions to address these intersecting problems in a high-variety way. We now call this approach "inclusive democracy," which, through its framework design, supports openers in creating a representative body, whether in a school, district, or community. We call it inclusive democracy to put special emphasis on the fact that the inclusive nature of the process amplifies and accelerates the democratic potential of the group. As background, in earlier stages of open system work we called this "radical inclusion," but we found that did not sharply engage the practitioner's understanding of the role of the group as a democratic catalyst. We then added the modifier inclusive to also address the fact that, for too many of our communities, democracy had failed to meet its promise, whether in classrooms and districtwide practices, or in our broader society in such areas as voting or civil rights. Inclusive democracy is therefore in alignment with Selznick's communitarian charge to build a space worthy of the people.

In Boulder, inclusive democracy was manifested as a breakthrough design in the equity council. From the very start, the group was anchored in the idea of democratic inclusion that would bring all different kinds of voices to the table. This was essential, as Boulder Valley equity director Amy Nelson shared with us: "Once the equity council was established, I think district leaders, the board, and community members recognized the importance of bringing folks together to really talk about the issues of equity within the district, and the forming of the equity council demonstrated its power in creating systemic change and bringing in voices that are historically marginalized."

When we started considering the challenge of building and designing spaces to interrupt closed systems, we sought out research on deliberative design, communitarianism, and cooperative structures. While we found much that was fascinating and compelling, it was mostly extremely time- and resource-intensive models that were poorly matched to the needs of education systems and the communities they served. In our experience, an unwieldy or extensive new community process is a hindrance to moving forward. It's simply not realistic in most systems.

Once we started to consider the *nature* of this challenge—designing a space to break through closed systems—we started to work out how to take the typical container leveraged by school systems, such as a task force or a committee, and place inclusive democracy within it, instead of asking the entire world to shift their schema. This became a high-variety redesign of the current construct, fostering an innovative and imaginative space for community dreams to manifest. We leveraged current constructs while embedding the possibilities of an open democratic model to build the full conditions for a body that would both withstand intense political pressure and represent the broader community. Therefore, the inclusive democracy framework was born, as shown in figure 4.2.

Figure 4.2 The inclusive democracy framework

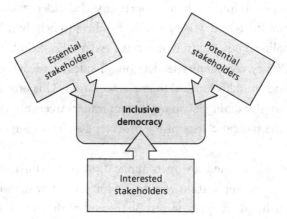

We believe that for open system processes to be successful, we first must understand who needs to be at the table. We've come to see that there are three strategic groups that it is possible to draw from: stakeholders you know need to be involved (essential stakeholders), those who want to be involved (interested stakeholders), and those whose participation is uncommon but necessary (potential stakeholders). This model is essential to addressing the challenge of elite capture, when particular groups commandeer democratic structures to pursue unrepresentative ideas or beliefs. The practice of inclusive democracy offers a way forward to mitigate this strategy. Marcus Bratton, director of implementation and partnership at CEI, shared his thoughts on how this model disrupts traditional closed system patterns.

> Often, we think it is sufficient to broadcast to a community that we are looking for volunteers to participate in a democratic process. However, typically in these cases, we end up getting a response from the same stakeholders who are always a part of the conversation, meaning that the end result may not truly reflect the diverse voices of a community. Instead, in Boulder we leveraged different strategies for each stakeholder, including the "jury duty" style approach, where we reached out directly to individuals in a randomly selected group and said, "Here is what's happening, and we are particularly interested in your unique perspective."

The first step was to build out the essential stakeholder group and to coordinate the naming of these important stakeholders with the superintendent and the board. (Using board members to help build this group increased political buy-in.) In Boulder, the essential stakeholders included the NAACP, key community leaders on all sides of the issue, and staff members who would be critical to implementation. This process also can create meaningful dialogue among system leaders to ensure they are still aligned on the radical clarity of the process, usually an important thing to revisit.

Next, BVSD created an open application to recruit the interested stakeholders. The application was online for just a few days before they had over one hundred applications. By the end of the first week, the district had over five hundred applications. At the end of the two weeks, they had over nine hundred applicants interested in serving on the equity council, the largest applicant pool the district had ever seen. Through coordination between the district and CEI, a shared rubric helped align the key aspects of the application. For BVSD, it was an inspiring moment to hear the stories of the folks who wanted to be on the council, why they cared about the issue, and how they saw it as important for their community.

After the application process, BVSD began the important work of re-cruiting the potential stakeholders. This is where and how many systems and processes fall apart. Instead of back-end recruitment that often fails to bring real perspective into the space, we tried a new method of random selection to pull students and families from across the Boulder Valley system into the process. Working with the district information technol-ogy and system team, CEI and BVSD devised an approach, akin to jury selection, in which we reached out to Boulder residents who might oth-erwise have never known about the process. We've come to see through Landemore's *Open Democracy* that leveraging random selection, or *sor-tition*, is both a historical foundation of democracy (seen in Athens) and an emerging innovation in the democracy space (in Iceland and across the US).[7] Together, district and school leaders worked to matriculate these randomly selected students, family members, and teachers into the equity council. Board vice chair Lisa Sweeney-Miran shared why this process shift was so important to BVSD.

> I think it became apparent very quickly that the missing component was hearing directly from folks who were immediately impacted, and who might have the most stories to tell or bear the greatest brunt of the dif-ficulties in terms of interactions with SROs and police officers generally. So, from there we were trying to figure out what's the best way to bring the community in to be a part of this conversation, to hear those experi-ences and to really make sure that their voices are heard in this process.

The results spoke for themselves: the group was 80 percent from com-munities of color, and it included parents, students, and a wide range of perspectives that had previously never been included in a district com-mittee. Through the process, this diverse array of perspectives combined

to give the group a strong sense of purpose and potential, answering
the question of "What kind of people do we think we are?" It created a
sense of empowerment among the leaders. Many times during the process the randomly selected group intervened to share perspectives that
many hadn't expected, shifting the discussion and creating an enriching
experience.

Building inclusive democracy to secure a breakthrough space is an important and critical objective for open system work. It pushes the boundaries of traditional system design, provoking capacity and high-variety
design questions throughout. As you pursue building your breakthrough
space it's important to return to the critical question of whether or not
the task force or committee or space is truly representative or exempli-
fying the community you're working in. If the answer is no or unclear,
you must continue to refine the space to ensure the promise of inclusive
democracy. Table 4.2 allows you to create and design your own inclusive democratic process, constructing a space to break through in your
community.

CADENCE FOR MAXIMUM IMPACT

Designing a process for maximum impact means building a cadence and
momentum that amplifies your open moment.

We've seen it a million times—the drip, drip, drip effect of a community process. The meeting occurs once per month, every month, all
year long. At the end of the process, no one is really sure what happened,
or why they met, or what they did. This "drip effect" robs our potential
open system spaces of their momentum, energy, and vitality.

If we conceive of breaking through closed systems as walls, barriers,
or structures resistant to change, then we need to think about ideas such
as momentum, amplification, and energy to fully maximize the potential
when designing a breakthrough space. Openers must resist the closed
system temptation to play the process out over significant lengths of time
and instead conceive and design for a cadence to get to action and impact.

In the Boulder process, Rob Anderson understood this from a few
angles. He was under political pressure to deliver from both the local
community groups and the board. To his credit, he committed to hold-

Table 4.2 Democratic inclusion: who are your stakeholders?

Essential Stakeholders	Interested Stakeholders	Potential Stakeholders
Individuals and groups that need to be included because the issue or politics demands they must be involved. Think of these as high-stakes enablers of your authorizing environment. *Examples: The mayor, the parent who is always involved, advocacy groups, the student council president, etc.*	Individuals and groups that want to be included (citizens, parents, etc.), demonstrate buy-in with the team goal(s), and have enough relational/social capital to know the process. *Examples: Members of citizen groups, involved parents, community organizations that want to be included, etc.*	Individuals and groups that have a stake in the team goal(s), but don't have the process on their radar or any social capital connections to groups that are close to the process. *Examples: Students who are working full-time jobs, parents who don't read the district emails, etc.*
Process: superintendent, board, and/or leadership team selection	Process: Process selection or an open application with a clear rubric	Process: Sortition—random selection akin to a jury selection
How could this work in your context?	*How could this work in your context?*	*How could this work in your context?*
What would be the opportunities or pitfalls?	*What would be the opportunities or pitfalls?*	*What would be the opportunities or pitfalls?*
Your essential stakeholders:	Your interested stakeholders:	Your potential stakeholders:

ing a three-hour meeting of the equity council every week for six weeks, a schedule that created real community, culture, and momentum, and brought the issue in front of the school board by November. This allowed for some flexibility for extra meetings in the process (which are usually always needed), and for the group to come together and do their work with a purpose and approach pitched to amplify the potential for change. He explains his reasoning:

Cadence is a critical component of co-creation. Lengthy and poorly timed processes are where a lot of good ideas go to die. Leaders need to find the sweet spot to understand the complexity without dragging it on so that people don't forget what has been said. By setting time-lines, i.e., not forever, but naming we are going to give this a couple of concentrated months, it helps the group to understand why they can't get off on tangents, so they have pressure to make a decision. We took three months and it gave folks enough time to consider complexity and absorb new content. We stated clearly that this was going to be a public recommendation and we let people know it was going to be in front of the board by November.

Cadence design can also be leveraged to build real community inside the process, like a design sprint or team-building process. You can't re-ally get to know a group and build trust if you only meet them for one hour, once a month. Instead, we need to be conceiving of these groups as places that build real connection, identity, and culture over the length of the process. Openers therefore should be intentional about designing activities, facilitations, and ideas that build the culture and connection of the group. Board vice chair Lisa Sweeney-Miran agreed.

> I think generally regardless of what the task at hand is, when folks work in a collaborative way where they're meeting each other once a month for an hour or two unfortunately so much of those meetings is trying to remember what happened last time, and trying to reset and starting over with expectations. Whereas on the sort of schedule where you're meet-ing for three hours on a weekly basis folks have to be focused [because] they're in it the whole time. There's no chance to sort of forget what was being worked on and to start over again. It's just a continuous process, of thinking and talking and having these feedback loops.

A thoughtful and urgent cadence also helps lead to impact. Moving toward a moment where a decision can be made by the leadership or gov-ernance of a system, whether it's a school board decision or a community decision moment, allows for a target on the horizon that a group can be motivated by. Openers must take the opportunity to design a break-through space for critical and open system change that doesn't turn into

---

Cadence Analysis

- *Culture cadence.* How are you going to leverage the speed and trajectory of the group to give it a sense of purpose and impact?
- *Schedule cadence.* How will you resist the drip effect of a typical process and design for momentum?
- *Impact cadence.* What is the target for impact? Is there a board meeting, a community event, or a separate process that if timed right, can create breakthrough potential?

---

another drip effect. Instead of losing and sapping momentum, they can create real potential for change.

Designing Amplification

In addition to cadence, openers must take special care to design for amplified spaces. This usually involves partnering with the communication or marketing teams, or with external media outlets or others who are interested in showcasing the effort over time. The amplification is not just for letting people know from a simple marketing orientation; it builds genuine community knowledge, both where it is and where it is going. Without the ability to tie amplification into the design of the breakthrough space, the potential for the process of opening to dissolve into the noise of the system or be deprioritized is much higher.

In the Boulder process, the school district paid enormous attention to shifting the narrative of how they were approaching the situation. From the very beginning, the chief communications officer of the district supported the project. The communications team worked with local and statewide media to highlight and feature the work, revamped the website to include key details on what was happening and why, and then continued to share information with their newsletters and communications. The result was a community that was highly aware about the work moving forward, which likely not only drove up interest and participation in the process, as evidenced by the submission of over nine hundred applications, but also helped shift the narrative that the district wasn't committed to community-driven change or shifts in equity-seeking systems.

Amplification Analysis

- *Internal communications.* What is your strategy to keep internal stakeholders connected and aware of the process?
- *External communications.* What is your strategy to keep the external community informed and abreast of the process?
- *Hanging threads.* How are you going to ensure amplification for community knowledge and accountability?

Our work in designing open systems and high-variety capacity is to transform and adapt systems—both inside and outside. This means that the work of designing spaces to get amplified ensures that people inside the system or organization are deeply aware of what is going on alongside the external community.

BREAKING THE ADDICTION TO CLOSED SYSTEMS

As you are designing for your breakthrough space, you will need to consider how you will attend to the closed system mindsets and addiction to current ways of working that are present in the system.

Throughout any process in which you are designing a breakthrough space, you will come face to face with elements of the closed system that will prepare in advance to resist the changes potentially proposed, even before the community co-creates ideas for moving forward.

In many of our experiences, this is where openers or community leaders start to get nervous or concerned about the potential for change in a process. They start to see the system manifest resistant behavior and get concerned about the potential for change. In many cases, these are the ~isms we've discussed in the sidebars on liberatory open system leadership, which must be confronted continuously with the leaders and systems who have committed to the co-creative moment.

Openers must take special time to notice the closed system behavior manifesting throughout the design of the process. In education, this could be resistance from district officials who run departments who may be implicated in the co-creative design or the work moving forward. We explicitly use the language of "addiction to closed systems" to showcase that closed system behavior has perpetuated for a significant amount of time, leading to resource allocations, actions, and events that benefit certain groups of people inside and outside of systems. Amy Nelson, equity director for BVSD, shared the importance of groups and individuals breaking this cycle: "It was critical to unlearn—we've all got to unlearn something, we all have unlearning to do. Through the process of listening, staff were learning what it means to be present in a school. What does safety mean? How do I really build relationships with students?"

Openers sometimes reject or push resistant individuals, organizations, and/or departments away—at our own peril. While it requires real courage and grace to include them (because indeed, they may be the most opposed to the process overall), by designing for their inclusion in the process, we actually reinforce the power of the space and its potential to break the addiction to closed system behavior. We want those individuals who are skeptical of community co-creation to be right there throughout these conversations, seeing highly effective practices, confronting these truths alongside the entire community, and, ultimately, alongside families, business leaders, and others in creating solutions together. It is harder to break the addiction by confronting people and asking them to change. It is better to approach it through attraction, modeling, and showing a better path forward that honors and recognizes everyone.

In the Boulder work, some departments were invested in the previous SRO process and idea. They had notions of success and failure that were tied up in personal identity, possibility, and what changes to the SRO process would mean for their jobs. The police departments were also on this list, having been perceived to have failed to partner with communities through the design of the SRO process for quite some time. In both cases, Anderson had the foresight to include these departments and individuals inside the process, not to exclude them. While it is normal to want to create separate processes, in our experiences, these are exactly the groups and individuals that need to be included in the journey. Over the course of the Boulder equity process, these leaders and partners heard the hard and tough stories of families and students and how they were affected by the current system. By designing for their inclusion and asking for their help in the process, the opportunity was created for a maximized attempt to include them in the further process outlined in later chapters. Superintendent Anderson shared his thoughts on why bringing in these voices mattered:

> Co-creation is sharing power and control. There is so much fear of change, so it takes courage and understanding to move forward. Leaders can't be afraid that people are going to disagree. These are complicated issues—if people are in agreement, then why have a process? The culture and system shift began at the top by embracing the idea that we are not going to walk past this problem anymore. You have to believe the process is going to get you better if you include the skeptics. If you exclude them, then you get pressure on the back end which then creates these flipping effects where the issue changes the next time the district looks at it. If you ground the process in the values and beliefs of the community and include all perspectives in that process, the decisions can and do stand the test of time.

Leaders and community members both have particular challenges in noticing the race, class, identity and other ~isms that are present in existing systems and are manifesting as resistance to potential disruption. Yet the leaders in both of these case studies did the important work of noticing, identifying, and asking for help to leverage the community process in order to illuminate and bring people along with a process that created a liberatory redesign along the way. In all of these cases, and in many more, political pressure could have threatened to scuttle or break the process, but the energy was manifest to transform the process.

Breaking the Addiction to Closed Systems Reflection

- In the design of your breakthrough open space, where do you expect or notice the most resistance?
- How would you characterize the addiction to closed system behavior?
- How can you design a space to include those affected by the process and to maximize their learning and work along the way?

CONCLUSION

Provoking open system change means challenging the dominant ideas of how we work with community. When we work with system and education leaders, their inability to imagine new people in the room is often shocking. They are deeply worried that any new process will be hijacked by the "same people" or "folks who just want to cause problems." We have noted that in such a scenario, even if they end up co-creating, they often end up recycling the same narratives and perspectives as before. If we are indeed committed to democracy building, then we must take the principle of designing breakthrough spaces seriously. If the authorizing environment we intend to build will be the one to interrupt the system, then it needs to be strong, diverse, and able to withstand the intense outside scrutiny that adaptive system change attracts.

Never forget that designing spaces such as these is a new muscle to most public education systems. This journey is one that many education leaders haven't taken or are afraid to take because they fear getting it wrong. They've seen their friends and other leaders face enormous political blowback for getting it wrong. Politics can be a blood sport in local communities. But instead of running away from it and wishing it away, your work to design breakthrough spaces gives you tools to maneuver and grapple, giving you the chance to model the creative democracy that can lead to redesign, trust, and transformation.

CHAPTER 5

Open Principle 4

Model Creative Democracy

Democracy cannot be static. Whatever is static is dead.

ELEANOR ROOSEVELT

Ours is a society struggling to become cooperative . . . all the thwarted motives of men cry aloud for it. But the way is blocked by the ideologies of the past buttressed by those who have grown strong in its favors.

REXFORD TUGWELL, QUOTED IN *THE CRISIS OF THE OLD ORDER*

The very idea of democracy, the meaning of democracy, must be continually explored afresh; it has to be constantly discovered, and rediscovered, remade and reorganized. . . . What direction shall we give to the work of the school so that the richness and fullness of the democratic way of life in all its scope may be promoted?

JOHN DEWEY

BIG IDEAS IN THIS CHAPTER

- Establishing shared reality
- Co-creation and reciprocity
- Repairing ruptures
- Consensus-driven decision-making
- Cultivating communitas

Figure 5.1

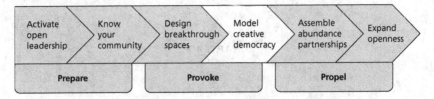

MODEL CREATIVE DEMOCRACY

The world is full of significant challenges that require the public to band together to solve them. And yet, our democratic institutions seem stymied again and again in the face of these challenges. Our democratic muscles have withered—we are in a rhythm where everything seems rote, even things as sacred as voting. We are surrounded by democratic engagement mechanisms that are atrophying through disuse.

Neighborhood committees, zoning boards, school councils—all of these are structures that people have been conditioned to see as perfunctory and vestigial. They have become an institutional version of an appendix. These tools are available to us, but we need to rethink how we use them. We need an injection of creativity to revitalize the act of citizenship, to inspire us to see participation as art.

Open leaders have now spent time committing to the leadership mindset, community knowledge, and designing of breakthrough spaces to disrupt the boundaries between systems, creating opportunities for openness. In this section, we will move deeper into the *provoking* phase, creating the potential for the breakthrough energy that disrupts the boundary between systems and their communities to be sustained, built deeper, and dynamically held. Like the previous chapter, these are practical ways to hold spaces that naturally gravitate to becoming closed and removed. The open leader must now turn to helping communities make decisions and chart a path forward that lights the flame of local democracy.

In this chapter, we will explore how openers might model creative democracy when opening systems. We will describe how openers can use the breakthrough space to model creative democracy by establishing a shared reality, fostering co-creation and reciprocity, repairing ruptures, using consensus-based decision-making strategies, and cultivating communitas. If open leaders can hold a space through this liminal and sometimes transformative experience, they may find, as we and others have, that there is a shared joy at the final stage of an opening that creates an inspired path forward.

One of our most exciting examples of a state system opening up and modeling creative democracy is playing out in the Commonwealth of Kentucky.

Open Vignettes: Kentucky

The Kentucky Board of Education appointed Dr. Jason Glass as commissioner in 2020. COVID-19 was raging through the commonwealth, and stability of operations was of critical importance. At a time of high anxiety and uncertainty, everyone was looking for a plan, an assurance of normality. Commissioner Glass worked closely with the office of Governor Andy Beshear to respond quickly and efficiently to the moment of crisis. At the same time, he was laying the foundation for a different approach to state governance of education—an approach that would be more responsive and collaborative with communities. As Glass says:

> When we would try to create regulation in the old model, we would start with the professional staff and what they think is best, then try to convince the Commissioner, then the Commissioner tries to convince the Board, then we'll get regulation that has the force of law, and all the districts will have to comply. What we imagined was a model where we are hearing from districts about what they need, then how do we adjust regulations based on what we have heard. We want this to come from the field, the experiences of people that are out working in and around our schools, rather from the policy elite's perspective.[1]

Glass's leadership of the department demonstrated many of the principles of open systems. He displayed open leadership in his commitment to listen and learn instead of imposing a plan. He sought to deeply know his ecosystem and community by engaging in an extensive listening and learning tour with thousands of participants, which was led by students from across the commonwealth. He designed a breakthrough space by creating the Kentucky Coalition for Advancing Education (KCAE) using the inclusive democracy approach, resulting in a statewide coalition that included students, caregivers, educators, district leaders, legislators, and business and community leaders. This coalition had nearly twice the percentage of people of color as Kentucky as a whole, and it reached across the entire length and breadth of the commonwealth.

The KCAE, supported by staff at the Kentucky Department of Education (KDE) and the Center for Innovation in Education (CIE), moved beyond traditional modes of community engagement to rethink how the department could partner differently with communities. The members of KCAE conducted empathy interviews with people in their communities, focusing on those who were traditionally marginalized. Members put their interview notes alongside the raw data from the listening tour and did real-time sensemaking about the patterns and themes that were emerging. They created "user profiles" of students, teachers, family members, administrators, community members, and district leaders that captured the variety of experiences and perspectives of people across Kentucky. At weekly meetings, coalition members took on one another's points of view and created products in real time that they then shared with their networks and communities for feedback, engaging even wider circles in the process. As we finalized our products, writing teams used a consensus-driven decision-making process to approve drafts and advance versions to the whole coalition. The coalition used the same processes to approve final versions, ensuring that these versions now spoke for the whole group.

The Kentucky Coalition for Advancing Education demonstrates how open systems can revitalize the practice of democracy in both structure and process. Throughout this chapter, we will describe how democratic institutions that creatively include diverse stakeholders in co-creation can dramatically shift the way they partner with communities. The first step is naming a shared reality from which to begin.

- Why is it important to move beyond equity and discuss systemic liberatory shifts?
- What can emerge from processes of co-creation that transform communities and build trust?
- How does modeling creative democracy reignite civic capacity building at the local level?

ESTABLISHING SHARED REALITY

Open leaders must create a shared understanding of reality and the problem, and this conception of the problem must be held by all members of the team.

Dean Williams, in his seminal book *Real Leadership*, talks about authentic leadership as the act of making people face reality.

> [T]he diagnostic work is to determine what aspect of reality is being avoided by the people. All factions embedded in a situation of irresolution hold a view of the problem that is limited, biased, and incomplete. That aspect of reality that the people are avoiding will be a piece of the puzzle that needs to be faced if progress is to unfold. The leadership task, therefore, is to detect what it is that the people are missing that, if surfaced and confronted, would enhance the people's capacity to solve their problems and advance.[2]

Establishing a common understanding of the current state of affairs and the problem you hope to solve together is a key component of extending the open moment you've identified. In any community and project, there likely exist many different viewpoints and perspectives through which to see the work. The work of the open leader is to help build a shared reality across a group of people that can be the container for collective work, building on the clarity you established in your breakthrough space.

While it can seem trivial, naming the current state and the problem statement is really the first act of co-creation, and by taking it on, a group can prove to themselves that they can do something meaningful together. A collectively developed reality is also an important part of avoiding a common problem of open systems work: the tendency for those with more power and influence to put their thumb on the scale and overly shape the terms of the work, even when a diverse set of stakeholders is involved. Establishing the shared reality together is a way to start practicing a few different muscles that are generally atrophied from underuse in traditional organizations and projects. Specifically, these processes help us develop the capacity to empathize with perspectives outside our own, looking at a variety of data and engaging people in the sensemaking of data (rather than just treating them like data themselves).

Building Empathy

The first challenge that openers often face when trying to establish shared reality is getting everyone to truly empathize with each other, especially when bringing in members and perspectives from traditionally marginalized groups. The worst possible outcome would be for their marginalization to continue in the denial of their experience, something that can happen without careful planning and execution of the empathy process.

In Kentucky, we asked every member of the coalition to conduct empathy interviews with people in their networks who often aren't included in decision-making processes. Many members reported that this was one of the most important elements of their experience. Why?

Part of the answer is offered up by Shane Safir, Jamila Dugan, and Carrie Wilson in their book, *Street Data*, in which they talk about three levels of data: satellite, map, and street data.[3] Satellite data is the quantitative data typically used to define a shared reality—high-stakes statewide assessments, for example. Map data is more granular, helping to make sense of the real-time status of the system—think formative assessments or quick surveys. Street data is the kind of data that comes from storytelling and observation, the constant flow of information that is all around us, if we take the opportunity to listen. All of these types of data are important, but our systems are designed primarily to collect and respond to satellite data. We have found that unless we organize to collect street data, it is impossible to establish a shared reality.

Members of the coalition worked in teams across perspectives to make sense of the data together. Teachers, students, community members, and district leaders together looked at interview data from a variety of stakeholders and distilled common themes. Most importantly, they were building a deeper sense of empathy for other members of the system and seeing that the challenges they felt were unique to their own experience were actually much more universal.

Whether you are choosing to do empathy interviews or gathering data about people's experiences in other ways, a critical question must be: where are your blind spots and how can you broaden the empathy process over time? In Kentucky, we looked at who we had interviewed and noticed that we hadn't yet talked to enough teachers, so we took extra care to go out and find teachers from underrepresented communities. This ended up being critical to our success and showed us that empathy and defining a shared reality is more of a process than a final state with a clear endpoint. As Audrey Gilbert, a student at Frankfort High School who was part of KCAE notes, "Through the process, I could see that other people in my community had the same thoughts as people who were exactly like them across the state in all different communities. It was just something really different that I hadn't seen before, and it was really powerful. There has been a lot of division in terms of conversations around education in Kentucky for a long time, so being able to see the commonalities together in one place was something I really enjoyed and was not really expecting."

Defining a Problem Statement

Empathy processes are powerful, but every attempt to define a shared reality must reach a point of finality. We have found that defining a very clear problem statement can be a critical lever in providing clarity and creating a clear point of intersection in our shared experience. Because we had engaged in statewide work and visioning, we synthesized these into ten key themes that defined the current state of education in Kentucky. For example, one of the themes states: "The system doesn't really know, see, or value each stakeholder as an individual. This was as true for students and families as it was teachers and leaders. There are similar feelings from communities—that the system doesn't adequately see, know, or value the aspirations, assets, and challenges of the community."[4]

In places like Burlington, Vermont, another city where we supported strategic planning with an open systems lens, we used the empathy process to develop this problem statement:

> The district has not yet created a culture based on values and beliefs that reflect how the community aspires to support the full range of student needs, especially those who are most systematically marginalized or outside of conventional expectations. This gap undermines trust with students, families, and educators. The gap occurs because the district lacks a shared approach for identifying root causes and generating a

---

Crafting a Problem Statement Activity

One format for drafting your problem statement could be: [user] wants [identified need]; however, [problem] because [issue].

- Who is the user/stakeholder?
- What does the user/stakeholder want or need?
- What is the core problem that needs to be addressed?
- Why is this issue a problem?

---

plan of action with clear lines of resources, responsibility, timelines, and accountability.[5]

By creating a problem statement, the project sets the stage for moving beyond analysis paralysis and toward a solution. Once we had established these statements, the stage was set for doing work in deeper relationships with one another. With the problem statement, the project reaches a sharp point, focusing its energy and intention for the constructive work to come.

CO-CREATION AND RECIPROCITY

Open leaders have the opportunity to co-create in ways that honor the diverse expertise of the team, but they must take care to establish reciprocal loops for information and products so that all members can lend their gifts to the work.

Establishing Shared Reality Reflection

- What data sources exist in your community and how might you make them accessible for everyone on your team?
- How can you create intentional spaces for participants in spaces to hear each other's stories?
- Who are some potential users of the system whose insights you must include in the work?

Representative democracy has been robbed of its energy because of an underdeveloped ability to harness the creative energy of citizens. In an open system frame, we come to see that this is the intentional choice of many public system leaders who prefer elite, removed, closed system technocracy. Too often, people feel as if policy happens to them, created by people far away—and they are not wrong! In education, families and students come to know, experience, and believe that leaders do not see their experience or effort in the systems that surround them. Too often, closed systems cultivate this distance by using expertise as a barrier to deeper engagement. We often hear people within the system say that it's not useful to have "regular people" at the table because they don't understand the issues enough to really contribute. But what does it say about our systems when we cannot process the lived expertise of the people who experience the system day in and day out?

This is not to say that traditional forms of expertise don't matter, but we too often lack the structures and routines for bringing traditional expertise into a more balanced relationship with lived experience and other forms of expertise. Indeed, open system creative democracy building requires an open leader who is willing to hold the complexity and dynamism of a community emerging into something new. Openers must help systems build capacity for creative work by utilizing breakthrough spaces and a shared definition of reality to cut through the false barriers between different kinds of expertise. When a community comes together and watches these barriers fall, creative capacity flows from the ability to co-create and act with reciprocity, in a truly responsive relationship with one another. Connecting back to the strategic triangle, the co-creation of public value unlocks operational capacity and legitimacy and support, but only if the terms of the reciprocal relationship are clearly defined.

What Is Co-creation and Why Does It Matter?

As we have shared throughout this book, co-creation is the process of building things with those who are affected by the issue. Openers thinking about co-creation may only see the downsides: the time required, the need for facilitation to ensure that everyone is working effectively together, the need to maintain relationships. What we have seen is that co-creation can change assumptions about operational capacity in dramatic ways. Sometimes quite suddenly, people involved in the co-creation will bring resources, time, energy, and partnerships to the table. This activation of new capacity is a hallmark of the co-creation process.

Karen Perry, a director at the University of Kentucky Center for Next Generation Leadership and a KCAE participant, observed, "There are 'Local Laboratories of Learning' that have spun out from that team. These local labs also have local coalitions that have a similar model of inclusive composition, so that local districts are engaged in this work. These districts are driven by their own coalitions that are also radically inclusive, especially toward historically marginalized groups of people." Through the KCAE process, Audrey Gilbert, a student representative on the coalition, also became involved in the design team for the Local Laboratories of Learning. We found out that Audrey was a leader in the Kentucky Student Voice Team, and she activated her network of student leaders to help us develop tools, resources, and approaches to sustain student voices in the local work. Both of these examples demonstrate the power of co-creation to activate capacity that might have otherwise gone unnoticed.

Additionally, it is hard to overstate the power that co-creation can lend to the legitimacy of the enterprise. Those who have a track record of being cynical around a topic become increasingly vocal champions because they are able to tell a deeper story about how the work was done. Instead of reaching the end of a project and facing an army of skeptics, co-creation can activate an army of advocates.

What Is Reciprocity and Why Does It Matter?

We define reciprocity as the habit of responsiveness and ongoing curiosity about the interconnectedness among parts of a system. Reciprocity helps us balance the community's expectations of involvement with the process. It's a structured give and take, with trust built on the transparency of who will do what and how the insights from the rest of the group will influence the emerging product. Reciprocity is about more than a division of labor, however. Reciprocity ensures that information flows back and forth between those who are doing work and those who will be affected by it. Reciprocity means keeping yourself open to new insights so that the work can evolve over time. Reciprocity requires clarity around how organizations hear and adapt to new information. Time and again, we see people engage communities and then retreat to expert-driven spaces. A commitment to reciprocity ensures that this does not happen and that the trust developed through co-creation isn't squandered.

Reciprocity creates a new kind of relationship between education systems and the community. As our friend Tony Monfiletto, executive director of Future Focused Education in New Mexico and one of the founders of the Reciprocity Project has written: "We imagine reciprocal relationships that measure school success based on whether the communities where they reside are better off because of their presence. The strategy rests on designing to be responsive to local communities and viewing young people who are offered thrilling and authentic learning opportunities as the very assets that become the change agents that their families, neighbors, employers, and civic leaders have been waiting for."[6]

In our work we have seen the combination of co-creation and reciprocity ignite the virtuous cycle of the strategic triangle. Any open moment must find a balance between co-creation and reciprocity. In some projects, it may not be feasible to co-create every product, and reciprocity can help sustain the work by creating transparent cycles of responsiveness. But how can leaders create the space for co-creation and structure reciprocal flows of information that build trust?

Collective Ideation

One essential aspect of building creative democracy is helping communities come to see that sharing ideas is not a high-risk affair. Many community members, families, and students have had experiences where they have put forward important ideas or initiatives only to be shot down by project leaders. Critical to the act of co-creation is modeling a collective ideation that can allow everyone to share and experience the potential possibilities ahead in a process. Once a team has created a shared problem statement, one of the most powerful ways to leverage co-creation with a diverse team is to engage in brainstorming or ideation. We have seen variations on these processes, but here we are borrowing from the design thinking process, using this protocol from the famous design thinking firm, IDEO.[7]

- *Defer judgment.* Creative spaces are judgment-free zones—they let ideas flow so people can build from each other's great ideas.
- *Encourage wild ideas.* Embrace the most out-of-the-box notions. There's often not a whole lot of difference between outrageous and brilliant.
- *Build on the ideas of others.* Try to use "and" instead of "but," it encourages positivity and inclusivity and leads to tons of ideas.
- *Stay focused on the topic.* Try to keep the discussion on target. Divergence is good, but you still need to keep your eyes on the prize.
- *One conversation at a time.* This can be difficult—especially with lots of creative people in a single room—but always think about the challenge topic and how to stay on track.
- *Be visual.* Use colored markers and Post-its. Stick your ideas on the wall so others can visualize them.
- *Go for quantity.* Crank your ideas out quickly. For any sixty-minute session, you should try to generate one hundred ideas.

As openers, the core addition we would make to this brainstorm process is the reminder to make your team as intentionally inclusive as possible.

After brainstorming, you could consider using an affinity process, grouping the sticky notes that seem connected. As a group, discuss which ideas could be developed into solutions to the problem statement. Identify the most promising ideas as a collective, ensuring equity of voice. Consider using a technique like dot voting in order to reduce the tendency for individuals with perceived power and influence to shape the direction. We frequently use "gut checks" as well at the end of a decision-making process to make sure that the choice we have made really gets at the heart of the issue. Sometimes, that can involve going back to the problem statement and asking each other, "Does this idea really address this problem?" In the spirit of focusing on the experiences of marginalized groups, it can be critical for openers to be intentional about asking those members who carry that experience to start these gut check reflections. Karen Perry shares how the empathy process can also enhance the gut check: "We had to check our own agendas and ask whether what was being proposed lined up with what was represented in the empathy data. We would ask ourselves, 'What would that person think about this idea?'"

Establishing the Desired Level of Co-creation

Co-creation can mean many things, and groups can benefit from establishing the extent of co-creation that would satisfy their need for involvement. Our colleague Gretchen Morgan described these levels of co-creation, including who does the work and how they will loop back with the broader coalition.

Level One: This work will be done by the lead team or lead individual. They will let the staff and community know when the work begins, and they will share the product of the work and the rationale broadly when they are done.

Level Two: This work will be done by the lead team or lead individual. However, unlike a level one action, before making a final decision or implementing at scale, the lead(s) will test their best ideas with relevant stakeholders and refine them if needed. Lead(s) will still communicate the product of the work and the rationale broadly when they are done.

Level Three: An inclusive team is formed. Together they either represent or seek stakeholder input, design a solution, test solutions with

---

Liberatory Creative Democracy

- As you assemble a shared reality, how are you ensuring that persistent ~isms are not manifesting through exclusion?
- Are there certain groups that are receiving more attention or deeper empathy than others?
- What are the protocols or scaffolds in place to ensure equity of voice and representation while co-creating? What are the norms and accountability for breaking those norms?

stakeholders, and ultimately communicate broadly about the product of their work and the rationale.[8]

This is built on the assumption that not everything can be at level three, at least at first. This is especially true in systems as complicated as a district or state agency. As organizations develop fluency in co-creation, more and more work might move from level one to levels two and three.

Defining Reciprocal Flows of Information

Even with level three co-creation, it is critical that openers be clear about empowering or authorizing work outside of the breakthrough space, and about how work done outside the collective space will loop back. Open systems of any size thrive with open flows of energy and information, whether they are four-person teams, a school, or a whole state. This is the heart of reciprocity.

In open systems work, it is all too easy to slip back into a mode of consulting a focus group and then sending the experts off to do the "real work." Experts within closed systems have a tendency to gather up insights and then go behind closed doors, with inadequate clarity about how they are supposed to honor the insights and power of the group. But lack of clarity about how the work will proceed weakens the breakthrough space. Lack of clear reciprocity undermines the trust that is the foundation of the public value, operational capacity, and legitimacy and support spiral. This will be important as we consider co-production, the next and ongoing stage to ensure reciprocity, in the expanding openness chapter.

In Kentucky, KCAE was tasked with creating several products, including what would become the *United We Learn* report, that set out the current state of education and the desired future vision. At the outset of the writing process, we clearly defined who was doing the core writing, who was giving feedback, and who was checking for whether the product addressed the insights we heard during the empathy process. We also defined when each of these processes would happen in the co-creation timeline. By defining these information flows, we set up a trust-enhancing cycle of reciprocity.

Examples of co-creation and reciprocity that deepen the practice of democracy are all around. We met Sam Battan and the Colorado Youth Congress (CYC) through our network of Open System Institute Residents. Their guidebook for youth-led systems change is nothing short of a revolutionary approach to how to engage young people as agents of change. Within the guidebook, they lay out what they call their "integrative decision-making process," used when there is lack of clarity surrounding the roles and responsibilities on the team.

Every governance meeting in the Colorado Youth Congress allows members to propose areas where there is confusion about their role or lack of clarity on the team more broadly. Each proposal is added to the agenda at the beginning of each meeting, and then processed individually in the following order:

A. Present Proposal: Whoever proposed the agenda item describes what tensions they're experiencing and states a proposal to resolve it. If the proposer doesn't have a resolution ready, they can request discussion to help craft the proposal.

B. Clarifying Questions: Anyone can ask a clarifying question to seek information or understanding. The proposer can always say they don't know. Pay attention to the intention behind your questions: this is not a chance to mask people's opinions/judgements as questions.

C. Reaction Round: Everyone has a chance to speak, one by one, to give their authentic reaction. Reactions must be made as first-person comments (i.e., try not to speak for the group).

D. Amend and Clarify: The proposer can clarify the intent of the proposal or change the proposal based on people's reactions.

E. Objection Round: The facilitator asks "Do you see any reasons why adopting this proposal would cause harm or move us backwards?" Objections are stated and captured without discussion. The proposal is adopted if no objections surface.

F. Integration Round: Focus on each objection, one at a time. The goal is to work collaboratively as a team to craft an amended proposal that would not cause the objection, but that would still address the proposer's tension. Once all are integrated, go back to the Objection Round with the new proposal.[9]

As you can see, the CYC is modeling creative democracy by creating processes that move beyond the traditional ways of decision-making. They are including young people in co-creative processes and structuring those processes for maximum creativity and clarity.

As we discussed creating breakthrough spaces in the previous chapter, we highlighted a number of pitfalls that can sabotage open systems work. Similarly, when clearly defining roles within the co-creation process and how flows of information will work in reciprocal ways, try to avoid these common pitfalls:

- *Experts shaping the process to give themselves control of the work.* It's a common thing to see the experts take over the detailed work where their expertise is allowed to rule the day, often relegating those they deem as nonexperts to advisory roles.
- *Cadences that convey inevitability.* When timelines are too short for meaningful input or responsiveness to any raised issues, it can feel like the train is already barreling along the track, moving too fast to allow any deviation.
- *Stacking the team to ensure approval.* Leaders start to bring new members into the group to "support" the work. However, participants can feel it when teams get loaded with supporters of the leader's point of view who can then begin to edge out dissenting voices. Remember the important work of inclusive democracy from the previous chapter and keep a keen eye on the composition of the group.

As teams work through the intense co-creation and reciprocity processes, they may notice that the density and pace of information can feel like too much to process. They may find it challenging to surf the information flows of feedback. One way to parse out the flows of feedback is to think through the lenses of "sufficiency" and "feasibility," a model developed by our colleague Gretchen Morgan at CIE. As planning and solution development progresses, different people can look at the solution

---

Fostering Co-creation and Reciprocity Reflection

- What kinds of expertise are required for your project and what kind of biases need to be addressed to unlock that expertise?
- How might you set up expectations around sharing insights, information, and products to build trust?
- As you create smaller work teams, are there some members you want to lend their insights (and ways of working!) to various subgroups?

---

and consider two questions: Does this plan sound feasible? Does this plan sufficiently address the problem? It would be tempting to put the experts in charge of determining the plan and being the ultimate judges of feasibility, and to put the community members in a position of determining sufficiency. We urge caution here, since that can run the risk of reinforcing negative patterns where the community might be perceived as not having enough expertise to weigh in on the planning. Put together diverse teams to determine the responses to both questions, and you might find that there are community assets that can be brought to bear on feasibility concerns and system-based members might demonstrate that they have deeper expectations for sufficiency than you might expect.

By taking on co-creation and reciprocity, you model a creative democratic process that is in stark contrast to the closed system behaviors of our modern institutions, which too often seem like black boxes.

REPAIRING RUPTURES

As we build a path forward, ruptures are inevitable. Our work must be to transform the space with new paradigms of healing to move communities forward.

Moving through the dynamic co-creation process requires a certain comfort with ambiguity, even as we work to provide the necessary clarity to move the work forward. Within ambiguity is the possibility for misunderstanding, hurt feelings, and broken trust. We call these injuries to the breakthrough space "ruptures," because they occur where there has been a breach in the boundary of the open system you have created.

Rather than something to be ashamed of or to avoid, we think creative democracy requires direct engagement of ruptures in the nascent open systems we are building. When we were both teachers, we knew that breaches of our classroom culture needed to be addressed directly, but always with care and compassion. Often, addressing ruptures made our classroom communities stronger, as they were opportunities to clarify and distill the essence of the space in which we wanted to work. We feel the same way about the open systems we create in other education spaces. Repairing ruptures can actually accelerate the crystallization of the openness we are seeking and can provide a proof point of the resilience of the system. Far from being signs something is wrong in the process, we see them as great examples that the possibility of healing can occur.

We take enormous inspiration from the TED framework, which inverts the traditional drama triangle. The drama triangle, originated by Stephen Karpman, helps us understand the patterns we fall into during conflict. We typically fall into three categories: victim, persecutor, or rescuer.[10] It is not only individuals who need to see these patterns; we need to see the patterns that emerge in our communities between groups, systems, and others. This is a powerful reflection that we've seen people get truly emotional over as they consider where they fit in the process.

The TED framework inverts the drama triangle to help us understand that when ruptures occur, we can approach them fundamentally differently. Instead of victim, rescuer, and persecutor, we have creator, coach, and challenger.[11] This inversion of the roles allows us to call out the creator of the rupture instead of the persecutor, and to see the victim as instead a challenger with agency in the process. Lastly, instead of a rescuer swooping in to solve the issue, a coach helps all parties navigate the process. Openers must see themselves as the coach through a process of modeling creative democracy.

The biggest question is almost always whether you repair the rupture publicly or privately. In the Colorado Youth Congress, members believe that "tension and conflict [are] a natural part of group dynamics and should be normalized. The overall framing for any conflict that surfaces is that it is a chance for us to grow as individuals and a community."[12] The CYC applies the following process to their ruptures:

I. Start one-to-one: If someone has an interpersonal issue with another person, or someone's actions (or lack of action) is causing harm, we ask everyone to start with a one-to-one conversation to try and resolve things. The person initiating the meeting shares how they feel, what they need, and asks the other person what they might need. They center their feelings and their needs, while doing their best to not assume anything about the other's experience or intentions.

II. Trusted mediator if needed: If the people involved in the conflict cannot find a resolution, they may ask for a (confidential) person to be brought in to try and mediate.

III. Panel: If there is still no resolution after a mediator has agreed to help, a panel of peers and adults in CYC can be brought in to help make recommendations as to how to resolve the conflict.[13]

There are times when repairing ruptures requires a more public approach—especially if the breach occurred publicly. In Kentucky, we had a moment when the ratified products of the coalition were edited for posting on the website. While this might seem minor, we knew that changing things after the whole coalition had co-created specific language would undermine trust and the participants' investment in the whole project. We reached back out to the whole coalition and shared the version on the website, compared it to the version they had ratified, and asked for their permission to allow the edited version to exist on the website. We also offered up our time to talk about the changes and any issues people might have with them. An important thing to note here is that because we had gone through the earlier steps of empathy, collective ideation, cocreation, and reciprocity, the trust we had built up was palpable. When we acknowledged this rupture, it drew on the bank of trust we had developed, and refilled it and then some. To the participants, it was almost like another example of reciprocity, a refreshing change to the lack of explanation they might have received under different circumstances.

Many writers and facilitators speak about "moving at the speed of trust." Repairing ruptures is about making that adage real—being aware of when trust is broken, addressing it, and moving forward with full consciousness of what has occurred.

CONSENSUS-DRIVEN DECISION-MAKING

Openers find that creative expressions of democracy, such as consensus approaches, may build stronger commitment and ownership of the path forward.

In our experience practicing creative democracy, a critical element is modeling better types of participation than just majoritarian democracy. Instead, we should all realize we need to practice a more robust type of democratic decision-making. Instead of fifty-plus-one majoritarianism, which in our experience has the potential to create factionalism, we instead need to promote a consensus approach that generates community bonding and bridging for open systems. In *The Moral Commonwealth*, Philip Selznick makes the case for a more consensus-driven approach to modeling democratic action that inspires us constantly.

> Among the foundations of communal democracy is the integrity of decision-making by "the people as a whole." This means, above all, that democracy cannot be equated with majority rule . . . The demand for consensus is a demand for inclusion. And the politics of inclusion are, in principle, a vindication of democracy . . . A mechanical majority—a faction large enough, cohesive enough, and enduring enough to shut

Figure 5.2 Open system "modified consensus" model

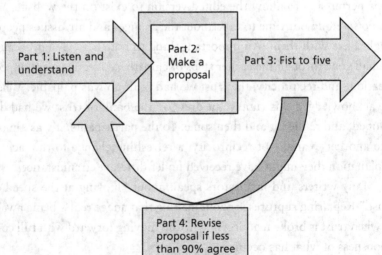

out or negate minority views—threatens both community and democracy . . . It is also an impoverished rendering of the democratic ideal.[14]

Open systems processes require that we explore new ways of democratic participation. We believe that consensus protocols are a critical method for deliberating and finding common ground. We must create a consensus model approach as opposed to the traditional deliberation approach of fifty-plus-one. Figure 5.2 illustrates how leaders need to achieve modified consensus to drive toward higher levels of agreement.

Open Systems Modified Consensus Approach

Overall process:

- Small group discussion and recommendation building
- Sharing round (one minute per person max)
- Proposal round (put aside nonpriority, friendly consolidation)
- Consensus round (two tries per proposal)
- If no proposals, begin again
- Advance recommendations to the whole group
- Whole group synthesis and advancing

Rules:

- *Small group building and advancing.* In small groups, we will do stakeholder-driven consensus to build recommendations that can advance to the full group.
- *Fist to five.* Five is strongly agree, one is disagree but not block, fist is block.
- *Modified consensus.* Recommendations cannot advance to the whole group if they are blocked by more than 10 percent of the small group.
- *Process.* The fist to five protocol measures consensus on the current recommendation.
- *Priority question.* You are free to discuss other recommendations, but your first recommendation *must* answer the question: "What is your recommendation regarding X?"

Open system practices like consensus-driven decision-making help us come together and create fractal patterns that exemplify the new world we seek. The "mechanical majority" (that is, fifty-plus-one) might be a necessity in the structure of a distant state or federal system, but it is poorly suited to the functioning of a local democracy like a school system. Indeed, while it seems impossible to imagine a federal or state system forging consensus instead of majoritarianism, we believe that if we commit to a different way of being in our work and lives at the community level, there may be a better future for consensus in our country.

In KCAE, we took on the challenge of setting a direction and focus for statewide change, especially around assessment and accountability. We utilized a modified consensus approach which created space for people to speak, listen to others, propose recommendations, and then adopt. Typically achieving 80–90 percent group approval (that is, no blocks from more than 10–20 percent of the group) is the threshold to aspire to, not full and complete consensus. Some would argue that this is not true consensus and yes, we concede. Some dissent is good and healthy! This consensus approach, with its 90 percent goal, pushes the group to the heart of disagreements and potential challenges. As a group moves forward, it becomes clearer that when recommendations and outcomes emerge, something different has been created—a proposal generated from within and backed by a nearly universal group of members. A truly radical idea for our fractured and lethargic democracy. As Commissioner Glass notes, "We made the effort to ensure that all of the recommendations were openly vetted, and an effort to develop consensus so that you weren't tallying votes and trying to develop a majority and minority and find ways to disempower and exclude the minority. It was a process of asking 'How can we take your perspective, work it in, and get everyone to a position of "yes"?' That is a very different power model compared to what happens where decisions are usually made."

The consensus-driven model can certainly create complexities, but even in moments of seeming deadlock, trust can emerge. In our work in Burlington, Vermont, when creating elements of the district's strategic plan through consensus, there was a moment when two members whose children had not been served well by the district objected to the wording of part of the plan and blocked its approval. As these two caregivers raised their fists to block, you could almost feel the groan move through the room. However, two things happened. These two members and a couple of others worked on alternative language. It came to reflect their needs, but more than that, it helped them feel deeply heard by the whole group once it was affirmed. Others would recall that moment as a significant turning point for the coalition—the moment when it was clear that the district was really listening to the voices of all members.

CULTIVATING COMMUNITAS

Open leaders must take time and care to name the hallmarks of the community experience and celebrate both the outcome and the feeling of doing the work in a more democratic way—a feeling we call "communitas."

The work of practicing a different kind of democracy is both energizing and draining. It can be fundamentally draining to run so counter to traditional ways of doing work, like constantly swimming upstream from the bad habits of closed systems. But the energy that naturally emerges from bringing diverse teams together and engaging them in creative work is thrilling. But that energy can easily dissipate as the project draws to a conclusion, as the work products get finalized, and as the process leads back into more traditional systems.

Communitas is the consolidation of that energy, the feeling of connection and accomplishment that can sustain openness. In her book *Communitas*, Edith Turner defines and explores the concept, saying that "Communitas is togetherness itself" and "Communitas occurs through the readiness of the people—perhaps from necessity—to rid themselves of their concern for status and dependence on structures, and see their fellows as they are."[15]

Too often, we rely on a brief retrospective moment in a meeting agenda and documentation of the decisions made along the way to serve as a chronicle. But meeting minutes are not stories, and documentation is not storytelling. And even stories alone cannot create sustained openness. The people who were involved in the process need to make sense of the experience together and create a sense of communitas.

Cultivating communitas can provide emotional liberation from broken ways of working that have done harm to traditionally marginalized communities. As members of these projects talk about how different the experience was, they are engaging in a healing process that can end with a sense of hope that the system might be changing for the better. As leaders in the emerging open system hear these stories, it can galvanize their resolve to sustain open practices, and inspire other leaders adjacent to the project to adopt these practices as well.

In the final meeting of the Kentucky Coalition for Advancing Education, we created breakout rooms with members from different roles where we asked them to reflect on this question: what have we learned about inclusion, empathy, co-creation, and reciprocity?

We used these guidelines, first developed by our colleague Jenny Poon, to shape the discussion:

- Take turns telling stories, making sure that each person has a chance to tell at least one story.
- Narrow your focus to a specific moment or moments; do not try to sum up the entire experience.
- Provide as much background information and context as needed so that we understand what's going on in your story.
- Only refer to someone by their real name if the moment you're describing was visible to everyone here. If not, then refer to people only by their role (such as student or teacher).
- If the story you want to tell doesn't match the theme of this room, that's ok. Tell it anyway!

When we brought everyone back together, we asked a member from each group to tell their stories to the whole coalition. The reflections were powerful. Penny Christian, a parent advocate from Lexington, Kentucky, shared: "Parents are brought to the table in this space in a way that I've

---

Liberatory Communitas

When you are celebrating communitas, is it a shared feeling? Is there a majority of one affinity pattern that is celebrating more than others? Or a minority?

Cultivating Communitas Reflection

- Have you felt communitas in any work you have done? What did you notice about the momentum it generated?
- Where might there be a natural place for communitas in your project?
- How might you capture the stories generated in the creation of communitas?

---

never seen. I've been asked I don't know how many times, 'Can you be the parent representative for this?,' which usually means you are checking a box for the female, the parent, the Black person. It never felt like that with this. We are literally in a space where we are going to change what education in Kentucky looks like. To be included at this level is rare air."

Through the stories we gathered alongside Penny's, the assembled members of KCAE were able to both celebrate their significant accomplishments and name how the process was different from other ways of working. By telling their stories to themselves, this nascent open system set the stage for more openness in the future.

CONCLUSION

As we close this chapter, we want to bring back the idea that public leadership is the act of focusing energy and attention. A cult of personality can focus collective attention but requires that the collective will submit to a singular vision, borne of a single person. What we offer here is an alternative that advances a more inclusive form of democracy—one rooted in cultivating collective insight *and* will.

What we have shared above can be understood as a recipe, but we implore you as a creative and democratic leader to take what's here and create a path that holds to the deeper intentions that we describe. Shape the energy that comes from the collective experience. Create flows of information that build greater trust. Call out problems with that process when they arise. Name the intention of the collective through a clear decision-making process. Celebrate joyously when wins happen and learn everything you can about how you got there.

The old Aristotle quote about habits rings true here: "We are what we repeatedly do. Excellence, then, is not an act, but a habit." If we agree that excellence and prosperity are rooted in our ability to create open systems that model creative democracy, then we must consider the habits of democracy that we are cultivating in our daily lives.

CHAPTER 6

Open Principle 5

Assemble Abundance Partnerships

We can all benefit if we work together. We can't afford not to because our children are suffering. This pandemic has really affected our community, so what can we come together on?

AMANDA FERNÁNDEZ, CEO OF LATINOS FOR EDUCATION

Abundance is not something we acquire, it is something we tune into.

WAYNE DYER

Community doesn't just create abundance—community is abundance. If we could learn that equation from the world of nature, the human world might be transformed.

PARKER J. PALMER, *HEALING THE HEART OF DEMOCRACY*

BIG IDEAS IN THIS CHAPTER

- Generating higher-order impact
- Short-circuiting scarcity with clarity
- Managing co-contamination

ASSEMBLE ABUNDANCE PARTNERSHIPS

We have now arrived at the third phase of open system design, the *propelling* phase. This work creates the potential for open systems to go beyond one-off breakthroughs and into a whole new realm of possibility.

Figure 6.1

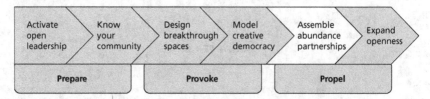

If leaders fail to leverage abundance partnerships and expand openness, they create an open island in a sea of closed systems that can eventually gravitate back to the closed system.

Assembling abundance partnerships involves a set of practices that will enable openers to share power in the long term and build even more opportunities for open system work across their local context. However, forces of scarcity await every open system process. Through the case studies in this chapter, we will explore the key practices for assembling: generating higher-order impact, short-circuiting scarcity with clarity, and managing co-contamination.

The chapter will highlight three different stages and types of abundance partnerships to help readers understand the linear stages of building such partnerships. The first, an early stage, is a nascent effort to bring communities together across the state of Georgia to build a new organization to enable new educational opportunities. The mid stage will be represented by the Sin Fronteras Education Partnership in New Mexico, bringing together national, regional, and local partners to co-create family partnership training grounded in local wisdom. The late stage will be represented by an inspiring story from the COVID-19 pandemic, when community groups in Chicago rallied to dramatically expand internet access for students in the city. An important question we will keep returning to in this chapter is whether you are building a standard partnership or one that creates abundance and potentially larger open system impact. In each of these cases, openers decided to build the latter instead of the former, and the results and momentum that emerged created opportunities for much larger system impact than an ordinary partnership.

It was not long into both of our careers in education that it became clear that it was not enough for organizations and institutions to commit to open system behavior. To sustain the level of impact we imagined, it required the commitment of others in their ecosystem to come together in ways that rejected dominant scarcity patterns of the past. In her book, *The Trance of Scarcity*, Victoria Castle compels us with the idea we are living under the sway of scarcity as a "semi-conscious state that operates in our lives without question or discernment."[1] Her book is a powerful meditation on the idea of scarcity, anchored by the resonant metaphor and resulting call to change the narrative. If we are to redesign education and reignite democracy, we need new partners who are willing to shake loose this trance, embrace abundance thinking, and rebuild trust inside communities.

Open Vignettes: Georgia, New Mexico, and Chicago; Early, Mid, and Late Stage Perspectives

Early Stage: Georgia

In December 2021, a group of district leaders, business partners, and leaders of education advocacy organizations from across the state of Georgia met to explore the question of why deeper learning was not a reality for every student, every day. Over the course of multiple convenings, the network engaged in deep open systems work. The network mapped the current ecosystem around deeper learning across Georgia. The members created a breakthrough space by inviting in significant student, teacher, and family voices. The network modeled creative democracy by naming a shared problem statement and co-creating a multipronged strategy to address it, establishing three working groups that would each engage a different root cause: a Practice working group that would support the field in deeper learning techniques, a Public Will working group that would shape public understanding of deeper learning, and a Policy working group that would consider the shifts in the policy environment needed to enable more deeper learning. In the words of Michael Duncan, superintendent of Pike County Schools and one of the founders of the network, "We were tackling something that has been unattainable in American education, which is scaling deeper learning. We have invited many people and organizations into that challenge and asked them to co-create and coauthor our strategy together. We have established a tone with all of these partners that we don't have all the answers, but we will figure it out together, and as a result we are not seeing people coming in with their own agendas."[2]

The assembled districts committed to creating at least one deeper learning experience in the coming year, with an associated student exhibition of learning. The entire network of organizations committed to "the roadshow"—attending these exhibitions and leading a conversation with students, families, and educators in each participating community about deeper learning. The insights from these conversations would then be utilized by the Public Will and Policy groups to shape their work. But as all of these organizations launch into this collaboration, with their different theories of action, service models, and funding streams, will they be able to move forward within a concept of abundance?

Mid Stage: New Mexico

In New Mexico, a group of community organizations came together to launch the Sin Fronteras Education Partnership (SFEP) to deploy high-impact, community co-created family partnership training across the state. Instead of bringing a boxed curriculum or a training series from another part of the country, the coalition committed to a community-driven process to design and build New Mexico guiding principles for family partnership work and then co-create the training alongside respected community leaders. One of the results was a trauma-informed relationship initiative called Partnership Circles, which helps students, families, and educators come together in a shared power context where they can process community trauma, generate empathy with each other, and co-develop next steps for success. "In Sin Fronteras, the partners have a shared value about transformation in our schools. We bring an asset-based approach to partnerships, always asking, 'What can each person contribute?' We know the answers exist in the community. We can co-build this together," shared Moneka Stevens, a leader in SFEP.

Meriah Heredia-Griego, cofounder of Levado, also understood this from her career leading community co-creation initiatives. The desire to include this type of statewide politically catalyzing leadership from students, families, and community leaders was an essential aspect of her theory of action. "We are building a partnership of collaborators who are willing to come together, bring their strengths, and put the hard work of transformation first. In doing that we are able to co-create thoughtful work and products for the community to own, not to sustain our organizations. Community and justice before organization."

In the Sin Fronteras project, the leaders of the individual organizations must keep open hearts at the forefront of their perspective. Not only for each other, to hold space for differing values and perspectives, but also for the communities they serve, ensuring that the programs and progress create the potential for community healing.

Late Stage: Chicago

In the early months of the COVID-19 pandemic, it was very clear that there was an urgent structural issue in providing internet services to families across the country. In every state and many localities, massive efforts were launched to bring the internet to families regardless of their socioeconomic status, to ensure their access to education and support services during the crisis. In Chicago, Kids First Chicago led numerous organizations (the city, Chicago Public Schools, and others) in coming together to launch a coalition initiative called Chicago Connected. Over the course of the pandemic, Chicago Connected provided internet access to over forty thousand households and nearly eighty thousand students, leading Bloomberg to declare this "$50 million four-year program to give free internet to low-income students . . . now the largest K–12 internet connectivity program in the country."[3] To make this incredible achievement come to life, the coalition brought thirty-five different community partners together to reject scarcity and build a world full of abundant access to connectivity for Chicago students. Daniel Anello, of Kids First Chicago, recalled the moment of potential, empathy, and urgency that called people to abundance: "I think the combination of the urgency of the moment, and also the feeling of shame on us for not paying attention to the urgent issue, catalyzed a feeling that everybody felt all at once—it created a sense of unified empathy, and that collective empathy was really important, because it meant that the mission, the getting the thing done was more important than any self-interest or personal agenda."

All of these case studies will be woven throughout the chapter so that leaders can experience the early stage, mid stage, and late stage design aspects of assembling abundance partnerships to sustain effective open system change.

GENERATING HIGHER-ORDER IMPACT

Open moments often expand into opportunities for broader impact. These require new partners, teams, and stakeholders to create impact they each could not achieve alone.

The fundamental rationale for creating abundance partnerships is the firm belief that multiple organizations and institutions working together can achieve something greater than they could ever have done on their own. We call this "higher-order impact" to show that the opportunity it represents is above the current capacity of any one organization alone.

We come back to the strategic triangle to begin the work of linking various triangles together through shared capacity and authorization environments. Each organization or institution represents a different and unique public value claim (such as organizing families or working with districts) that operate independently from each other. When you build a normal, technical partnership you are joining the unique operational capacity of each organization. This is a challenging and important process, but it essentially leaves the public value and legitimacy and support components still distinct. Imagine a school district working with an afterschool program. The extended capacity is clear and distinct, adding to each other's work. They are mutually reinforcing but fundamentally different still.

On the other hand, when you seek to assemble abundance partnerships you are joining both the legitimacy and support and operational capacity functions. Coming together, both groups name a new public value opportunity, which can only be achieved if they work together at a deeper level. Figures 6.2 and 6.3 illustrate the differences between technical and abundance partnerships and their relationship with creating higher order public value.

Figure 6.2 A traditional technical partnership sharing capacity

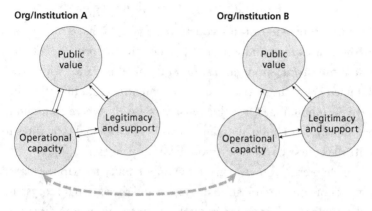

While organizations still have unique individual public value proposi-tions, the sharing of legitimacy and capacity functions creates upward pressure inside the public value propositions of each organization, shift-ing the way they operate moving forward. The end result is shifted mind-sets, beliefs, and capacity. The energy that results from an abundance partnership has enormous potential to transform institutions and orga-nizations through combined co-creative momentum.

Figure 6.3 An abundance partnership sharing capacity, legitimacy, and value

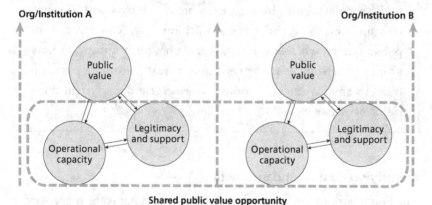

Consider Entry Directionality

An important question for consideration is, "What are the roles of the institutions and external partners in the process?" Is this *inside to outside*, an organization building abundance with external partners to dramatically shift the potential of an initiative they have been building? Or is this *outside to inside*, where community partners need to build abundance within institutional structures to shift the course of the institution toward openness?

In chapter 3, you were given the opportunity to map the closed features of your organization or system and the external ecosystem. Revisiting that analysis again is helpful in examining the directionality of the abundance partnership.

Inside to Outside Partnership

Is the type of abundance partnership you are trying to create beginning inside an institution such as a school system or agency? With the type of partnership that begins with leveraging institutional power and moves toward the outside ecosystem, there is an opportunity to accelerate openness through partnership in the broader space.

Outside to Inside Partnership

Is the partnership beginning in the broader ecosystem? Through moving from the broader community into the school system or public system, whether through organizing, philanthropy, or nonprofit partnership, your partnership can create enormous opportunities to amplify the opportunity for emergent open system shifts inside of a system.

Identifying Your Abundance Action

The first questions leaders need to speak to are: What is the higher-order impact you seek? Is this amplifying the results of a process that just unfolded? Is it developing new capacity that is clearly needed in the ecosystem? Is it seeking to seize an opportunity that just emerged? Or is it a long-festering issue that can only be addressed through multiple organizations coming together?

In New Mexico, the leadership of the state education agency leveraged federal dollars to create a request for proposals (RFP) for a family partnership initiative. The problem could have been solved by one organization, but the leaders of four organizations—the Colorado Education Initiative, Future Focused Education, Levado, and Abriendo Puertas—saw a potentially transformative opportunity. Katie Avery, former director of strategic outreach for the New Mexico public education department, realized that this was a crisis opportunity and that a call for a higher-order impact in family engagement work was needed.

> During the height of the COVID Pandemic, there was a lot of crisis management work being done at the agency at that time. As things evolved, we learned of the federal funding that was going to be available for pandemic relief and recovery efforts. The federal funds are not long-term, but because authentic family engagement work is more a way of being and a paradigm shift for district and school leaders, my hope is always that once you plant the seed and nourish the soil a little bit, that the flowers will grow, and they'll continue to grow, and folks will see how beautiful they are, and they'll say yes, we want this garden to thrive forever, and we'll figure out a way to make that happen.

When the RFP came out, the four organizations came together as Sin Fronteras with the goal to assemble an abundance partnership to achieve what the education agency sought. The agency, in turn, realized this was an opportunity for abundance and larger scale change, leading them to seek dramatic transformation along an open systems approach, and eventually to select SFEP as the partner. Katie Avery shares:

> We kept asking ourselves: "How does the delivery of that content and the content itself encourage the dismantling of systems, structures, and practices that perpetuate those barriers?" I had been talking to and doing some empathy interviews with folks in the community in New Mexico, and heard repeatedly that it was really important to support something that was not a one-size-fits-all model. I think a couple of

things were compelling about the Sin Fronteras application. One, it was
not pre-scripted. They were seeking to build a statewide task force or
advisory group that was going to engage in a co-creation process. This
was super compelling as we considered how we lift up work that's been
done for generations. The other piece that was super compelling was
this notion of it being sort of a cooperative approach that these four entities came together because of their various skill sets and their various
expertise and access within community and proximity to community. I
frankly had not seen anything like it.

In the Sin Fronteras work, there was a recognition that a regular,
strong partnership could have done some of this work, but only an abundance partnership could have seized the opportunity in this way. As you
are working through what it means to build higher-order impact, continue to interrogate that important question—does this need to be an
abundance partnership?

We offer a reflective activity aligned to this framework to assess
whether an abundance partnership is the way you can generate higher-
order impact. Table 6.1 offers various questions you ought to consider in
building higher-order impact, starting at a personal reflective level and
then moving up to organizations, sectors, and beyond.

Once you've explored generating higher-order impact in the type of
abundance partnership you're building, you need to map the critical aspects of each set of partners.

- *Rationale analysis.* What are the specific reasons for each partner
  to join? Divergent reasons for participating in a partnership are often an excuse for scuttling the entire project. We would argue that
  in fact they are needed and essential to break the affinity and mental models to truly produce abundance. Interest convergence is in
  fact a necessary and critical aspect to moving forward in reordering
  and challenging scarcity. We need to play and partner with those
  from different perspectives and rationales. It is not the difference
  in rationale that is the challenge—it is the avoidance of seeking to
  understand why two groups ought to work together in partnership.
  Interest convergence need not be 100 percent alignment, but open-

Table 6.1 Higher-order impact reflections

Personal Abundance	Organizational Abundance	Sector Abundance	Potential Conflicts
• What would you learn or how would you grow with this partnership? • How could you personally become a more abundant leader through this work?	• How would your organization or institution change as a result of this partnership? • If your organization operated more abundantly through this partnership, what else could be possible? • Is this an inside-out or outside-in partnership?	• How could the sector change as a result of the partnership? • How would this model new ways of operating?	• How could this challenge existing notions of how people approach this problem in your community? • What would the potential break-downs be between organizations? Where will scarcity be the most present?
Set a clear aspiration for one year from now:	Set a clear qualitative aspiration for your shift:	Name aspirations for ways in which the sector will have changed in one, two, and three years as a result of the abundance partnership:	How can you notice and seek to address these potential conflicts?
	Set a clear quantitative target for your shift:		

ers need to seek healthy overlap so that they can be sure that strong interest keeps all groups at the table.

- *Resource analysis.* What are the unique resources each partner is bringing to the table? Whether dollars, time, expertise, or perspectives, each partner has a unique set of assets they are holding, and these must be explored. As the partners will share operational capacity, it is essential to begin the process by sharing an understanding of the various resources around the table.

- *Relationship analysis.* What are the discreet relationships each partner brings? This goes beyond who authorizes, funds, and supports them. What's needed is a deeper understanding of their profiles, networks, and the groups that they have natural and extensive affiliations with. This is also a place to start to identify potential issues that could threaten the partnership in the long run.

The last question that must be addressed is who plays the role of trusted convener. In any partnership there must be a named trusted convener who can hold the partnership together, who exemplifies the open leader traits we discussed in the introduction, and who can hold the complexity and potential for multiple paths and perspectives to emerge. This can sometimes be a member of the partnership, such as Levado and Meriah Heredia-Griego in the Sin Fronteras project, or an outside entity, such as Kids First Chicago. In either case, a trusted convener ensures that some of the worst challenges to abundance partnerships that we discuss throughout this chapter can be mitigated. The reflection questions in table 6.2 are great protocols for new partnerships coming together and exploring their "Why" in the partnership.

SHORT-CIRCUITING SCARCITY WITH CLARITY

As new partnerships emerge, they will face numerous scarcity issues that will sabotage the efforts unless addressed directly, early, and often.

We've all seen it happen a million times. "Why did *they* get that grant?" "Why is that organization partnering with them?" We've all heard the story about the bucket of crabs, all pulling each other down. Our society is steeped in scarcity, and like fish in water, we don't even know we are as deep in it as we actually are. It's fundamentally one of

Table 6.2 Exploring and discussing: launching abundance partnerships

Mapping Topics	Essential Questions for Each Partner to Answer
Reasons	• Why are you interested in this shared endeavor? • How much overlap and interest convergence is occurring in the partnership? Is it enough to sustain the larger higher-order impact you all seek?
Resources	• What is the expertise you are bringing to the endeavor?
Relationships	• Who are your natural networks? • What are the networks that you don't typically access?

Trusted Convener: Who will be your trusted convener? One of you? Another partner outside of the space?

the largest and most challenging problems that closed systems perpetuate—the idea that there is not enough for everyone. It's socialized deep inside our mindsets and behaviors. As leaders who have attempted to build entire careers around abundance, we would be lying if we didn't find ourselves trapped by its enormous gravitational pull sometimes. There have been times when people wanted to build abundance with us when we weren't ready. We tried, but scarcity dilemmas forced us to abandon the cause.

In our experiences with partnerships, there is always an unnamed question or persistent named challenge that looms over the entire project. For example, whether everyone on the project has the same beliefs about standards or the appropriate role for businesses in education policy can be flashpoints for a team. These challenges or questions jump to the forefront when times are hard, money goes away, or personalities clash. This may manifest as all sorts of problems or issues, but many times it all comes back to what we refer to as the "original sin" at the start of the project.

Humans can be opportunistic and avoidant creatures, willing to make things work and paper over problems. This instinct will lead to compromises or accommodations to launch exciting endeavors. These become the original sins of partnership that threaten the shared, reimagined public value and haunt the work moving forward. In every one of the projects described herein, there has been an original sin that lingered through the length of the project. Some of the largest manifestations of this involve time, credit, resources, framing, approach, and more. In our experience, sometimes there are many at the same time!

As the Georgia work is getting started, leaders are taking time to interrogate some of the potential challenges that may emerge in the long term. When the network considered the strategy around the deeper learning roadshow, a number of participants brought up how we would measure the success of the approach, reflexively bringing up the need to anchor success to traditional standardized testing. The moment was a test of the emerging idea of a different articulation of public value, and it required the network to name the larger paradigm shift that deeper learning would require. By choosing to discuss the issue directly, rather than paper over it, the network was able to hold it as a point for ongoing inquiry. As Leslie Hazle Bussey, executive director of the Georgia Leadership Institute for School Improvement, the trusted convener of the network, notes, "We are not directly neutralizing those doubts, but this is the 'Deeper Learning Network.' Through the design and the invitational culture, we are being intentional about modeling what we want to see happen in the classroom through our own adult behavior and interaction with each other. I think we want to invite some of that critique, and our DNA should be about surfacing and intentionally creating the space to hear these issues."

As you assemble abundance partnerships, you should begin with an assumption that the project has an original sin. What are you avoiding or failing to resolve that could come back to rear its head later in the

---

Original Sin Reflection
- What are you saying "yes" to that you have second thoughts about?
- What are you avoiding that your gut is telling you may become a problem?
- Are there personality triggers in the project that you are concerned about or challenged by?

process? Assume there is a problem present at the beginning of the work that participants see as a problem but decide to avoid for the sake of the project going forward. Notice these, because they will reemerge later in new forms. Given the sharing of operational capacity and authorizing environments, these original sins have the potential to evolve into major destabilizing challenges.

Openers need to understand that just as the potential for maximized impact in the endeavor grows through designing and assembling abundance partnerships, so do the dangers and potential destabilizing factors. This can mean dramatic impact or dramatic conflict. Watching and considering the potential challenges of the original sin allows openers to be vigilant in the early stages and throughout, and it gives them a chance to repair any faulty electrical wiring before it overloads the system.

The roots of scarcity run deep in our society—and why not? Our society is organized around resources—their extraction, collection, and maintenance. Many of our ancestors came from societies where the preservation and ordering of those resources was an inherently finite affair. Therefore many of us are socialized to accept scarcity as a precondition for living and working. Victoria Castle suggests that "we break the trance of scarcity every time we interrupt the deeply inculcated messages we have been trained to accept as Truth and intentionally replace them with new, life affirming Stories."[4]

In the Chicago Connected work, they fought this scarcity mentality by keeping themselves grounded in co-creation. Daniel, from Kids First

---

Noticing and Interrupting the Original Sin Reflection

- Are you clear about the impact you can achieve through an abundance partnership?
- As you mapped reasons, resources, and relationships did you have any second thoughts about the partnership? Is this really an abundance partnership or a regular partnership?
- What are the potential original sins that you see emerging in this abundance partnership?

Chicago, gave this perspective on fighting scarcity with clarity by keeping those most impacted close to the process.

> Once things started moving, they moved so fast that having people who are directly impacted guiding all the decision-making was a lot harder to do than it typically would be, because that takes time. So if you're going to open up the system, you got to take the time to do it. That means meeting people where they are, helping them get up to speed on the issues in a way that they can be really productive contributors. We knew it was critical to keep parents and people directly impacted by lack of internet at the table.

Yet the idea that all of our ancestors lived this way is a convenient fiction that encourages this worst instinct. Indeed, collaboration and co-ordination are more the norm than our modern society gives them credit for. Is it hard and challenging? Absolutely. But it's not impossible, and examples abound of how groups have come together to challenge the dominant assumption. As brilliantly explained in *Gardens of Democracy*:

> A fundamental assumption of traditional economics is that competitiveness creates prosperity. This view, descended from a misreading of Adam Smith and Charles Darwin, weds the invisible hand of the market to the natural selection of nature. It justifies atomic self-seeking. A clearer understanding of how evolution forces work in a complex adaptive human society shows that cooperation is the true foundation of prosperity (as does a full reading of Adam Smith's lesser-known masterpiece *A Theory of Moral Sentiments*). Competition properly understood—in nature or in business—is between groups of cooperators. Groups that know how to cooperate—whose members attend to social and emotional skills like empathy—defeat those that do not. That's because only cooperation can create symbiotic, nonzero outcomes. And those nonzero outcomes, borne and propelled by ever-increasing trust and cooperation, create a feedback loop of ever increasing economic growth and social health.[5]

Much of Chicago Connected's success rested on breaking through assumptions of scarcity—from internet providers, organizations, nonprofits, families, and communities—in how internet access could be scaled and achieved to really provide help for all students. This required constant dialogue about money, resources, and results to keep interrupting the traditional scarcity patterns that existed. The end result was a dramatic expansion of connectivity and a shining example of abundance thinking transforming how kids were served. The critical issue is getting clear on the specifics—the cost, the players, the structure of what is and isn't on the table. For Chicago Connects, this clarity cannot be underestimated in the effort to bring about abundance. As Daniel Anello says, "We had this aligned group of Internet service providers, the City, Chicago Public Schools, United Way, philanthropy . . . just about everybody seemed to be aligned because they understood the mission—we are focused on connecting families to the Internet, and that issue is defined. There is a scale, there is a cost, etc. Most importantly, our alignment was founded in what the community wanted."

The Chicago example shows that we have an extremely powerful tool in our arsenal to build abundance and fight scarcity—clarity. It is our belief that much of the scarcity we face in public education results from a lack of clarity across many entities, leading to confusion, confrontation, and ultimately conflict. As we noted in discussing the idea of radical clarity, it is a gift you give yourself and other people. In each of these following scarcity situations we see an opportunity for powerful clarity interruptions. It may not be enough to resolve every scarcity challenge, but in our experience, clarity will solve a significant number of the issues inside and outside organizations as they seek assembling abundance. It may not ever be fully solved, but many times it can be managed.

Scarcity Challenges

- *Interest divergence.* Over time, it's possible that interests will diverge inside the partnership between institutions or organizations. The result is a scarcity concern around the current capacity deployed to the project and the leveraging of shared authorizers. In some cases, it's one partner who decides another project is more relevant and urgent. In others, it's a partner deciding that the work of abundance is too tiring and draining. Maybe they don't like where the revised direction or shifts are occurring in their organization—or within themselves.

- *Resource dilemma.* In the Chicago example, dollars had to be shared across a variety of organizations and partners. Indeed, trusted community partners were key players. The Chicago mayor's office, a key leader in the effort, said "Community partners make this entire initiative work," and resources were a key factor.[6] From paying individuals and groups to get the word out, to training the newly connected families how to navigate the internet, there had to be a constant focus on the budget and on establishing clarity.

- *Capacity differential.* All abundance partnerships must accept a very hard reality: there will be a capacity differential between groups and individuals. Certain organizations or groups in the partnership will do more than others. Scarcity thinking wires us to think we need equivalent or equal capacity inside the partnership. Like partners in a marriage who are keeping track of who takes out the garbage, it's a fallacy when striving to build real abundance. It's a fallacy at the outset because it assumes that we know everything that every partner is doing. Just because we don't see capacity being deployed in other organizations does not mean that it is not being deployed. Abundance assemblers must first admit the limitations of their visibility. In many cases, work is hidden or not evident for many good reasons. Maybe while one organization is building training infrastructure, another is working with key political leaders inside the authorizing environment to build the case for the partnership. One shows up on Google docs; the other does not.

The way to confront scarcity is not to fight back with more scarcity, with avoidance, or with hostility; it is with clarity. The deep, ingrained socialization of scarcity runs so deep that one must consciously turn to the "clarity cycle": a process of naming the scarcity challenge, sharing and building awareness of it with the broader audiences involved, resolving it as best as possible, and then continuing to return to it over and over again. These scarcity challenges are by no means exhaustive and comprehensive, but they are the ones we find most likely to emerge in the wiring of abundance.

Scarcity thinking leads to avoidance, which leads to ambiguity, which then leads to communication breakdowns in budgets and resource con-

---

Short-Circuiting Scarcity with Clarity Reflection

• What personal experience with scarcity do you have that you need to interrupt or interrogate?
• Which of the scarcity dilemmas discussed has shown up recently in a project, or which do you anticipate may show up?
• How can you continuously hold abundance when faced with these dilemmas?

---

versations. This is not to assume every project is going to create real transformational abundance across all partners, indeed far from it. Instead of imagining plentiful resources or fighting over obscurity in the budget, instead lean deeper into the work of getting clear about the realities of the budget, understanding what is actually possible, and creating visibility for how to address the issue.

All of these can also be symptoms of an original sin. If uninterrupted, it usually means that the potential for higher-order impact cannot be achieved. Who does what and how it gets done are essential and defining questions of every partnership. In our experience, people are often extremely avoidant, delayed, and fragile when it comes to naming this issue. This is where the clarity cycle is critical. Find all the information early and often so you can name the problems and challenges in the capacity situation.

MANAGING CO-CONTAMINATION

All stakeholders have distinct agendas that can create fear and concern from others; this must be managed to sustain the partnership.

Through the course of this chapter and this phase of open system work we have been discussing propelling the work forward with the power of abundance partnerships that can give new energy, ballast, and lift to open system redesign in communities. What we must turn to is a major issue in the building of partnerships, a real source of real frustration for openers everywhere: co-contamination.

Co-contamination means individuals or groups joining your project that corrupt the essential shared public value proposition and disrupt the binding together of capacity and support. Why is co-contamination such a problem? If not dealt with, co-contamination essentially risks destroying everything you've worked for.

Co-contamination manifests as either the entry of new actors into the space, a shift in the behavior of current authorizers or participants, or the appearance of subversive members of a process who seek to challenge the outcome or legitimacy. This is a wide range of negative or destructive behavior that can severely damage or sabotage a process. It is bigger than co-opting a process—it is the disruptive breakdown of the co-creative space that has been held to open the system. In the article "(Co)-contamination as the Dark Side of Co-production," the authors give this understanding of the concept: "Co-contamination results from the misuse of resources during the interaction between service providers and service users . . . the main idea is that public value is negatively affected when resources are used in a manner that is considered unexpected or inappropriate by the activities of either system."[7]

In politically critical co-creation spaces, it can mean resources depleted, shared rationale obliterated, and relationships ruined. This could be the new partner who commandeers the steering committee toward their ends. It might be an organization who joins the partnership but saps capacity and funding toward another project. It may be a new leader inside the abundance partnership who rejects the shared vision entirely, but because they are at the helm of a current partner, they hold the whole project captive.

Openers need to realize that generating abundance that achieves higher-order impact will inevitably create a lot of noise and therefore draw attention. People notice. In Sin Fronteras, their audacious goal is to transform family and community partnership. Once they started making this happen, and it was clear that they had the resources to achieve it, other organizations wanted to be a part of it. That's the goal! Yet openers need to be thoughtful and cognizant of how to manage the potential deleterious impacts of co-contamination. As Brian Williams and his coauthors state, "To address the co-contaminating opportunities and effects on the regular producer side of the equation, organizations must commit to self-reflexivity. Managers must engage in a critical review of their professional norms, organizational or institutional processes, and past and present policies and practices."[8]

Openers in this moment need to manage the fear and reality of co-contamination. Here, we intentionally use the term *manage* instead of *solve*. Like a lot of other big ideas in this book, there is not a solution to co-contamination; it is always a tension that needs to be explored in the context of open system partnerships. We also need to note that co-contamination can occur at any stage in an open system process. At any moment, openers need to leverage key reflection and actions to manage

---

Ten Frequent Examples of Co-contamination

- *Reasons:* New members want to join but demand excessive shifts in already agreed upon ideas.
- *Reasons:* Current members start to use "outsider" language (such as stepping back on ownership and using "we" in the project).
- *Reasons:* Partners have a subversive, undisclosed reason for entering the abundance partnership that becomes known.
- *Reasons:* Mission drift occurs in the shared value agreement for all partners, changing the commitment scope.
- *Resources:* Outside pressure from philanthropy or other partners aims to change the shift or focus of the mission.
- *Resources:* Partners shift the original terms of sharing capacity (time, money, etc.) without full agreement.
- *Resources:* Partners exit over conflict over capacity (time, money, etc.).
- *Relationships:* Outside advocacy groups demand changes from the process before it's finalized or complete.
- *Relationships:* New partners demand entrance into the partnership without a clear commitment to share capacity or support.
- *Relationships:* Key political stakeholders shift the terms of the partnership, corrupting the authorizing environment.

co-contamination: maintain your core focus, reject simplicity and embrace empathy, and say no when it matters.

Core Focus

In any co-creation process, whether it is a small group of families deciding the path of a school or a larger network of partners working toward abundance across an entire ecosystem, there are core members. They may have equality in standing with everyone involved with the project, but they represent the leaders and organizations most committed to the project and the shared value proposition. In any stage where there is movement from new members or current members toward co-contamination of the process, openers must establish a core focus. In SFEP, the leaders were careful to establish a shared set of values and impacts for the task force early in the work. Bringing new partners together for the first time is an enormous challenge from a co-creative perspective, opening up all sorts of new energy and information into a process. It is a key moment that can destabilize the process or propel it forward.

Instead of just jumping right into content co-creation with the task force, the Sin Fronteras team spent extensive time and energy on a shared co-creative act of building the core focus by establishing guiding principles for all new partners to create together, to share, and to build. These principles created connective tissue among the group by establishing shared language around the project for the first time. The guiding principles also offered natural entry and exit points for members. And they served as a powerful alignment activity when new partners or energy arrived inside the partnership, creating and deepening connections among leaders and participants. Existing members who might sense misalignment could use that as an opportunity to name a reasonable cause for separation from the work.

The power of these community co-created guiding principles inspired the design of the content, helped smooth over disagreements, and also helped to ensure that new partners (such as trainers) were very clear on the core values of the project. In this case, leveraging a core focus activity like the guiding principle process created a powerful space for clarity to manage the potential for co-contamination in the project as new and old partners struggle through challenging questions.

Sin Fronteras Guiding Principles

- *Begin with community assets.* We anchor our work in the history and future of work that currently exists in our communities.
- *Grounded in local wisdom.* We place and understand our work in the unique knowledge and truth of our communities.
- *Co-creation and co-ownership.* We build and share the work alongside those in the communities we serve.
- *Transformative healing.* Our work should enable restoration and reparative experiences, allowing the opportunity for growth in a community to move beyond past trauma.
- *Community reverence.* We honor, recognize, and cherish the communities we serve.[9]

Returning to Empathy

One of the major challenges of co-contamination is not even co-contamination—it's actually the *fear* of co-contamination! This is where scarcity once again rears its ugly head and creates mental models, beliefs, and assumptions that create the perception of a problem before it even starts.

We've been involved in countless projects as facilitators where people eagerly tell us which "problem partners" or facilitators are blocking the process. We've watched as people assume the worst of partners before we even get started, ready to balk at even the smallest notion of accommodation. As we discussed in the process of creating a shared reality in chapter 5, empathy work is a critical component of co-creation. Empathy often means spending one-to-one or small-group time with those most passionate and connected to the current co-creative endeavor. In these conversations, openers must ascertain how the core group feels about the new or shifted conditions associated with expanding abundance partnerships—the people, ideas, and resources. Sometimes their entrance means the abundance will be accelerated dramatically. In other cases, personalities may clash and competing relationships could doom the partnership.

In the Sin Fronteras project, there have been multiple cases where Meriah Heredia-Griego has played the role of trusted convener, building empathy and understanding across the group as challenges or the potential for challenges mounted. "I start by having conversations individually to understand everyone's needs and interests. Once we are in a gathered setting, I can drop a nugget that everyone understands. We often don't have to dig into an issue all together because we've had individual focused conversations about these ideas. That makes the group conversation smoother and aligned, because we've already worked through the challenges earlier."

As openers, we must always be highly attuned with empathy for all the participants or partners we are working with. In many cases, like the Sin Fronteras example, the fear of co-contamination was actually greater than the actual risk. And in our experience, this can be just as dangerous or more dangerous. Unless openers and leaders are not prepared to listen, learn, and make shifts necessary, the challenges will emerge.

Say No When It Matters

Openers must be prepared to say no to partnerships that don't make sense. As projects undergo the threat of co-contamination, usually participants or partners make requests or shifts, and openers must determine if they are the right path forward for the work. Saying no to new partners doesn't come naturally to openers. We have found that openers by nature are includers who see the potential in many partnerships, arrangements,

---

Liberatory Abundance Partnerships

Openers must directly confront affinity bias in themselves and in their partnerships to lead to true abundance, ensuring that new patterns of resource sharing, relationships, and perspectives can shift behavior and systems. Note: we use affinity instead of identity in this section because we have found that some leaders are naturally talented at reaching across identity barriers and not necessarily across affinity. For example, a white leader may feel comfortable with her Latino community, but not with her Ethiopian one. While there is work happening across identity, there is still an affinity pattern that needs to be interrupted to maximize the openness in the school community.

- **Generating higher-order impact**
  - Are you considering organizations outside of your affinity patterns to partner with and to assemble abundance with?
- **Identifying your abundance action**
  - As you are targeting a potential action for abundance partnership, how are you considering the implications of the abundance you are considering generating?
- **Reasons, resources, relationships**
  - Have you excluded groups from other affinity patterns because they do not (or do) share the same reasons as you? Why?
  - Have you excluded groups from other affinity patterns because they are (or are not) bringing resources to the conversation?
  - Have you actively pursued groups with relationships with other affinities to add value to the partnership?
- **Noticing and interrupting the original sin**
  - In the design of the partnership, are you being more avoidant or more confrontational with groups with different affinities?
- **Short-circuiting scarcity with clarity**
  - Are you perpetuating scarcity patterns with groups outside your natural affinity?
  - Are you only building abundance and interrupting scarcity thinking inside your affinity?
- **Managing co-contamination**
  - How are you ensuring that potential partners outside of your affinity have the potential to join the group? Or, if they will not be able to join the group, can you create other vehicles for partnership?

and opportunities. However, at some point openers need to be very clear about the dangers of failing to say no when it matters.

If openers pursue core focus and embrace empathy to manage these tensions, they often find ways through the co-contamination dilemma. Yet still, even through all of that work, there will eventually be a line that has to be drawn to preserve the power of the open transformation that is occurring. Failure to say no can lead to destabilizing the shared vision of partnership, introducing unfaithful actors into the project, and the worst-case scenario—causing animosity among the core abundance partnerships, ensuring the failure of the project.

It's also important that openers recognize the difference between *no, forever* and *no, for now*. In some cases, *no, forever* is saying that this is just not a fit and it doesn't make sense for us to join capacity and impact. There is little to no possibility for the interest convergence work to manifest. It would be too hard, we are too different, and our visions don't align.

Sometimes the answer is *no, for now*. Maybe the project is at a pivotal inflection moment where the process of assembling abundance may be too destabilizing for a project. Maybe it is clear there is enormous long-term potential, but it just doesn't make sense right now. *No, for now* is an important frame to bring to these moments because it creates a potential for deeper future partnership that could manifest later in the project but makes it clear that right now it just doesn't make sense.

In SFEP, numerous opportunities were presented to the group to expand the scope of the project with new partners. In some scenarios, the partnership just didn't make sense to enter into the abundance model SFEP was building. In one case, the project was too new, too fragile to introduce new opportunities—SFEP still needed to focus on its core work. In another case, it was clear the partner had a completely different

---

Managing Co-contamination Reflection
- What potential threats for co-contamination exist in your partnership or process?
- What would be the result of co-contamination if left unchecked?

vision for what the project could lead to, and the interest convergence just wasn't aligned. In the first case, it was a *no, for now* and in the latter, it was *no, forever*. In both cases, the *no* was leveraged to ensure the success of the project at important inflection points.

If you have to say no to a current participant or new partner, do you have a sense of how you'd leverage core focus and embrace empathy to say *no, forever* or *no, for now*?

CONCLUSION

In the path to propelling the momentum for co-creation and open systems across entire organizations, networks, and ecosystems, assembling abundance partnerships is a critical first and very challenging step. We must confront the scarcity-dominant cultural patterns in our society and remodel, rewire, and reimagine partnerships for abundance.

At the heart of this chapter's propelling work is the idea that we must assemble new arrangements and partnerships with clarity and transparency to amplify the potential for open systems transformation. If we can do this work, we can transform individual values into shared values and opportunities for a higher-order impact we could not do alone.

The work of this chapter is grounded in the idea that we can imagine a better way. The next step in the work is expanding openness inside of a system or among partnerships. This final step then allows us to zoom out and consider the potential for openness across our entire society and the implications for shifting systems in this direction.

CHAPTER 7

Open Principle 6

Expand Openness

Democracy, then, must begin at the start and never cease. It must be open.

HÉLÈNE LANDEMORE

How we are at the small scale is how we are at the large scale. The patterns of the universe repeat at scale. There is a structural echo that suggests two things: one, that there are shapes and patterns fundamental to our universe, and two, that what we practice at a small scale can reverberate to the largest scale.

ADRIENNE MAREE BROWN, EMERGENT STRATEGY

It's always around me, all this noise, but not nearly as loud as the voice saying,
"Let it happen, let it happen (It's gonna feel so good) Just let it happen, let it happen."

TAME IMPALA, "LET IT HAPPEN"

BIG IDEAS IN THIS CHAPTER

- Sustaining co-production
- Identifying and integrating slipstreams
- Translocal adaptation
- Lifting up openers and open narratives

Figure 7.1

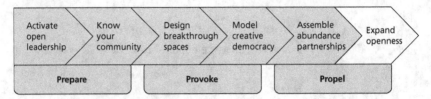

EXPAND OPENNESS

We now arrive at the final open principle. Since the very beginning of the book, we've discussed the tension of presenting a linear path given the interconnectedness of open system redesign and co-creative work. We hope that we have shown what it means to prepare for open system work, both personally and within a community, and to see these principles as interconnected rather than linear. Now we are asking readers and leaders to imagine building the significant propelling power to sustain and expand openness through systems and across ecosystems.

Throughout the book, we have sometimes described building the open system or open ecosystems as creating an electric current. If the current gets blocked at any stage of the process, it could stop all the positive energy from building in the system. A virtuous cycle has the same connotation—if the flow is broken or blocked, we lose momentum. This chapter is dedicated to the work of openers leveraging the momentum and breakthroughs they have experienced to now expand openness. This is the work of ensuring the open moments they've built become standard features, not a blip or bug of the system and ecosystem they work in.

We begin with sustained co-production, the critical work of keeping the community deeply involved in implementation to enact deeper system change. We then move to identifying and integrating slipstreams, which helps openers identify opportunities that emerge in the system as further vehicles for change. How should the work of openness spread? To answer this question, we adapt and bring in the concept of translocal adaptation, borrowed from Margaret Wheatley in *Walk Out Walk On*, to explore why replication is a failed concept and how communities learning together can grow openness.[1] Revisiting our first principle, a key leadership move for openers is understanding the critical role they have in lifting up openers and open narratives—seeking and sustaining others in their communities who can share in the important work of system change, and shifting the discourse within communities that partnership and redesign are not Sisyphean affairs but rather projects with real, tangible results.

In every case study we've presented, we've intentionally featured only a slice of the work. In this chapter we return to many of the open vignettes, following their stories further to understand how they are expanding openness inside their system. You'll learn about Boulder's efforts to expand the impact of their school discipline reform with deeper co-production, hear how the Homegrown Talent Initiative spurs replication for adaptation as it expands to new communities and regions across the state, and explore how Kentucky is amplifying the creative energy from their initiative to build new visions of possibility, Burlington is creating durable structures to sustain involvement and mutual accountability, and Chicago leveraged their relationships and networks to break through on assessment and accountability with new slipstreams in the city.

While we have arrived at the last open principle in our book's path toward fostering more openness, we need to decidedly and unequivocally state that expanding openness is not the end—it really is just the beginning. If we are to fully conceive of how many closed features exist in the systems that surround us, we must fully accept that the work is never truly done. This daunting reality is the real truth of the opener: through embracing the never-ending opportunity ahead of you, closed systems around you may begin to fall away and communities' hopes will rise up.

SUSTAINING CO-PRODUCTION

Openers should attend to maintaining reciprocal relationships with the community throughout the process of implementation.

Throughout this book, we've talked a significant amount about the need to catalyze and sustain co-creation to create open systems. In chapter 1, on understanding the theoretical underpinnings of co-creation, we also discussed co-production, the work of long-term capacity creation with the community and key authorizers. We grounded the discussion in the following definitions:

Co-creation: In the genesis of assembling a public value proposition, members of the authorizing environment are given the ability to shape the design and final product, producing they believe is needed. *Example: A community design team is formed to guide a turnaround process. This design team gets to name the school and the type of program involved, and they build the blueprint with the school leader.*

Co-production: In the ongoing work of producing public value, members of the authorizing environment help and are involved in the organization directly. This can range from being deeply involved in directly running the operation to simply having oversight and steering responsibilities. *Example: The school district appoints a citizen oversight council which helps place new schools, guides the chartering of new options, and advises the board and superintendent on critical issues.*

In Boulder, after the conclusion of the first equity council process in the fall of 2020, the district board and the leadership team knew that the work was only just beginning. Immediately after the recommendations were approved by the board in October, the district stated directly that they were going to take the community momentum from the process and go deeper into design and implementation. Superintendent Anderson explained his thinking about co-production moving forward in the process.

It was important to be inclusive every step of the way. So we turned back to community and essential thought-partners at each step of the process, not cutting one corner. Once you get started with opening, that's not the time to stop—you have to double-down, you have to keep engaging. As we were designing the new School Safety Advocates, every question was on the table: Who should be at the interview for the candidates? What should we call them? What training should they have? What should they wear? We became incredibly precise at being inclusive. Once we opened up the system, it was easier to keep it open. Now we continue to share the results and continue to be open to new perspectives because tomorrow might bring us a new problem which means we may need to re-engage folks tomorrow, and our team has embraced that idea.[2]

As Superintendent Anderson and his team showed, co-creation wasn't the end—it was just the start of co-production. They decided to launch a youth equity council that would go deeper on advising the district on the key questions that had been discussed along with the school safety advocate issue. They sought community partner feedback on the design and ongoing implementation, critical co-production structures. Equity director Amy Nelson shared her thoughts on how the opportunities for co-production began to emerge around the equity council and the youth equity council.

> I think something that's important to note is a lot of our decision makers such as the board see an initiative that's new, [and] they want to know "Well, what does Equity Council think about this? What does the Youth Equity Council think?" It's really a wonderful thing to have a board that recognizes the importance of community and student voice as we're talking about initiatives that will impact them and our communities.

Across this expansion of openness, you can see how the voices and perspectives are leveraged for deeper understanding, implementation, and perspective. We must take a closer look, however, and understand how in these examples we see fractal evidence of every single one of the open principles. In table 7.1 we share how BVSD continued through their on-going co-creation work manifested each of the principles.

To expand open system change in institutions and in new partnerships, openers must understand how to shift from co-creation to co-production in the ongoing work of implementation. In our experience, too much open system change work stops after co-creation. Openers and community members are inspired and excited by the incredible potential of co-creation: vision, design, catalytic collisions, and emergent new ideas. After the exciting launch, openers fail to attend to the deeper and ongoing work of keeping the community involved in the project in a meaningful way. Some find implementation too hard, too boring, too tedious. Yet it is the grinding but essentially propelling work of co-production that keeps the system open even when it inevitably wants to close and revert to the old ways of being. Superintendent Anderson names a deep truth in pursuit of co-production: "Nothing is forever. The world

Table 7.1 How BVSD continued co-production across all open principles

Open Principle	Co-production Manifestation
Activate open leadership	• Continuing to exemplify open minds, open hearts and open paths with regards to new initiatives • Exemplifying democratic leadership in the empowering of community voices • Encouraging leadership and board members to prioritize co-creation
Know your community	• Continuing to partner with community groups for perspective on critical issues
Design breakthrough spaces	• Strengthening the equity council with new opportunities to weigh in • Establishing a youth equity council to hold breakthrough spaces
Model creative democracy	• Empowering groups to make decisions that have impact
Assemble abundance partnerships	• Partnering with local and national organizations to train School Safety Advocates
Expand openness	• Continuing to co-create with groups

changes. The people in your community change. This is continuous improvement—open systems and co-creation create alignment with what you do and what your community cares about."

Similarly in Burlington, Vermont, the district leadership team has embodied a spirit of continual evolution and co-production with the community, sparked by the initial act of co-creation. The district is creating a strategic plan guiding coalition that will use the same inclusion model to deeply involve students and families in the implementation of the strategic plan. Members of the guiding coalition will be compensated for their time and will meet regularly to review progress on the strategic plan and identify ways for the community to support the work. The district identified the moment of transition from the co-creation to the co-production process as an opportunity to rethink the membership of the group. In the words of Victor Prussack, engagement director for the Burlington schools:

As we got to the end of the strategic planning process, fewer members of our coalition were showing up because we had gotten to the "edu-speak" world of implementation. We needed to step back and rethink where we needed the community to be participating. We will be reforming the guiding coalition to hold the district accountable to doing what we had written in the strategic plan.

Throughout this book we have mentioned the concept of fractals, of patterns that recur on small and large scales throughout systems, our lives, and the cosmos. Instead of succumbing to the numbing vision of implementation offered by closed technocratic systems, openers must embrace the idea that each move in the long-term co-production of a breakthrough space or creative democratic moment can be a fractal representation of all of these principles together. By doing so, they are ensuring that the line between the system and the community remains in a dynamic state of exchange, energy, and potential. Figure 7.2 reinforces our discussions about co-creation, showing how it's critical to ensure that the operational capacity remains tethered to the authorizing environment.

Sustaining co-production through deep implementation with the community is a challenging and grinding process that many leaders and openers struggle to complete. Yet, if we are to truly reignite democracy through open system work, we must understand that co-creation and democratic action must be an ongoing process to fully embed the democratic spirit in the project, continually reinforcing the key principles we've seen throughout the book. We must reimagine how co-production, instead of a grinding implementation, can become a fractal manifestation

Figure 7.2 Moving from promise to commitment: co-producing capacity

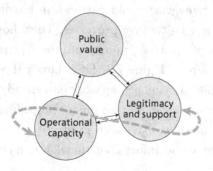

Sustaining Co-production Reflection

- How have you seen co-production falter?
- How can you design for co-production to ensure long-term open system impact?
- How can you embed all the open principles into your co-production structures, ensuring a fractal manifestation of openness?

---

of the spirit of each of the principles we've discussed, continually reimagining and reigniting the work moving forward.

IDENTIFYING AND INTEGRATING SLIPSTREAMS

As new opportunities for openness emerge, leaders must cultivate them and weave seemingly disparate initiatives together.

In any system or organization, there are numerous change initiatives happening all the time. This might be a new organizational initiative, a concerted effort in one region of a city, or another wave of new programs to focus more targeted efforts. In the wake of the success of an open moment or co-creative process, new initiatives will emerge. Openers ought to think of these as the slipstreams of energy occurring throughout an organization that create the potential for new co-creation or co-production with the community. We call it a "slipstream" to invoke the idea of flows of water, energy, or momentum moving in the wake of larger movement that can carry opportunities to expand openness. If they adopt this frame or mental model, openers can begin to see these slipstreams as necessary and critical arenas for ongoing impact.

Specifically, slipstreams are system or community work that, through effective change management and partnership building, can converge with or emerge new co-creative processes. This allows an opener (or hopefully, a team of openers) to jump into the slipstream, building the case for more openness. Figure 7.3 shows how a slipstream can be an opportunity to build system opening work into already existing or newly emerging processes, and can create a unique propelling momentum.

One brilliant move we have seen in identifying slipstreams in systems is making the opportunities invitational. Karen Dodd, the chief per-

Figure 7.3 Merging open system work with slipstreams

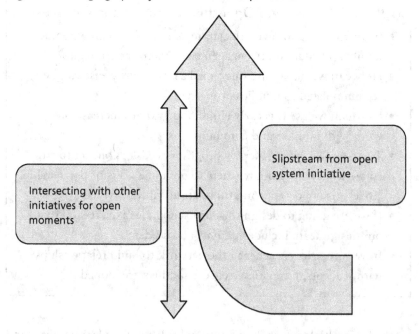

formance officer for the Kentucky Department of Education, oversees the strategic planning process for the agency. As she led the process, she sought to incorporate greater openness in how different departments engaged in their strategic planning. Rather than mandate that departments co-create everything with their constituents, she asked them to choose an initiative that might be done in a more open way. Karen says, "I recently led a KDE leadership team meeting and started to share with them the ideas of inclusion, empathy, co-creation, and reciprocity. I asked them: 'How can you take the work that you do in your everyday processes, your initiatives, and make that more co-creative? How do you open it up beyond the walls of the state department or even just beyond the walls of your own office? How might you co-create with the other offices within KDE?' I would say that this is just the beginning within the department."

The sidebar list contains slipstream examples we have seen that can create momentum for open system change. These could be in communications, afterschool programs, assessment, or many other areas. Consider the building of a new strategic plan. This represents a new slipstream of

Potential Slipstream Opportunities to Expand Openness

- If we are going to revise the strategic plan, how can we embed family and community engagement into all the strategies?
- How can we make sure this timed assessment release can be communicated to families properly?
- How can we use this early childhood grant to increase our work with families and communities?
- This new secondary literacy program needs to connect to parents—what if we train teachers to do home visits or partnership circles to support meaningful relationships?
- If we are going to design this new school, let's make sure that our design team includes parents and students.
- If we want every teacher in the network to build relationships with students, how can we ensure families are looped in?

work that multiple internal and external folks will be leaning into, and is therefore a place where opening work can be really powerful. Or consider an initiative to roll out a new communications strategy for schools, a new afterschool program, a new grant to be applied for. In these cases, openers can see and create opportunities for these change initiatives to find ways for the energy they've created in other areas to be lifted up for potential new open system change.

In many of these cases, the goal of the opener is to integrate these slipstreams with open system work already in practice, external partners who are excited about the possibility of change, and new opportunities for modeling creative democracy. Then, by converting the potential within the slipstream, an adept opener can catalyze the opportunity to provoke a new open moment.

In chapter 6, we shared the inspiring story of Chicago Connected. Not long after Kids First Chicago supported the breakthrough in connectivity and internet access across the city, they were asked to support building a new initiative around assessment and accountability. Often the third rail of politics in education, the relationships and energy created through the open system work created slipstreams toward partnerships with the city, communications about the future of education, and leaders interested in what the next phase of the work could adapt into.

Natalie Neris, an opener-in-residence with the Open System Institute and chief community engagement officer with Kids First Chicago said, "Chicago Connected is a really great example of how listening to people, engaging communities, and partnering with the right people can create changes." They seized the opportunity to merge various efforts from across the city, including both district and community leaders to create a shared vision for the system moving forward.

Throughout the COVID-19 pandemic, Kids First Chicago conducted a radically inclusive design process to bring community partners together to converge these slipstreams of possibility into a larger, community-wide conversation for the future of education. Led by Natalie, the efforts created breakthrough conditions for new co-creative energy. Natalie shared some of her vision for the project and bringing all these new partners to table.

> We needed to make sure that they were a part of the conversation proactively but also recognizing that it is the combination of all of those groups that ultimately, if we could get those groups to buy in, and again to be part of this design, then they would be more likely to embrace our radically inclusive theory of action. Then they would be more likely to support the implementation of the policies.

Natalie's process mirrored the principles embedded in this book—the need for open leaders, designing a space to co-create, modeling creative democracy in the process, and assembling abundance partnerships—to catalyze a real shift in this controversial topic.

She convened what she called a "radically inclusive" stakeholder engagement design team, ensuring they had diversity from a variety of backgrounds and viewpoints on the issue. She committed to building their capacity and knowledge on the complicated topics of assessment and accountability, and worked tirelessly on her open moment—to redesign the system of accountability and assessment in Chicago. This was a consequential inversion of power. The stakeholder engagement design team was able to design outreach and coanalyze data findings for more than twelve thousand respondents to surveys they themselves designed and focus groups they were a part of. Instead of being told what the accountability framework would be, they are able to say, "Here is what we want." Through the process, the system that usually dictates (Chicago Public Schools) was a listener, ultimately tasked with developing a framework that reflected what they heard from stakeholders.

At the end of the process, Chicago Public Schools and the city of Chicago had something unlike anything they had before—a shared community vision and plan for reimagining assessment and accountability, co-created and co-produced with the community. Natalie shares the impact: "The beauty of it is that not only has trust been able to increase with the district but we're also seeing the district place a greater value on this infrastructure for radical inclusion. That's really what the stakeholder engagement design team is—it's infrastructure."

Liberatory Expansion of Openness

- As you take opportunities to co-produce, have you been honest with yourself and others about the challenges from the first round of co-creation? Were there affinity groups that were not included or sought out that should be included in this next phase?

- As you seek to merge slipstreams with other projects, are you considering real opportunities for communities and students furthest from opportunity to gain access to openness?

- As you are considering adaptation across communities, are you seeking communities with similar affinity or identity, or seeking to bridge differences to bring openness to communities that may not be immediately considered because of a closed system mentality?

- How are you lifting up stories of openness that involve communities and identities that can tell different stories from the dominant stories usually told about these places?

Slipstream Reflection

- What are the upcoming or available slipstreams in your current systems that you can jump into right now?
- Where can you de-prioritize changing existing structures and instead prioritize finding the new and more dynamic change management processes that you can tag on to?
- What are the dangers of jumping into slipstreams for openness?

Kids First Chicago leverages these provocations routinely to ensure systems are responsive to community, creating conditions for more slipstreams to emerge. This work was an inspiring step forward in a fractious time and topic. Through leveraging slipstreams emerging inside and outside the system, Natalie and her team created real convergence for an open system process that led to the potential for real system change.

The danger in this process is attaching too late in the game (showing up at the end when the process is already designed), or demanding too much of an opening in the process. Think about weighing the opening as proportional to the scale of the slipstream: small slipstreams, small openings; big slipstreams, big openings. But as always, manage the pace of change. The problem with attaching openings to slipstreams is that it can potentially weigh down an already heavy change management process. Put too much on it, and the drag means that the slipstream slows, dries up, or changes course completely.

As openers seek to expand openness in and across systems and communities, considering how slipstreams can create possibilities for additional open system work is an essential path forward. The examples of Kentucky and Chicago highlight work inside and outside of systems to create slipstreams for community co-created work. As we discussed in chapter 3, advocacy work can be a critical way to highlight and provoke the system change that openers seek, and it requires open-minded leadership inside the system to address the issue.

TRANSLOCAL ADAPTATION

As openness expands, leaders must be cautious to resist scale and instead consider growth and adaptation.

Now that we've explored understanding and defining community, building a recognition of the importance of your external environment and your ecosystem context, we need to shift to talk of how to conceive of expanding openness and why scaling or replication are inadequate matches for open system work.

The typical ed reform or social innovator approaches a new opportunity and says, "How can I scale this up to reach more people?" or "How do we replicate this?" In many cases, openers will find some success with a new way to bring voices into the fold and the next idea will be to say, "How many more people should this impact?" This is an inspiring question, but also a daunting one for social impact researchers and practitioners across the globe. There are many books written on scaling and building out exciting work. However, we want to start from the very beginning by saying that scale and replication are fundamentally incompatible with open system work.

Why do openers need to be very wary of questions of scale or replication? Yes, we need more open systems—schools, districts, communities, and more. But we need to remember that the critical component that openers need to operate within is the idea of local context being the grounding factor (as highlighted in chapter 3). Growth is, in many ways, an obsession of our society. If we do it in one place, we must do it in others, right? Not necessarily.

We have found that scale and replication are actually powerful and subversive ways to reinforce closed system structures. While separate concepts, the idea of scale (growing an initiative to support more students, families, etc.) often contains overtones of replication (taking something that worked over here and moving it over there). Even if the original breakthrough was an open system design, the quest for scale and replication as a mental model for growth means that you shortcut the open system design work that we've discussed throughout the entire book. Openers must always question the knee-jerk desire for scale and replication. How can you really support open leadership in replication given the unique perspectives of each leader? How can you scale given the unique features of each community? How will you replicate breakthrough spaces given time constraints? Can you really model creative democracy when you are mostly concerned with growth?

In their book, *Walk Out Walk On,* Margaret Wheatley and Deborah Frieze propose the term "translocal learning" to guide us toward a more sophisticated understanding of how change spreads. This reframing aligns to open system thinking and helps us understand that if indeed there is an opportunity to explore bringing the work to more communities, a better way is possible.

> Scaling up creates a monoculture that relies on replication, standardization, promotion and compliance . . . Community is nothing like a machine, and citizens rarely surrender their autonomy to the expert's advice. In fact, it only takes a little bit of digging to discover that even in corporations, exchanging best practices often doesn't work. What does work is when teams from one organization travel to another, and, through that experience, see themselves more clearly, strengthen their relationships, and renew their creativity.[3]

Open system growth is predicated on the belief that it must move (if indeed it makes sense to move) *authentically* from community to community and from believer to believer, with a slow, steady pace that allows for the adaptation to evolve. Therefore, in open system work, we propose the term *translocal adaptation.* Understanding and connecting open system work to translocal work is essential for system leaders or education advocates. So many education advocates promote policy shifts, claiming they will solve many problems across many different contexts. Yet, as we've discovered, the radically decentralized nature of our American education system is designed especially to prevent this.

Throughout this book we've cited *Gardens of Democracy* as critical to our thinking as leaders. One of the fundamental core concepts of the book directly relates to translocal adaptation, the shift from "machine brain" to "garden brain," which is a recognition of the organic nature of systemic change.[4] Instead of mechanical replication and scale, we need leaders, networks, and communities insistent on learning and adapting from others who are in this work. This could be scaling or replicating inside a community (such as moving from one classroom to another or one school to another) or across communities (moving from one context to another). A leader who understands the community, the environment, and the ecosystem must come to the inevitable conclusion that the next step isn't going to a new community right away—it's building a deeper openness within your current community and then exploring what it would mean to learn from others together.

In chapter 2, we showcased the Homegrown Talent Initiative in rural Colorado. This project is a great example of leveraging translocal adaptation in two unique and distinct phases. In the first phase, the work was about fostering learning and adaptation across the original eight sites. Next, through an expanding openness move, the districts leveraged shared advocacy to expand the work to more than fifty rural communities across Colorado in order to revitalize the educonomy in each town.

As the HTI project came into its third year, and the immediate challenges from COVID-19 had waned enough to allow for travel and exploration again, the HTI leadership was very interested in creating a model for learning across the sites. In the spirit of translocal adaptation, they knew the work was varied and distinct in each community, so talk of replication was off the table. Instead, they wanted to build a structure for leaders to explore each community, getting a flavor and taste of each place while inspiring new thinking for them to bring home. This eventually manifested into a CEI initiative called "discovery site visits," which designed the conditions for each community to learn and share with each other. Over the course of the 2021–22 school year, each community hosted a discovery site visit that welcomed members from across the entire HTI community to see, experience, and give constructive feedback to the home community. The resources, materials, and guidance allowed the communities to interrogate their assumptions and then bring the ideas they saw in various communities back to their own communities. Over the course of the year, the HTI initiative saw marked growth and learning across these communities, creating more energy, personal relationships, and local adaptation.

Around the same time as the launch of the discovery site visit process, there was a major conversation around how to spend the enormous amount of new federal funding that was flowing into Colorado from the American Rescue Plan. Colorado Succeeds organized the HTI communities and other rural advocacy organizations to put together a joint letter to the Colorado Department of Education (CDE) requesting that they leverage these new resources to fund the expansion of community-driven workforce redesign in Colorado. In response to their shared voice and advocacy from the field, CDE created a new initiative, called Rural Coaction, calling for regions of districts to come together to build a shared vision for workforce development and advocacy.[5] Districts were asked to come together to build a plan to seek significant new funding. By July 2022, many of the original eight HTI districts were included in awarded coaction grants, creating the opportunity for more than fifty districts to participate in community-driven educonomy work. In addition, many new communities were included in these grants that had not been part of HTI originally. This second phase of translocal adaptation shows the power of shared advocacy to create the conditions for scaling open system work. Through collective voice, communities came together not to ask for money for themselves but for resources for collective opportunity. This is a critical difference that ensures that translocal adaptation isn't just a self-seeking measure, but instead exemplifies an emergent or shared value across a community or set of communities. The challenge is now manifesting translocal adaptation at a much more significant scale. The discovery site visit model, which enabled powerful learning and adaptation across sites in the first phase of the project, will have to be modified and shifted to consider regions, statewide networks, and the various stages of development that are represented in the new open challenge. Figure 7.4 shows the significant expansion of HTI and community-driven educonomy work in Colorado.

Translocal adaptation is a rejection of the typical scale and replicate talk that we hear too much in education and system change discourse. It asks a different set of questions aligned to open system work—who are the leaders, what are the unique features of the community—and then asks leaders to consider the unique features that make sense for their context, and not to place other communities' structures on top of their own. It asks them to consider additional co-creation for full implementation

Figure 7.4 Expanded map of HTI communities

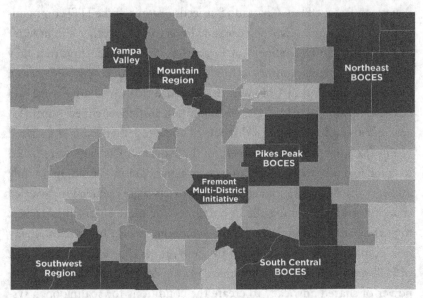

Source: Homegrown Talent Initiative, www.homegrowntalentco.org.

and new co-production mechanisms to ensure that full community buy-in continues in the process. Yet, as the HTI example shows, if done very well, it can lead to a metaphorical "dog catching the car" moment, where the many communities are now at the table to make it work for their context. This requires new complexities, new challenges, and new thinking to take the open system design work to new levels of expanded potential.

Translocal Adaptation Reflection

- How have previous efforts at scale and replication furthered closed system thinking or behavior in work you've participated in?
- How can you imagine translocal adaptation as a structure to expand openness in your effort?
- How can you leverage advocacy to gather resources for translocal adaptation?

LIFTING UP OPENERS AND OPEN NARRATIVES

Open leaders have a responsibility to elevate the visibility of leaders within their own and partner organizations and to share stories of open change.

Openers need to understand that as they are lifting up their community to achieve new opportunities for open system work, they need to seek out and identify others who are particularly inspired by the work of opening systems and share the narratives of change broadly.

In many ways, this practice is the main reason we wrote this book, why we've worked with residents and leaders across the country, and why we are so convinced that open system work must be the future of education and public system design. We need to change the narrative that closed system structures are the only way forward and that community-driven work is mystical or hidden. We have brought folks together in particular because we see enormous intersection between so many groups.

In any open system endeavor, openers will be surprised to find others in the process who are thrilled for the different types of conversation, the energy that co-creation stimulates, the possibilities new partnerships foster. We call this practice "lifting up openers" because openers must see their work as nurturing, sustaining, and supporting these leaders they meet along the way.

Shifting Narratives Checklist

- Are you leveraging all of your communications infrastructure during the open system process?
- Are you creating methods to highlight and feature your community and their aspirations in the process or afterward?
- How are you regularly and continually updating the community on the progress?
- Are you considering new ways of informal sharing of new narratives?
- How are you lifting up the individual stories of those involved in the process?

In chapter 4, we learned about Kentucky and the Colorado Youth Congress, and about their efforts to build spaces that shift the way we think about democracy, creating potential for open system redesign. In Kentucky, leaders of the districts redesigning local accountability through the Local Laboratories of Learning (L3) work are also embodying new habits and accelerating fractal change. Jim Detweiler, deputy superintendent and chief academic officer of Boone County Schools, embraced inclusion and empathy in his work beyond the L3 initiative. As the school year kicked off, he and his community partners through the L3 work organized a Spanish-language panel of families for their systemwide principal training so that leaders could better empathize with their experience, a first-of-its-kind event for the district. As the state lifts up stories of leaders like Jim, and further connects these leaders in communities of practice, these habits spread and become more commonplace.

In the New Mexico Sin Fronteras project, one of the most important moves made in the project was the recognition that the core partners could not do this work alone, committing to the important work of building a training corps across the state. The community movement builders and training leads were given real responsibility for working with local communities across the state and for leading training efforts on behalf of the collective. They were additionally charged with driving design over the next generation of the trainings, ensuring high-variety dynamic interaction with community needs. This is an unusual posture

---

Lifting Up Openers Nationally: Seek Common Ground

Often, openers and open system leaders think and consider the work of lifting up others as proximate and local. While that is usually true, we think it's important to name an important example of an organization lifting up openers all over the country—Seek Common Ground. Launched in 2018 to be a space for community leaders from across the country to come together to solve local problems, learn from each other, and engage in deep reflection, the organization runs "actions accelerators" to create catalytic exchange from community and coalition leaders on topics as diverse as social-emotional and mental support, leveraging federal rescue funds (ARPA and ESSER), and direct COVID response.

CEO Sandy Boyd explained their approach:

> We do a lot of dot connecting. There's so many people creating a lot of good things out there, most are community state-based groups that don't need to start from scratch every time. So we're constantly looking for resources that we can bring to people so that they can see what other people have done, and have something for you which they can build, do their own thing, or whatever they want. But fundamentally, they see what else is out there and how we actually bring the community together.

Claudia Quintero, senior director, shares the questions she considers regularly as she builds and fosters openers across the country:

> We are asking folks to be in that constant space of interrogation with curiosity: "What is special and unique about the place and community in which I work? What does this community need right now? How can we, and others, work together to be a part of the solution?" It is a constant conversation that needs to happen with trusted community leaders, and that includes families, teachers, students; in other words, everyone that is a part of, and impacted by, that community. The shift that needs to happen is moving towards an ongoing conversation so that those mechanisms exist to have consistent space for dialogue and feedback as circumstances change, as they always do.

It's important to understand the national camaraderie that is a benefit of belonging to networks that bring together openers. As we've shared before, openers are often lonely individuals—and often people of color and female—who operate in silos inside larger organizations where they are hoping to shift the culture. By creating networks where openers get to share language and perspective, the isolation within can be balanced by the connectivity across.

Lifting Up Openers and Open Narratives Reflection

- How do you see your role in fostering the leadership of other openers in your community?
- How can you create conditions to learn from each other as you all seek to expand openness?
- How can you place or nudge openers to take on new roles or leadership positions in other places aligned to their purpose, passion, and place?

in which to position a training cohort, empowering them with real community-opening leadership.

Long recognized as a critical strategy for organizers and learning efforts, distributing and lifting up the voices of these other openers creates new conditions for change that the core group could never lead. As we discussed in chapter 2, a tremendous amount of the work of openers is to align their purpose, passion, and place. These new openers each have their own open leadership story, their own commitment to place. By activating and empowering others in the process, new efforts will emerge, colliding and confronting closed systems.

Lifting up other openers must mean you take an active role in helping others become energized across these aspects of their life. We all benefit when other openers have been sustained and supported in their potential paths to open other systems.

To fully propel the exciting open system change that leaders have fostered, they need to be committed to changing and promoting open narratives to help the broader community not only understand that open system change is possible, but that it can happen in their community. This means seeking those other leaders who want to build the open future and lifting up their narratives.

CONCLUSION

We have now arrived at the end of the open system principles and the cycle of *preparing, provoking,* and now *propelling.* In this chapter, you've seen evidence and examples of how leaders from across the country have continued to expand the work of open systems in their context. We can find no better fitting end to the principles than to leave you with these examples to show that not only does the work continue, but openers must find new ways to navigate complex contexts, transform their landscapes, and create open futures. Many of these examples end with the somber but important caution that slow, steady system change work over time is what will create real progress for students and communities—not the celebration and frenzy that some would want, but a realistic take on the challenges moving forward.

As clichéd as it sounds, expanding openness is really just the beginning. In the opening chapters of the book we discussed much about how to not see this work as a linear line but as a spiral and a set of fractal patterns. As you now arrive at the end, we must reinforce this again. You've worked through this book's concepts and have arrived at this chapter to see that the work begins again—in new slipstreams and new methods of co-production to keep community and institutions together, in new methods of adaptation, with new friends, and with new narratives proving what is possible.

And powerfully, *The Open System* begins again, in each heart and soul ready to build and serve their communities to reimagine what is possible and ignite a new spirit of democracy.

An Open Future

Recommendations for Building the Open System

I am the seed of the free, and I know it. I intend to bear great fruit.

SOJOURNER TRUTH

At a time of radical historical change, the concept of courage will itself require new forms. This is the reality that needs to be faced—the call for concepts—and it would seem that if one were to face up to such a challenge well it would have to be done imaginatively. Courage, as a state of character, is constituted in part by certain ideals—ideals of what it is to live well, to live courageously. The ideals are alive in the community, but they also take hold in a courageous person's soul.

JONATHAN LEAR, *RADICAL HOPE*

We are then compelled to face without equivocation the most profound issue which this new order of society has raised . . . the issue of the control of the machine . . . If the machine is to serve all . . . it cannot be the property of the few.

GEORGE COUNTS, *DARE THE SCHOOL BUILD THE NEW SOCIAL ORDER?*

IMAGINING AN OPEN FUTURE

At the end of our first open system convening in 2019, the final session was titled "Imagining an Open Future." Participants at the event spent time visioning, imagining, and dreaming what it would mean to co-create such a future with our families and communities. All of them, in each of their own ways, were and are working on similar projects in their respective spaces. This book, an outgrowth of that convening and conversations, contains just a bare snapshot of the possibilities that emerged in that space and since that time.

As we did in the opening chapter, we once again dedicate and anchor this book to the incredible leaders operating across the country and globe who seek to build a better world within their communities. While we have strived to bring many of their voices into this text, we know it is only a sliver of those serving their communities as openers. Therefore, at the beginning of the conclusion, we once again note that while these are some of the possibilities for an open future we see before us, we know that so many more exist. So let us move to the realm of imagining the future—one where more and more openers like those we profiled in this book come together to co-create, co-produce, and build a just, more open world.

BUILDING AN OPEN FUTURE

To commit to open system work, at any level or analysis, to find your open moment and build the capacity for a system to change, to partner, to transform with its community is a powerful and transformative experience. The chapters before have been dedicated to how to bring that work up, around, and beyond—to new levels of impact, to new paths inside systems, to new leaders who can carry the torch—and ultimately to change the dominant narratives of closed systems. For a variety of reasons, the focus of this book has been dedicated to the practices and reflective activities necessary to give openers the insight to move through these challenges in a distinct context—education.

Yet, if we were to be honest with ourselves, too few of our public systems are designed to achieve the high-variety, adaptive, and open models we are proposing. Indeed we must come to the real conclusion that in too many situations and in too many aspects of their current design, large American public systems remain in various states of closure.

We believe the January 6 insurrection and concurrent institutional democratic decline call for a democratic "Sputnik moment" in education and society more broadly—a challenge to live up to our full potential as a society. This moment must be seen as a trans-partisan opportunity to build the future of American democracy: a clarion call to serve, to invest, to support, and to reimagine our democracy.

On the right, we are compelled by Niall Ferguson's book *The Great Degeneration,* which makes the case for institutional renewal across all of society and argues historically that (after a myriad of factors) "countries arrive at a stationary state . . . when their 'laws and institutions' degenerate to the point that elite rent-seeking dominates the economic and political process . . . civil society withers to a no man's land between corporate interests and big government."[1] On the left we are inspired by Ta-Nehisi Coates's challenge to the current state of American democracy: "The vote is only as good as the citizens who believe in it . . . And when you have—let's be clear, a minority of Americans, but a highly motivated minority of Americans—who are intent on either having themselves at the top of the hierarchy, or [rejecting the state], you've got a problem."[2]

Democracies designed with highly adaptive, resilient, and reliable public systems—education, health care, government, and the rest—must be the dream of every opener. We consider this book a beachhead for the assault on closed systems across our society, beginning with education because it is the critical forge for our democracy and the future of our society.

In an ominous recent study released by RAND, significant research was done to understand the challenges facing our country in this important moment. They identified the following characteristics that help ensure the success of a nation:

We believe that there is substantial historical and research-based empirical evidence for the importance of a specific set of societal characteristics—and, critically, the way they work together in a synergistic mix—in providing national competitive advantage. They are

1. national ambition and will
2. unified national identity
3. shared opportunity
4. an active state
5. effective institutions
6. a learning and adapting society
7. competitive diversity and pluralism.[3]

In their report, they conclude that "multiple trends are working to weaken traditional U.S. advantages . . . These and related trends raise a worrying prospect—that the United States has begun to display classic patterns of a major power on the far side of its dynamic and vital curve."[4] We believe that open system work has a significant amount to offer our American society given this analysis, in particular the emphasis on effective institutions, a learning and adapting society, and competitive diversity and pluralism—central components of open systems and key to building renewal within our public systems.

To imagine this open future, we offer a set of thematic and short considerations that could serve as a catalyst for promoting even more openness across our public institutions, society, and beyond.

First, we want to dream inside education itself. What is the new and systemic open education sector that we must build and invest in to ensure education is maximally positioned to best leverage community co-creation?

Second, we will begin to move from education into adjacent public systems. What would it mean for us to imagine democracy-expanding infrastructure that would work cooperatively and collectively to amplify and reignite democracy in our local communities?

Lastly, we will end with emerging thinking around openness across public systems such as health, food, and safety. We believe that there is incredible opportunity to leverage co-creation and co-production in these other public systems.

We recognize that these are limited, short proposals that cannot in any way capture the full nuance of complexities in full sectors or industries. We offer these to provoke connections, thinking, and the exploration of future work. We are excited to hear from others in the field about what this could mean and how we can converge to build an open future together. Let this be the beginning of a conversation on how open system change may be able to deliver on the opportunity of a reignited democracy.

OPEN EDUCATION SECTOR

In our first theme, we want to explore how education should consider the long-term transformations that must occur in the education field to sustain the openness that we encourage leaders to seek in this book.

Open Investment and Technology

We first and foremost need philanthropic efforts to invest in open system infrastructure. Significant funds are needed to support the strategies outlined in this book and initiatives to bring more families and communities to the table. While it is clearly a trend in education, there must be sharper and more collective effort to invest in the intensive, focused work of open system design.

Philanthropy has a long track record of investing for one to three years in a particular focus area to provoke change and then, when they fail to see the change, the philanthropists depart from the scene. We need philanthropic leaders to step up and commit to the hard, challenging work of institutional redesign and democracy building through open systems in education. This requires trust and important conversations, and will likely require assembling abundance partnerships between philanthropic entities, such as those that produced projects like the Homegrown Talent Initiative, to sustain and cultivate deeper levels of open system change. In that partnership, five foundations came together to share resources and dollars, and they then trusted the organizations to assemble their own abundance partnerships to work together for the benefit of their communities. This is all too rare in our field, and we will need more collective investments such as these to catalyze cross-sector and open system change.

Opening systems also means looking at how technology can facilitate more open systems. We can use technology tools to advance dialogue, participation, and inclusion in schools for families, students, and staff. One example of technology being used to open systems is the Possip platform. Founded by opener-in-residence Shani Jackson-Dowell, the platform shifts the paradigm of a typical once-a-year feedback survey and transforms it into an ongoing open system dialogue between educators, decision makers, and caregivers. Without needing to download anything, families, students, and staff are able to contribute their ideas, needs, feedback, and celebrations for their schools and districts.

The technology uses AI-assisted chat in hundreds of languages to seek and discover what families and parents care about, to check in on them, and to support educators in having an ongoing dialogue and understanding about caregivers' needs. The Possip "pulse check" also creates the capacity to aggregate the results and themes so that educators can address common problems in their classrooms, principals can do so in their schools, and districts can do the same across their entire system. Shani explains, "instead of forcing people to show up to a school board room or statehouse to express their ideas, we can use technology to give a parent or caregiver the opportunity to share from their own home—or wherever they are. This helps systems and families build a bridge together and partner on celebrating what's going well and making adjustments where needed."[5]

These examples are just the beginning of what it means to shift the investment and technological space to facilitate more openness in education.

Open Capacity Builders

In each state or community, we believe it's important for one or more trusted education organizations to commit to open system capacity building inside their work. Ideally, this is an organization that can work between philanthropy, local, and state systems to coordinate effort.

These organizations (sometimes called intermediaries at the state or district level) should consider ways to support open system efforts across all education stakeholders, including leaders, organizations, and institutions. By leveraging this framework and this approach, new and exciting efforts will manifest creating new innovations, community efforts, and collective action. Each community will have a local, community-driven discussion about how to produce effective and strategic open system change. We have both been lucky to work for organizations (Colorado Education Initiative and the Center for Innovation in Education) that have made this commitment, leading to much of the work detailed in this book. We have been inspired by organizations as diverse as Kids First Chicago and Seek Common Ground as they embrace opening as their work, catalyzing change locally and nationally. An open future is not possible without daring entrepreneurs working inside existing organizations to change their culture from closed to open, and exciting entrepreneurs daring to challenge the closed order of things with a new open system–minded start-up.

A Bold Call for Civic Education

This book stands as a recipe for how to open up public education to the communities it serves, hold spaces for adaptation and redesign, and foster enduring openness. We need to model creative democracy in our systems, yes, but we also need to sustain calls to expand the current civic discourse and education in our public education system. Openness must begin with a clear and deep assertion that democracy and education are joined together at the foundation.

At the school, district, and education sector levels, there must be a new commitment to the teaching, study, and practice of civics across all grade levels. A new generation of "action civics" practitioners has emerged and should be encouraged, exemplified by the Colorado Youth Congress and the Kentucky Student Voice Team. Students should start early and encounter frequent learning opportunities to understand what it means to practice and live in democratic structures. In their 2012 article critiquing our current education system, leading educators shared a sentiment we wholeheartedly agree with:

> This count-the-widget evaluation of public schools has undermined the American education system. America's greatness is reflected in our ability to innovate, analyze complex problems, ask cogent questions, assemble and evaluate data, and seek creative solutions, not recall factual information. These are the skills of a democratic citizen, and failure to teach them imperils the future of the republic.[6]

Students, families, and communities should be brought into schools to model democracy on important community issues. Students should vote early and in every grade on important school issues. Students should be included on councils, task forces, and committees on a whole range of topics. Educators should see it as their role to steward these young openers.

Schools should think about the supports, mindsets, and practices required for educators to take on this new challenge. One small change that Doannie is exploring at his children's school is how we might use consensus decision-making instead of contests to make classwide and schoolwide decisions. Debate, a passion of Landon's, might also be practiced early and across grade levels, brought to a prominence alongside athletics.

Local counties and state agencies should work with schools and nonpartisan groups to ensure 100 percent of eligible families and students are automatically registered to vote and have access to ballots. Public celebrations should be thrown for students who cast their first local, state, and national votes. Students should be encouraged to participate in community service as often as possible, and it should be linked directly to issues they are discussing in class to heighten relevance.

We are also aware that in our efforts to consider reigniting democratic potential in this book we do not make any specific connections to civic curriculum and instruction. There are authors far more credentialed and steeped in this research than us, but it is beyond clear that our civic education infrastructure is in dire need of repair. Between the decline of civics and social studies and the lack of rigorous practice in action civics, we must ask our public leaders to support dramatic increases in K–12 social studies and civics–related investment.

We are compelled by Meira Levinson's argument of a "civic empowerment gap" in her book *No Citizen Left Behind,* in which she goes into great detail about these challenges and how deeper civic-focused redesign of schools can make progress.[7] The deep, calcified ~isms we have discussed throughout this book create real barriers for the flourishing of democracy, and we need a systemwide effort to activate all citizens to build a better democracy. Policymakers need to think about how they can invest massively in civics education, incentivize local partnerships between education systems and election officials, and stimulate the energy that this foundation requires.

In recent years, the debate around social studies has felt extremely political, with charges about critical race theory, for example, abounding. While some have admitted that most of this has been ginned up controversy for political machinations, we do not disagree that inside and outside of our public systems we often lack the ability to discuss tough historical or social issues.[8] We have also seen firsthand that the failure of systems to take parent and family concerns seriously on this issue can lead to enormous distrust, when, in many cases, conversations and community dialogue could have opened a path forward.

We applaud the recent efforts of groups like Heterodox Academy, who seek to avoid some of the challenges facing democratic debate and civic education by building a protocol and method for creating space for debate and discussion across all viewpoints. The "HxA way" (see sidebar) is a norm protocol that we find to be very effective at setting the table for these conversations.

It is also critical that these efforts do not end up creating space to limit or break down discourse, but rather to amplify and expand. This is a complicated moment politically in our country, with many competing viewpoints and ideas. In democratic discourse, we must reject any effort to raise up ideas that promote violence or suppression of groups, in particular those furthest from opportunity, as protected speech. No one can cry fire in a crowded theater, and in a diverse democratic republic, no one should be able to threaten the lives or question the humanity of others.

Our experience working in schools tells us that inflammatory speech exists on the left, the right, and sometimes independent of political identity. As fellow community members, we must accept that history and society is never fully set, so we must embrace debate and expression as the path forward to understanding. People have questions, they will stumble, ruptures will occur, and we must strive to ensure that in pursuit of expanding democratic, open systems, we must not choose to silence some over others. Fully living the spirit of pluralism and democracy in this moment requires grace and patience. It is a tension as old as democracy itself, and there are no easy answers—yet we are certain that openers will lead the way.

The Heterodox Academy Way

- Make your case with evidence
- Be intellectually charitable
- Be intellectually humble
- Be constructive
- Be yourself[9]

Open Educator Training

We need a meaningful and purposeful reframing of our educators beyond a narrow professional status and into a fuller vision of educators as our frontline democracy builders.

Higher education, teacher training programs, and alternative certification programs would be well-advised to shift their framing toward open system community-driven change and help educators understand the powerful role they play in revitalizing our democracy. Most higher education institutions, which train our educators, spend almost no time at all on family partnership and no time on practicing the skills of opening. Who trains teachers to redesign schools alongside families? Who trains teachers to visit the homes of families and partners and interrupt biases? How are we helping teachers get coached, in real time, in facilitating community meetings? If this is done, it is often through nonprofit or for-profit partners and seen as an add-on. An open future would embed these supports directly into the system.

This goes beyond higher education. Family partnership or community engagement, when present on teacher rubrics, usually shows up as a small, discrete strand of work. Opening, sharing power, practicing liberation—these must be integrated across the entire thread of educator work. If they are frontline democracy builders, educators must be both supported and held accountable. Schools and systems need to rethink structures about teacher performance vis-à-vis relationships with families and students.

Policymakers should demand a massive overhaul of our teacher and leader preparation programs in terms of building relationships, sharing power, and training for co-creation and co-production. Policymakers should also resist efforts to simply demand openness because nothing would squash this approach more than mandates. Instead, policymakers should create incentives and offer supportive, feasible guidance.

Open System Leaders as Democracy Builders

Extending out from the broader work of reimagining the role of the educator, we need to take our cues from our first open principle, activating open leadership, and spend serious time and energy reframing the role of the system leader (such as a superintendent or principal) as a central democracy builder and public leader. In our experience, too few current training programs conceive of education leadership in this light. We ask that the next generation of openers and leadership development conceive of this as a central responsibility and task.

In CEI's Rural Superintendent Academy, former Cañon City superintendent George Welsh spends a significant amount of time anchoring leaders in open system theory and practical implications, lessons he firmly believes in after decades in system leadership. He trains and commits leaders to not run away from local democratic systems such as school boards and community partnerships, but instead see that one can go nowhere without them. We have also been inspired by the recent efforts of the Yale Broad Center to invite us to support their cohort in open system theory, case studies, and developing leaders reimagining their roles.

The next generation of openers must move beyond traditional notions of a family engagement office, which is too often a separate, underfunded office or, even more likely, a sole individual responsible for too much of the opening across an entire school system. Openers must look at *every* department and ask how opening up to the community would look. How can we open up academics, finance, transportation, and nutrition? Applying these guiding principles of co-creation, co-production, and building abundance may matter even more to some of the more operational components of our school systems. This isn't more task forces (an easy out), but rather digging deep into the closed architecture of the current systems to examine and rethink a significant amount of the settled work inside a system. Smart openers will use their open moments to take on sacred cows and calcified problems, creating pressure for them to transform the system and build trust at the same time. Mark Warren shares a similar thought in his "Communities and Schools" article:

> [E]xperts and educators acting within the four walls of the school cannot solve the problems of . . . schools and . . . communities, because these problems are the result of fundamentally unequal power relationships in our society. We need an active and engaged citizenry to build the kinds of relationships and the type of power necessary both to transform education school by school and to address the broader structures.[10]

We concede that there is much that education leaders must also know and commit to in their work running schools and systems. Yet too few programs help new, emerging, or current leaders reconceive of their roles in this way. There is much to do in this arena and significant work to further a transformation in the way education system leaders operate.

DEMOCRACY-EXPANDING INFRASTRUCTURE

In the effort to maximize the reignition of democracy and trust in our public institutions, we should seek to consider what it means to create and foster integration of democracy across various public systems. As we have shared throughout this book, we are compelled by Hélène Landemore and her book *Open Democracy* and suggest that leaders and readers take her work seriously. We need more leaders to commit to innovating in the governance space through open democratic methods, such as using the lottery methods for recruitment that we advocate as a part of a mixed model, and leveraging her learnings from the work she has done from Iceland to France. We are inspired by a global community of organizations working on this, such as Democracy Next and others. We also believe there are some very tactical maneuvers that could make a big difference.

Elections and Voting

Throughout this book, we've touched on the issue of elite capture of democratic institutions. While we have described ways to remedy this issue through open system practices, we believe there are other ways to adjust the electoral system to generate elected officials and democratic structures that more represent the communities they serve. For instance, in many cities and towns across the country, there are literally elections every six months for public offices. We ought to prioritize consolidation and elimination of election cycles into fewer for the voting public.

The impact for school systems could be enormous. Often school board races happen "off-cycle," that is, not during general congressional or presidential election cycles. This creates extremely low-turnout affairs which create opportunities for individuals and groups that may not represent the full spectrum of views in a community. Aligning city, county, state, and school board elections into "on-cycle" elections creates an opportunity to maximize turnout among all advocacy groups and civic-minded folk. Research suggests that in places where elections are on-cycle, there have been spikes in the election's ability to produce community alignment. "Local officials who are elected in on-cycle elections are more likely to hold political preferences that align with their districts than officials elected in off-cycle elections. . . . Candidates who deviate too far from their constituents in on-cycle districts are significantly less likely to win office."[11]

Beyond aligning election days, voting should stop being a separate public institution from our American education and public systems. Students should practice voting and democracy-building practices throughout their entire education system. They can be empowered to make a plethora of decisions, ranging from informing educational actions to investment in vision and dollars through projects such as participatory budgeting. As a student approaches legal voting age, schools and local communities should honor and celebrate the right to vote and the responsibility it entails. These issues cannot be partisan affairs and must be seen as structurally central to rejecting closure in our democracy.

We could continue down this path and advocate for a number of democracy-based reforms, such a ranked-choice voting and voting access expansion, but we assume readers get the picture. We cannot see our democratic infrastructure as distinct or separate from our education systems—we should interrogate where it's not producing desired community effects and where integration can be useful.

Public Systems Integration and Cooperation

In too many of our communities, public systems act as a multilayer cake where everyone at the party chooses different flavors, diluting the full impact of voter choices. Schools operate as islands within counties and city governments, creating redundant budgetary, programmatic, and directional challenges. Mayors and superintendents often spar in cities, creating discord where alignment could maximize support for families and students. Many education reform advocates champion mayoral control as a remedy, and while we see both pros and cons to this structure, we instead are advocating for more community alignment. In our opinion, the concept of mayoral control often exacerbates authoritarian or closed leadership dynamics, so instead we should seek a fuller vision of community and system integration, even if ultimately a mayor is in charge.

To achieve this vision, we could imagine deeper integration across all public systems in a locality, eliminating redundant systems and creating fully integrated data systems operating within counties or cities. This could allow school systems to save significant cost overhead, provide even more budgetary capacity to manage financial controls and operations, and produce a stronger collective public value offering for local taxpayers. Combined with aligning elections and voting, this would allow voters' sentiment to maximally impact the future direction of a city instead of splitting it across various public sector layers. We imagine this issue will be hotly debated, but it ought to be considered, given funding constraints and the potential for catalytic cooperation.

If political or pragmatic resistance or lack of relevance blocks a path toward system integration, one could imagine still separate but more fully intersecting systems. These could be deliberate efforts such as regional institutions or cooperative structures, or further funding of pooling efforts for regional cooperative school districts, or the local county running budgets for multiple school districts to save costs. If well-funded and invested in, these regional cooperatives or systems-integrating measures could create new momentum and make more resources available to communities, while also having the side benefit of involving fewer bureaucratic checks on collective action.

Open Society Investments

Similar to our call for open system philanthropic support in education, we need a transformative effort to expand philanthropic investment in democracy building in the US. For too long in our country, we've seen open society initiatives as something US foundations commit to in foreign countries. Our entire adult lives have been spent on the bitter irony of democracy promotion abroad and the decline of democracy at home. This democratic Sputnik moment must be a collective effort of philanthropy, business, the nonprofit sector, and government—grounded in an expanding open education system. To that end, we are compelled by a myriad of organizations such as the Brennan Center, the new private sector Stronger Democracy Award, the Open Society Foundation, the MacArthur Foundation, Freedom House, and the Partnership for American Democracy, all of whom have committed to investing in American democracy at this critical juncture.

To fully meet this challenge we will need a collective learning agenda to glean what we can learn from decades of commitment to open society investments around the world in order to fund a civil society that commits to pluralism and civic engagement. These investments, whether in speech and debate (a major investment in post–Cold War Europe), investment in public goods (like community centers or other common spaces), or facilitating access to power and money for traditionally marginalized citizens and communities, must be reflected now here at home in the United States.

American philanthropy should commit its considerable investments into fostering a healthy exchange of ideas, discussion, and deliberation. We cannot long foster open systems in our American education system unless it is a full, society-wide commitment to openness and democracy building. Investments should be leveraged with afterschool programs and summer school to stitch together opportunities for youth and family voices, civic engagement, and participation. If we pursue this effort, we can imagine the next decade as one of genuine democracy building at home, from town centers to state capitals, and inside classrooms everywhere.

OPENNESS ACROSS PUBLIC SYSTEMS

In this section, we explore nascent and emergent efforts, thoughts, and concepts which may pave the way for considering open system work across other public systems.

Redesigning Public Safety

Throughout the course of writing this book—before, during, and after the pandemic and the racial awakening across this country—there arose a massive focus in the country as regular citizens asked important questions about the responsiveness and openness of our American policing and justice system.

Since the 1980s one of the most powerful and effective innovations in policing and justice has been the practice of community policing. Community policing was defined by a US Department of Justice 2014 report as "a philosophy that promotes organizational strategies that support the systematic use of partnerships and problem-solving techniques to proactively address the immediate conditions that give rise to public safety issues such as crime, social disorder, and fear of crime."[12]

We see enormous connections between community policing and open systems. Community policing, where police and localities work together to solve problems, serves as an open system example already in the field, creating opportunities for co-creation and co-production in public safety. Yet sadly similar to community schools in education, there are many that claim to represent the practice and far too few who manifest the potential for co-creation in reality or take it to the deeper and more powerful opportunities that it presents. Therefore, community leaders should push for deeper commitment and investment in community policing through real interrogation and commitment to the ideal and practice.

Policing, however, is only one slice of the public safety sector. Increasingly there is a realization that also, as in education, we put too much into one operational model to solve all our issues. In response to public demand for different models, cities and community leaders elsewhere are designing other opportunities to co-create in the space. The city of Denver recently launched an innovative community-demanded project called STAR to create a social and mental health delivery model that runs parallel to but in coordination with the police department, inspired by a breakthrough effort in Eugene, Oregon. Described by a new study from Stanford, STAR "provides a mobile crisis response for community members experiencing problems related to mental health, depression, poverty, homelessness, and/or substance abuse issues. The STAR response consists of two health care staff (i.e., a mental health clinician and a paramedic in a specially equipped van) who provide rapid, on-site support to individuals in crisis and direct them to further appropriate care including requesting police involvement, if necessary."[13]

The STAR model has now been sought by many more cities, creating a new, more community-centered model for responsive public safety.

There is significant opportunity to consider what the path of co-creation and community building would offer the American public safety community to redesign public safety and move beyond tired debates of the "thin blue line" versus "defund the police." Importantly, the research study looked at a significant range of the program's impact, eventually concluding:

> The evidence in this study indicates that the STAR community response program was effective in reducing police-reported criminal offenses (i.e., both reducing the designation of individuals in crisis as criminal offenders and reducing the actual level of crime). These results provide a compelling motivation for the continued implementation and assessment of this approach.[14]

Imagining future possibilities through community-driven system redesign, we could dream of going even farther. In large, complex cities or even small towns, efforts could be made to redesign public safety systems with more community ownership. Imagine devolving power inside of a massive citywide policing system toward something akin to a charter or innovation school—a neighborhood public safety structure that is managed and held accountable by that community. These would not be rogue operators, but rather the devolution of power to the communities to operate more nimbly and responsively. Additional benefits could include local recruitment, local culturally responsive training, and shifting narratives away from historical challenges. They could likely implement community policing more faithfully and become innovation labs within cities. And if they failed to serve the community, they could be revoked by the larger city structure.

If rebuilt in a new structure, the power of voice and redesign could provoke important questions on how local communities may want to imagine their public safety. In this model, local communities would authorize and select the best public system that matches their needs. If well designed and managed, it would create opportunities for local communities to name the style, content, and vision for their police system instead of the stale, problematic public monopoly we now experience in too many contexts. Akin to the local community who wants an arts-focused school

Openness in the Private Sector

While the focus of this book is leveraging open system redesign in public systems, we do not believe that open systems work is fundamentally limited to public endeavors. In his provocative book *The Open Organization*, Jim Whitehurst, former CEO of Red Hat and IBM, details his determination to build what we would see as an open system in the private sector. He speaks to the operating principles of the work:

> Red Hat's open organization operates using unusual management principles that leverage the power of participation—both internally and externally—to generate consistent financial results. It uses open sourcing to tap a massive, disparate community of people, all with different skills and motivations, to make super-high-performing products capable of running some of the most secure and mission-critical computer systems in the world. . . . We have leveraged these components to create a new sort of company—an open organization—a rebooted, redesigned, reinvented organization suitable for the decentralized, empowered digital age.[15]

We believe openers everywhere should take special notice of this evolution in the private sector. What would it mean to value and cultivate this sort of system redesign in the private sector? It would have incredible and significant spillover effects into our public sector, potentially creating mutually reinforcing systems.

or a STEM magnet as diverse options for kids, communities would be involved in the co-design of the future of their community and types of community justice they would prefer. And like a charter or innovation school, if these systems failed to perform their task, local communities could revoke their mandate and design a new system. Instead of accepting the closed monopolistic public option as the only path, local communities could co-create open public safety systems that can shift the debate toward community solutions and away from problematic slogans and reactionary sentiment.

Open Health

Alongside education and policing, health care represents the third pillar of the public system that must build an open future. Local community clinics, community partnerships—these can all be reimagined to build health infrastructure that is not a leviathan unmoored from the communities it serves but redesigned and built up alongside communities.

The narrative about openness in health care has focused too narrowly on individual control and portability of health data. However, if health care was leveraged by dramatic co-creation and co-production with communities, what might we see? "Patient-centered care" is a common buzzword in health now—responding to the concerns of the individual and partnering with them to achieve common aims. While there are many individual physicians who believe in this idea, there are few health systems that encourage these habits across all their staff. Even more rare is the health system that intentionally engages *communities* as true partners in advancing common wellness.

There are a number of promising health initiatives and organizations that are pioneering partnership, and as a provocation, we offer up ways in which they might model greater openness.

Community health workers use shared language and cultural background to build trusting relationships with members of the community. They use these relationships to deliver care and encourage healthy behaviors, yet they are still too often utilized as an arm of the medical establishment rather than cultivating deeper reciprocity between the community and health professionals. In the spirit of openness, we can imagine community health workers at minimum intentionally bringing insights from the community to health system leaders. Even better would be the deliberate inclusion of both community health workers and community members in the strategic decision-making about approaches to population-level health initiatives.

Hotspotting initiatives, like the one pioneered by the Camden Coalition of Healthcare Providers, provide comprehensive services to superutilizers of healthcare resources. As described by Finkelstein and others in 2020, "In the months after hospital discharge, a team of nurses, social workers, and community health workers visits enrolled patients to coordinate out-patient care and link them with social services."[16] We see this as deeply community-connected work, and the integrated and collaborative nature of the service delivery is something to be applauded. As we think about how to make the system more open, how might a broad coalition of community members be involved in co-creating and co-directing more systemic solutions that interrupt the cycles that cause extreme utilization of medical services?

A number of health systems have experimented with value-based con-tracts, where systems only get paid if they keep people healthy according to the terms of the contract. These value-based contracts establish goals that incentivize a negotiated set of outcomes that must be met in order for the system to be compensated. Industry groups advocate for creat-ing contracts that "support population health management and other value-adding activities" and doing so with the critical partnership with physicians and other providers.[17] They talk about networks of service providers collaborating to provide comprehensive care in alignment to the contract. We wonder what it might look like for community-level aims to be included, and for the contracts to be negotiated in partnership with the community. What kind of operational capacity might be un-locked if community organizations are included in the network of care?

OUR OPEN MOMENT

At the end of the book, it's important to express our deepest apprecia-tion for you, the reader. Thank you for opening this book, and therefore opening your mind to the possibilities that may emerge. We cannot wait to learn from you.

The message we have attempted to share, in our own imperfect way, is that there is an urgent need in front of us to redesign our public educa-tion system with communities and that instead of the common refrain that this approach will always fail, it instead can yield transformational and actionable results. We see as critical to the Open System Institute that there are so many more stories out there of opening in the world, and that through learning these new truths, we will adapt our own. *The Open System* will not be a closed system. We have strived to hold our multitudes together to manifest this one book, in one language, at one moment in time, knowing that our perspective will grow and expand as more openers seek their own open moment.

We now close this book anchored in a renewed sense of possibility. While writing this book, so much has happened in our society that urged us onward. Around the country and world, we have been inspired by even more examples of communities co-creating their future. The democratic decline that looked so impossible to overcome in 2020 now, in 2023, shows signs of small progress. Nevertheless, openers must remember the present is not necessarily a prologue; progress is not guaranteed. In many ways the closures and fractures in American education have become even more pronounced since we started writing, urgently making the case for the reignition of local democracy and redesign of systems that we believe is possible through open system principles.

We hope you are inspired to seek your own open moment in your community, to work alongside others in the task, and keep your heart, mind, and path open along the way. We know firsthand that if you commit to this course of action, you will join and be joined by so many others across the country who are seeking the same transformation. To them, to you, and to those who are yet to find their way to this work, we commit to building that open future together.

APPENDIX

Open Principle 1 Activate open leadership

Macro Questions
- Why must open systems begin with open leaders?
- Why is education a critical venue for building open system capacity? If we get it right, what are some of the downstream effects?

Practices	Questions
Energizing Purpose, Passion, Place Open leaders generate sustained open systems when they build energy between their professional *purpose* and their *passion*, in a *place* they deeply care about.	• Why do leaders need to be sustained in their practice of co-creating public value? • Why is the sustaining of open leaders necessary for long-term open system change? • How does the "spinning wheel" across all three sustain leaders as they attempt to co-create within traditionally closed systems? • How can leaders continually reflect on their alignment between purpose, passion, and place to maximize their sustained impact? • How did you conceive of your purpose in open system work across your career? • How does it feel when your passion is flowing or at full power in your role working with communities? • How did you come to understand your place where you sought to make community-driven work happen?
Democratic Leadership Open leaders resist traditional authoritarian leadership practices and build an inclusive, pragmatic sense of possibility through their work.	• Why is it important that open leaders resist traditional or authoritarian conceptions of leadership in favor of broader, democratic conceptions of leadership? • How do democratically minded leaders build shared, pragmatic approaches to improve systems? • How does democracy get strengthened as leaders integrate various perspectives and ideas within their leadership endeavors? • How have you had to shift your leadership practice in discrete ways to include more democratic practices? • How have you struggled with "moralizing upon it"—naming the problems in society while rallying others to solve the problem? How is this different from others who seek alternatives to building an open system?

Practices	Questions
Open Hearts, Open Minds, Open Paths If open leaders are to truly live in the spirit of the work, they must be prepared to open the deepest parts of themselves—their hearts, their minds, and their paths—in order to press themselves and others to maintain openness to challenging narratives and ideas.	• Why is it critical for open leaders to open up fully within themselves to manifest the possibilities of open system work? • How do open leaders serve as conduits for the expression of community will, even those that may be deeply challenging? • How do leaders ask themselves "Am I really here for everyone or just those I want to work with?" • How do open leaders sustain political courage to co-create when so much closed system schema exists? • How have you as a leader struggled with opening within yourself in complex processes or community moments? • How can you help others around you understand the shift this requires?
Liberatory Leadership Finally, open leaders must consistently be primed to interrogate their own biases and assumptions, observe the intersectional ~isms in their context, and create space for others to do the same.	• Why must open leaders consistently interrogate and pressure-test their leadership to ensure all voices are being heard? • How do leaders interrupt their own natural biases and perspectives consistently? • What does it mean for you to approach each aspect of openness with a liberatory frame? • What are the biases and ~isms that are likely to hook you the most or be held within your blind spots? • How do leaders create environments where ~isms can be openly discussed by participants in the process?

Open Principle 2 Know your community

Macro Questions
- How do openers redefine their conception of community?
- How do successful openers or open system leaders spend time understanding their community or ecosystem?
- How do openers identify their open moment to target the right opportunity for co-creation?

Practices	Questions
Redefining Community Openers must embrace the dynamism and complexity of communities to build adaptive, responsive open systems.	• Why does a dynamic definition of community matter for open systems work? • Why should we resist traditional "otherization" definitions of community as immovable or abstract concepts? • How can open leaders support communities to explore this definition to shift closed systems or mental models in their context? • How can a more dynamic definition of community aid an open system opportunity? • How have you shifted your conception of community over time? • How have others you've worked with, both inside and outside the system, been trapped or held within traditional definitions of community? How has this impacted the work?
Mapping Open and Closed Ecosystems Open leaders must analyze the closed or open structures within and outside their institutions or organizations.	• Why do leaders need to be clear-eyed about the open or closed nature of the systems and/or ecosystems they are a part of? • Why would failure to diagnose the system or ecosystem frustrate open system opportunities? • How did other open structures of systems support the development of this experience? • How can open systems partner with other open partners to maximize impact? • What are the dangers of closed systems interacting with closed ecosystems? • How have you as a leader conceived of the openness of your system and partners? • What have you done to maximize your awareness of open and closed system dynamics in your context?

Practices	*Questions*
Identifying Your Open Moment Open leaders identify opportunities for cracking open the system when the leadership, governance, and community align in their aims and capacity.	• Why is it important to build alignment between leadership (superintendent), governance (school board), and community to maximize the impact of the open moment? • How can a failure to align democratic structures for open system change in the end reduce trust or capacity in the system (such as, "Lets just do what the community wants no matter what the school board thinks!")? • How can well-intended openers actually create more closed system behavior by failing to meet their open moment? • Where do you see your "open moment," the space where liberation from closed systems is most possible? • What is the critical level at which to target the opportunity for open system design: learners, schools, districts/networks, or systems? • Where do you see the open moment on a spectrum from informing to empowering?

Open Principle 3 Design breakthrough spaces

Macro Questions
- Why must we see designing breakthrough spaces as a foundational element of building open system capacity in education?
- Why are our traditional, closed systems addicted to task forces and committee structures that often degrade system trust? Share your experience.

Practices	Questions
Radical Clarity To fully break open closed systems, leaders must be exceptionally clear about the parameters of the space they are seeking to hold.	• Why is a breakthrough space needed to provoke "cracks" in closed systems? • Why is it critical that open system processes must be anchored in the hyperlocal context of that community and push back on narratives from other communities or places? • Why is it important for open leaders to remain vigilant against misinformation and disinformation in the designing of breakthrough spaces? • How can breakthrough spaces be strong enough holding environments to sustain the intense political pressures required to achieve the aims of open system redesign? • How does sharp and focused clarity about the purpose or target help create more depth, as opposed to blurry breadth in the co-creative project? • How do leaders get into trouble when they fail to achieve radical clarity at the start of their open system process? • How will you frame and name the breakthrough space to convey the impact you seek? • How can you get even clearer on the question at hand—taking your open moment to reality—to ensure an effective trajectory of a breakthrough space?
Inclusive Democracy To achieve significant breakthroughs, leaders must build responsive democratic spaces that include and represent community voices.	• Why have traditional task forces and committees become ineffective and in some cases, even degrading of trust in democratic processes? • Why have previous mental models of design failed to solve this dilemma? • How can the inclusive recruiting process create stronger spaces? • How might each group of stakeholders (essential, interested, potential) offer a different perspective that adds value to the entire process? • How will you work with your local leadership in your open moment to help them understand the need for discrete outreach and design for each stakeholder group? • How will this require confronting biases about each group inside and outside the system?

Practices	Questions
Cadence for Maximum Impact Designing a process for maximum impact means building a cadence and momentum that amplifies your open moment.	• Why does establishing a cadence for maximum impact fundamentally shift the potential of breakthrough? • Why do the traditional drip-drip methods of closed system processes often fail to produce breakthrough outcomes? • How can spaces have strong momentum or intentional cadences that offer culture building and connection for participants? • How can you align stakeholders in your open moment to understand the need for intentional cadence and trajectory? • What is the trajectory to create maximum impact for your open system breakthrough? • How will you build momentum instead of a drip-drip approach?
Breaking the Addiction to Closed Systems As you are designing for your breakthrough space, you will need to consider how you will attend to the closed system mindsets and addiction to current ways of working that are present in the system.	• Why must open leaders ask for help to shift the dynamic in traditionally closed environments? • Why must leaders often make amends for previous closed system actions or behaviors, even when they were not in a leadership role during that time? • Why do breakthrough spaces need to accept progress over perfection? • How do open leaders continually and intentionally interrupt the closed system dynamics during a co-creation process? • How can open leaders and systems help their communities accept progress over perfection? • What are the impacts of making amends and moving beyond the closed system behavior? • What are your personal closed system addictions and behaviors? • What are the issues that need to be made amends for in the systems you've worked in or currently work in? • How do you need to accept progress not perfection?

Open Principle 4 Model creative democracy

Macro Questions
- Why is it important to move beyond equity and discuss systemic liberatory shifts?
- What can emerge from processes of co-creation that transform communities and build trust?
- How does modeling creative democracy reignite civic capacity building at the local level?

Practices	Questions
Establishing Shared Reality Open leaders must create a shared understanding of reality and the problem, and this conception of the problem must be held by all the members of the team.	• Why is a shared understanding of the current state and the problem so important in open systems work? • How do leaders confront uncomfortable realities and support others to confront them as well? • How might leaders think about different kinds of data to establish a shared reality—from empathy interviews to quantitative data? • How might members of the team be involved in co-creating that vision of the current state? • How do leaders create a sharp description of the problem? • What data sources exist in your community and how might you make them accessible for everyone on your team? • How can you create intentional spaces for participants in spaces to hear each other and others?
Co-creation and Reciprocity Open leaders have the opportunity to co-create in ways that honor the diverse expertise of the team, but they must take care to establish reciprocal loops for information and products so that all members can lend their gifts to the work.	• What are co-creation and reciprocity, and what do they look like in practice? • Why are co-creation and reciprocity so critical to the process of unlocking creativity and reigniting democracy? • How can leaders create the space for co-creation and structure reciprocal flows of information that build trust? • How is co-creation an important tool for reinvigorating local democracy? • What kinds of expertise are required for your project and what kind of biases need to be addressed to unlock that expertise? • How might you set up expectations around sharing insights, information, and products to build trust?

Practices	*Questions*
Repairing Ruptures As we build a path forward, ruptures are inevitable. Our work must be to transform the space with new paradigms of healing to move communities forward.	• Why do we need to prepare for ruptures and repair work? • How can we see ruptures as powerful opportunities to grow in important ways?
Consensus-Driven Decision-Making Openers find that creative expressions of democracy, such as consensus approaches, may build stronger commitment and ownership of the path forward.	• Why do we need to seek more creative forms of democratic engagement to reignite democracy? • How does the move from fifty-plus-one decision-making to consensus processes aid in the strengthening and durability of the final recommendation? • What does it feel like to be in a process that seeks consensus from a group? What does it change about listening, working together, and building shared understanding? • How does the search for consensus transform the internal mechanics of processes, eventual recommendations, and political impact of said recommendations? • How might you introduce consensus-driven decision-making in your project? • How might you build up commitment to consensus as you introduce your project?
Cultivating Communitas Open leaders must take time and care to name the hallmarks of the community experience and celebrate both the outcome and the feeling of doing the work in a more democratic way—a feeling we call "communitas."	• Why is it critical that leaders celebrate open system work and its success to build muscle to further other opportunities? • What does emotional liberation through communitas do for a team's sense of possibility? • Have you felt communitas in any work you have done? What did you notice about the momentum it generated? • Where might there be a natural place for communitas in your project?

Open Principle 5 Assemble abundance partnerships

Macro Questions
- Why do open leaders and open systems need to embrace abundance to transform long-term capacity and public value?
- Why are abundance partnerships critical to breaking down silos between institutions (such as K–12, higher ed, or business) or organizations with potential higher-order impact (two orgs with different values or missions, etc.)?

Practices	Questions
Generating Higher-Order Impact Open moments often expand into opportunities for broader impact. These require new partners, teams, and stake-holders to create impact they each could not achieve alone.	• Why must leaders identify opportunities to expand the impact of their projects? • What does it look like to identify leaders, systems, and capacities that can be linked to create higher-order impact than any of them could do alone? • What does it look like to reset a team or coalition and prepare it for work beyond the original scope of the project? • What are the opportunities in your project for deeper or wider impact? • What additional partners might be required to achieve this broader vision? • Where have you seen this play out, and what can transform through this process?
Short-Circuiting Scarcity with Clarity As new partnerships emerge, they will face numerous scarcity issues that will sabotage the efforts unless addressed directly, early, and often.	• Why is it so easy to slip into scarcity in community or education work? • What does it look like to reframe in order to address scarcity concerns? • How does providing clarity about roles, resources, and responsibilities help address the scarcity dilemma? • What are the drivers of scarcity thinking in your community (such as money, publicity, or control)? • How might you reframe these issues to alleviate concerns?
Managing Co-contamination All stakeholders have distinct agendas that can create fear and concern from others; this must be managed to sustain the partnership.	• What is co-contamination and how can it threaten initiatives as they are expanding? • Why does co-contamination have to be managed rather than solved? • As abundance begins to manifest, new actors often co-contaminate with different values, goals and capacities—how can this be addressed and dealt with? • Consider a potential partner organization—what sources of potential co-contamination might they bring into the work?

Open Principle 6 Expand openness

Macro Question
• As open system efforts move into long-term efforts or endeavors, how should leaders or communities sustain, expand, and integrate open system efforts?

Practices	Questions
Sustaining Co-production Openers should attend to maintaining reciprocal relationships with the community throughout the process of implementation.	• What are co-production and reciprocity and how do they differ from co-creation? • Why must leaders who achieve breakthrough openness with co-creation shift to sustaining co-production with their community? • Why is sustaining community partnership in co-production critical to long-term efforts and sustaining dynamic community participation? • How can leaders sustain reciprocity with communities even if implementation requires different levels of activity from different partners? • Where do you see co-production being necessary and where might other mechanisms for reciprocity be sufficient for maintaining trust?
Identifying and Integrating Slipstreams As new opportunities for openness emerge, leaders must cultivate them and weave seemingly disparate initiatives together.	• What is a slipstream, and what does it look like to cultivate and integrate one? • In service of greater openness, why are slipstreams important for leaders to identify and amplify? • How should leaders leverage open system wins in one part of their system to expand or integrate new slipstreams for open system opportunities? • Where are emergent opportunities for openness that you may want to cultivate in your organization?
Translocal Adaptation As openness expands, leaders must be cautious to resist scale and instead consider growth and adaptation.	• How can you reject scale and replication for growth and adaptation? • Where is "machine brain" pushing you in the process and where can you embrace "garden brain"?

Practices	Questions
Lifting Up Openers and Open Narratives Open leaders have a responsibility to elevate the visibility of leaders within their own and partner organizations and to share stories of open change.	• Why is it so important for open leaders to find other openers in their broader ecosystem and lift them up as part of the long-term success of the work? • How can leaders effectively amplify the stories of openers around them? • How can leaders create opportunities for openers to share their moves over time to help others join in the work? • Who in your organization or network is already demonstrating openness and how might you partner with them to tell their story? • Why is storytelling and narrative shifting about open systems critical in the movement to build open systems? • How do we gather and tell stories that shift narratives about what is possible? • How does storytelling about open system progress accelerate movement building and set the stage for other opportunities? • What channels exist for storytelling in your context? • What stories from your own work do you want to lift up?

NOTES

INTRODUCTION

1. George S. Counts, *Dare the School Build a New Social Order?*, reprint ed. (Carbondale: Southern Illinois University Press, 1978), 54–5.
2. Ruben Bermea, "What Does 'Progress Not Perfection' Actually Look Like in AA?" Alcoholics Anonymous, March 9, 2022, https://alcoholicsanonymous.com/progress -not-perfection-aa.

CHAPTER 1

1. Katherine Schultz, *Distrust and Educational Change: Overcoming Barriers to Just and Lasting Reform* (Cambridge, MA: Harvard Education Press, 2019), 16.
2. 2022 Edelman Trust Barometer, https://www.edelman.com/trust/2022-trust -barometer.
3. "The Trust 10," 2022 Edelman Trust Barometer, https://www.edelman.com/sites /g/files/aatuss191/files/2022-01/Trust%2022_Top10.pdf.
4. "The Trust 10."
5. Saki Kumagai and Federica Iorio, *Building Trust in Government Through Civic Engagement* (Washington, DC: World Bank, 2020), 14, doi: 10.1596/33346.
6. Ernesto Dal Bó, "Regulatory Capture: A Review," *Oxford Review of Economic Policy* 22, no. 2 (2006): 203–25. http://www.jstor.org/stable/23606888.
7. Ezra Klein Show, "Transcript: Ezra Klein Interviews Jerusalem Demsas," *New York Times*, July 23, 2021, https://www.nytimes.com/2021/07/23/podcasts/transcript -ezra-klein-interviews-jerusalem-demsas.html.
8. Hélène Landemore, *Open Democracy: Reinventing Popular Rule for the Twenty- First Century* (Princeton, NJ: Princeton University Press, 2020), 11.
9. Kumagai and Iorio, *Building Trust in Government*, 15.
10. This concept is based on Stafford Beer's work on system design.
11. This aspect of our definition is from Mark Moore's work on public value creation.
12. W. Richard Scott and Gerald F. Davis, *Organizations and Organizing: Rational, Natural, and Open System Perspectives* (Hoboken, NJ: Pearson Prentice Hall, 2007), 3.
13. Scott and Davis, *Organizations and Organizing*, 87.
14. Scott and Davis, 95.
15. Margaret J. Wheatley, *Who Do We Choose to Be?: Facing Reality, Claiming Leadership, Restoring Sanity* (Oakland, CA: Berrett-Koehler, 2017).
16. Dennis Sherwood, *Seeing the Forest for the Trees: A Manager's Guide to Applying Systems Thinking* (Boston: Nicholas Brealey Publishing, 2002), 15.

17. Stafford Beer, *Designing Freedom* (Berkeley, CA: House of Anansi Press, 1993), 11.
18. Beer, *Designing Freedom*, 99.
19. Mark H. Moore, *Creating Public Value: Strategic Management in Government* (Cambridge, MA: Harvard University Press, 1995).
20. Mark Moore and Andrés Alonso, "Creating Public Value: School Superintendents as Strategic Managers of Public Schools," PEL-081 (Cambridge, MA: Public Education Leadership Project, Harvard University, March 1, 2017), https://scholar.harvard.edu/files/markmoore/files/superintendents_as_strategic_managers_of_school_systems.pdf.
21. William H. Voorberg, Victor J. J. M. Bekkers, and Lars G. Tummers, "A Systematic Review of Co-creation and Co-production: Embarking on the Social Innovation Journey," *Public Management Review* 17, no. 9 (2015): 1333–57, doi: 10.1080/14719037.2014.930505.
22. Voorberg, Bekkers, and Tummers, "Systematic Review," 1346.
23. Jal Mehta, *The Allure of Order: High Hopes, Dashed Expectations, and the Troubled Quest to Remake American Schooling* (New York: Oxford University Press, 2015), 42.
24. Mark R. Warren, "Communities and Schools: A New View of Urban Education Reform," *Harvard Educational Review* 75, no. 2 (Summer 2005): 133–34, https://eric.ed.gov/?id=EJ738665.
25. Eric Liu and Nick Hanauer, *The Gardens of Democracy: A New American Story of Citizenship, the Economy, and the Role of Government* (Seattle: Sasquatch Books, 2011), 50.
26. David Osborne, *Reinventing America's Schools: Creating a 21st Century Education System* (New York: Bloomsbury USA, 2017), 11.
27. Kara Bobroff, founder of Native American Community Academy (NACA), communication with the author, 2022.
28. Community Engagement Partners, *From Tokenism to Partnership* (Pickerington, OH: Community Engagement Partners, January 2020), https://static1.squarespace.com/static/5d9b6448c92b0a1a86ee3c65/t/5e911f88e6e60e693ce99909/1586569099466/Tokenism-to-Partnership_CEP_2020.pdf.
29. Jeff Archer, *Funders' Playbook: Tools for Thinking About Family and Community Engagement* (New York: Carnegie Corporation, 2019), 3.
30. Marc Porter Magee, *The 50CAN Guide to Building Advocacy Campaigns* (Washington, DC: 50CAN, 2017), 15.
31. Karen L. Mapp and Eyal Bergman, *Embracing a New Normal: Toward a More Liberatory Approach to Family Engagement* (New York: Carnegie Corporation, June 2021), https://www.carnegie.org/publications/embracing-new-normal-toward-more-liberatory-approach-family-engagement.
32. John Dewey, *America's Public Philosopher: Essays on Social Justice, Economics, Education, and the Future of Democracy*, ed. Eric T. Weber (New York: Columbia University Press, 2021), 33.
33. Drew Schutz, presentation at the Beyond Equity: Liberation and the Open System conference, Denver, Colorado, 2019.

CHAPTER 2

1. All interviews quoted in this chapter were conducted by Matt Klausmeier in the spring of 2022.

2. Colorado Education Initiative and Colorado Succeeds, "Homegrown Talent Initiative: Coaction Launch" (HTI presentation, Frisco, CO, July 26, 2022).

3. Brian Danoff, *Why Moralize Upon It?: Democratic Education Through American Literature and Film* (Lanham, MD: Lexington Books, 2020), 9. Danoff notes in his book that the term "moral artist" comes from Plato's dialogue *Gorgias*.

4. Danoff, *Why Moralize*, 3.

5. Danoff, 33.

6. Danoff, 33.

7. Danoff, 33.

8. Danoff, 33. As Danoff notes, the concepts of a "raft of hope" and "the democratic ideal" are taken from Ellison; specifically, the quoted phrases are from Ellison's introduction to the thirtieth anniversary edition of *Invisible Man*.

9. Danoff, 87. Danoff notes that "convulsion of the world" is a phrase from Robert Penn Warren's *All the King's Men*.

10. C. Otto Scharmer, *Theory U: Leading from the Future as It Emerges* (San Francisco: Berrett-Koehler, 2009), 24.

11. Scharmer, *Theory U*, 24.

12. Peter Senge, Hal Hamilton, and John Kania, "The Dawn of System Leadership," *Stanford Social Innovation Review* 13, no. 1 (2014): 27–33, doi: 10.48558/YTE7 -XT62.

13. Scharmer, *Theory U*, 32.

14. Parker J. Palmer, *Healing the Heart of Democracy: The Courage to Create a Politics Worthy of the Human Spirit* (San Francisco: Jossey-Bass, 2011), 10.

CHAPTER 3

1. A+ Colorado, *¡Ya Basta! Enough Already!* (Denver: A+ Colorado, October 1, 2014), https://apluscolorado.org/reports/ya-basta-enough-already.

2. Jaclyn Zubrzycki, "In Southwest Denver, Calls for Change but Clashes on Details," Chalkbeat Colorado, 2014, https://co.chalkbeat.org/2014/10/30/21092645/in -southwest-denver-calls-for-change-but-clashes-on-details.

3. Interviewed by Landon Mascareñaz for The Open System Podcast, February 2018. Adjusted slightly by interviewee and author in 2022 for inclusion in this book.

4. A+ Colorado, *Denver's Next Journey: School Improvement* (Denver: A+ Colorado, March 5, 2019), https://apluscolorado.org/reports/denvers-next-journey-school -improvement.

5. This and following interviews quoted in this chapter were conducted by Matt Klausmeier in the spring of 2022.

6. Mark R. Warren and Karen L. Mapp, *A Match on Dry Grass: Community Organizing as a Catalyst for School Reform* (New York: Oxford University Press, 2011), 20–21.

7. David Mathews, *Politics for People: Finding a Responsible Public Voice*, 2nd ed. (Urbana: University of Illinois Press, 1999), 130–31.

8. Anne T. Henderson et al., *Beyond the Bake Sale: The Essential Guide to Family-School Partnerships* (New York: The New Press, 2007), 15.

9. Henderson et al., *Beyond the Bake Sale*, 15.

10. Henderson et al., 15.

11. Henderson et al., 18.

12. Mark R. Warren, "Communities and Schools: A New View of Urban Education Reform," *Harvard Educational Review* 75, no. 2 (Summer 2005): 137, https://eric .ed.gov/?id=EJ738665.

13. "Strive Together Theory of Action," Strive Together, https://www.strivetogether .org/wp-content/uploads/2021/10/ST_TOA-Overview-102021_Final.pdf.

14. Eric Liu and Nick Hanauer, *The Gardens of Democracy: A New American Story of Citizenship, the Economy, and the Role of Government* (Seattle: Sasquatch Books, 2011), 145.

CHAPTER 4

1. All interviews quoted in this chapter were conducted by Matt Klausmeier or Landon Mascareñaz in the spring and summer of 2022.

2. Boulder Valley School District, "Report on Strategic Plan Metrics," June 30, 2022, slides 14 and 15.

3. adrienne maree brown, *Holding Change: The Way of Emergent Strategy Facilitation and Mediation* (Oakland, CA: AK Press, 2021), 106.

4. Philip Selznick, *The Moral Commonwealth: Social Theory and the Promise of Community* (Berkeley: University of California Press, 1994), 384.

5. Hélène Landemore, *Open Democracy: Reinventing Popular Rule for the Twenty-First Century* (Princeton, NJ: Princeton University Press, 2020), xvii.

6. Landemore, *Open Democracy*, 3.

7. Landemore, 90.

CHAPTER 5

1. All interviews quoted in this chapter were conducted by Matt Klausmeier in the spring of 2022.

2. Dean Williams, *Real Leadership: Helping People and Organizations Face Their Toughest Challenges* (San Francisco: Berrett-Koehler, 2005), 83.

3. Shane Safir, Jamila Dugan, and Carrie Wilson, *Street Data: A Next-Generation Model for Equity, Pedagogy, and School Transformation* (Thousand Oaks, CA: Corwin, 2021), 55.

4. Kentucky Coalition for Advancing Education, *United We Learn: Hearing Kentucky's Voices on the Future of Education* (Frankfort: Kentucky Department of Education, 2021), https://education.ky.gov/CommOfEd/Documents/United%20 We%20Learn%20Report.pdf.

5. Burlington [Vermont] School District, *Finalized Strategic Plan* (January 18, 2022), https://go.boarddocs.com/vt/bsdvt/Board.nsf/files/CASNFA5FB040/$file/For%20 School%20Board%20re_%2021_22-25_26%20Strategic%20Plan%201_18_21.pdf.

6. Tony Monfiletto, "Primer: The Reciprocity Project," https://thereciprocityproject trp.org/wp-content/uploads/2021/01/The-Reciprocity-Project-primer.pdf.

7. "7 Simple Rules of Brainstorming," IDEO U, https://www.ideou.com/blogs /inspiration/7-simple-rules-of-brainstorming.

8. Gretchen Morgan, personal communication with the authors, spring 2022.

9. "Youth-Led Systems Change: A Guidebook," Colorado Youth Congress, September 2022.

10. Stephen B. Karpman, "Fairy Tales and Script Drama Analysis," *Transactional Analysis Bulletin* 7, no. 26 (April 1968): 39–43.

11. David Emerald, *The Power of TED: The Empowerment Dynamic* (Edinburgh: Polaris Publishing, 2015).

12. Sam Battan, interviewed by Matt Klausmeier, spring 2022.

13. Battan, interview.

14. Philip Selznick, *The Moral Commonwealth: Social Theory and the Promise of Community* (Berkeley: University of California Press, 1994), 504.

15. Edith Turner, *Communitas: The Anthropology of Collective Joy*, Contemporary Anthropology of Religion (New York: Palgrave Macmillan, 2012), 1, 4.

CHAPTER 6

1. Victoria Castle, *The Trance of Scarcity: Stop Holding Your Breath and Start Living Your Life* (San Francisco: Berrett-Koehler, 2006), 25.

2. All interviews quoted in this chapter were conducted by Matt Klausmeier in the spring of 2022.

3. Amy Yee, "Chicago Offers a Blueprint for Expanding Urban Internet Access," *Bloomberg*, May 31, 2022, https://www.bloomberg.com/news/articles/2022-05-31/how-chicago-connected-64-000-students-to-high-speed-internet. Originally published as "How Chicago Connected 64,000 Students to High-Speed Internet."

4. Castle, *Trance of Scarcity*, 48.

5. Eric Liu and Nick Hanauer, *The Gardens of Democracy: A New American Story of Citizenship, the Economy, and the Role of Government* (Seattle: Sasquatch Books, 2011), 37.

6. Yee, "Chicago Offers a Blueprint."

7. Brian Williams, Seong-Cheol Kang, and Japera Johnson, "(Co)-contamination as the Dark Side of Co-production," *Public Management Review* 18, no. 5 (2016): 700, doi: 10.1080/14719037.2015.1111660.

8. Williams, Kang, and Johnson, "(Co)-contamination as the Dark Side," 710.

9. "Guiding Principles," Sin Fronteras Education Partnership, 2022.

CHAPTER 7

1. Margaret J. Wheatley and Deborah Frieze, *Walk Out Walk On: A Learning Journey into Communities Daring to Live the Future Now* (San Francisco: Berrett-Koehler, 2011).

2. All interviews quoted in this chapter were conducted by Matt Klausmeier or Landon Mascareñaz in the spring and summer of 2022.

3. Wheatley and Frieze, *Walk Out Walk On*, 35.

4. Eric Liu and Nick Hanauer, *The Gardens of Democracy: A New American Story of Citizenship, the Economy, and the Role of Government* (Seattle: Sasquatch Books, 2011).

5. "Rural Coaction," Colorado Department of Education, https://www.cde.state.co.us/caresact/esser-ruralcoaction.

CONCLUSION

1. Niall Ferguson, *The Great Degeneration: How Institutions Decay and Economies Die* (New York: Penguin Books, 2012), 150–51.

2. Max Witynski, "For Ta-Nehisi Coates, Telling the Truth About America Means Confronting Black Oppression," *UChicago News*, June 3, 2021, https://news

.uchicago.edu/story/ta-nehisi-coates-telling-truth-about-america-means-confronting
-black-oppression.

3. Michael J. Mazarr, *The Societal Foundations of National Competitiveness* (Santa Monica, CA: RAND, 2022), 27, https://www.rand.org/pubs/research_reports /RRA499-1.html.

4. Mazarr, *Societal Foundations*, vi.

5. Communication with the authors, spring 2022.

6. James E. Davis et al., "Restoring Civic Purpose in Schools," *Education Week*, March 6, 2012, https://www.edweek.org/leadership/opinion-restoring-civic -purpose-in-schools/2012/03.

7. Meira Levinson, *No Citizen Left Behind* (Cambridge, MA: Harvard University Press, 2012), 31.

8. Charles Siler, "The Right-Wing Furore over Critical Race Theory Is Manufactured, Says Charles Siler," *The Economist*, July 14, 2022, https://www.economist.com /by-invitation/2022/07/14/the-right-wing-furore-over-critical-race-theory-is -manufactured-says-charles-siler. Siler, a former conservative think tank leader, argues that CRT is mostly a manufactured attack on public systems.

9. "The HxA Way," Heterodox Academy, https://heterodoxacademy.org/library/the -hxa-way.

10. Mark R. Warren, "Communities and Schools: A New View of Urban Education Reform," *Harvard Educational Review* 75, no. 2 (Summer 2005): 167–68, https:// eric.ed.gov/?id=EJ738665.

11. Michael T. Hartney and Sam D. Hayes, "Off-Cycle and Out of Sync: How Election Timing Influences Political Representation," *State Politics & Policy Quarterly* 21, no. 4 (December 2021): 13, 16, doi: 10.1017/spq.2020.6.

12. Office of Community Oriented Policing Services (COPS), *Community Policing Defined* (Washington, DC: US Department of Justice, 2014), https://cops.usdoj.gov /RIC/Publications/cops-p157-pub.pdf.

13. Thomas S. Dee and Jaymes Pyne, "A Community Response Approach to Mental Health and Substance Abuse Crises Reduced Crime," *Science Advances* 8, no. 23 (June 8, 2022), doi: 10.1126/sciadv.abm2106.

14. Dee and Pyne, "Community Response Approach."

15. Jim Whitehurst, *The Open Organization: Igniting Passion and Performance* (Boston, MA: Harvard Business Review Press, 2015), 9–10.

16. Amy Finkelstein, Annetta Zhou, Sarah Taubman, and Joseph Doyle, "Health Care Hotspotting—a Randomized, Controlled Trial," *New England Journal of Medicine* 382, no. 2 (January 9, 2020): 152–62, doi: 10.1056/NEJMsa1906848.

17. Jacqueline LaPointe, "Value-Based Contracting 101: Preparing, Negotiating, and Succeeding," RevCycleIntelligence, June 1, 2021, https://revcycleintelligence.com /features/value-based-contracting-101-preparing-negotiating-and-succeeding.

ACKNOWLEDGMENTS

We first would like to thank the Center for Innovation in Education and the Colorado Education Initiative, our partner districts, and all the communities who were wonderfully supportive and involved in the writing and design of this book. Thank you to Harvard Education Press for all of your support throughout this process and your commitment to bringing this book into the world.

We also would like to thank each of the openers-in-residence, our first group of dedicated individuals who committed to reviewing early chapters and ideas, giving us feedback and ensuring co-creation in the process. Thanks to Lauren Bryant, Sam Battan, Reilly Pharo Carter, Cliff Chuang, Shani Jackson-Dowell, Kate Garvin, Nick Gesauldi, Natalie Neris, Claudia Quintero, and Kerry Whitacre Swarr.

We also want to extend deep gratitude to the attendees of the first open systems convening in 2019 for helping us get started on this co-creative journey, and for all those who attended in 2020 to keep the work moving forward.

We are also beyond grateful to our families and friends who supported us throughout, who are truly too many to name, even as we felt their care and love throughout this process. As descendants of Mexican and Vietnamese people who struggled against colonialism, we want to take special care to thank the indigenous leaders on whose land all our work exists and acknowledge their struggle with closed systems since colonization. We want to especially thank Kara Bobroff for her mentorship and her sacred work to open up the education space to possibilities that will unfold for generations.

Finally, we want to acknowledge the readers of this book—the leaders who are just beginning to consider opening your hearts and systems. It is for you this book is truly meant—you are consequential beyond measure. It is you we are here to serve; it is you who are deserving of grace and support; and it is upon you the future of our democracy rests.

ABOUT THE AUTHORS

Dr. Landon Mascareñaz

Landon is an educator, writer, and democracy builder. As cofounder of the Open Systems Institute, he co-creates with leaders around the country to encourage an emerging discipline for openers everywhere. He partners with the Colorado Education Initiative (CEI) where he is responsible for community-driven economic development through breakthrough partnerships in the Homegrown Talent Initiative, working in sixty rural districts across eight regions of the state. At CEI he helped assemble the Sin Fronteras Education Partnership, a coalition of local, regional, and national organizations co-creating family partnership strategies for New Mexico communities, and he supported the launch of Colorado's Statewide Family Engagement Center.

In 2019, he was appointed by Colorado Governor Jared Polis to the state board for community colleges and occupational education, and now serves as the chair. He also serves as chair of the Reisher Scholarship Fund, supporting students across the state to achieve their higher education goals. During the first six months of the COVID crisis, Landon worked with community organizations to deploy the Denver Metro Emergency Food Network, which delivered over 320 thousand free meals to families and elderly people in need.

He has previously led partnerships at A+ Colorado, served as a leader in the family engagement department in Denver Public Schools, co-designed the launch of the NACA Inspired Schools Network (a network of indigenous serving schools), led Teach For America–New Mexico, and taught first grade on the Navajo Nation. In 2015 he completed his doctorate at the Harvard Graduate School of Education with a focus on boundary-spanning leadership.

Landon was born in California, raised in Colorado, attended college in Oregon, and began his professional career in New Mexico—leading him to consider the western United States his home. He lives in Denver, Colorado, with his wife and enjoys traveling, learning about ancient history, and developing his meditation practice.

Dr. Doannie Tran

Doannie is the partner for liberatory co-creation at the Center for Innovation in Education (CIE), continuing his commitment to building the future of education with communities. He taught middle school and high school science in both Oakland, California, and Boston, Massachusetts, before leaving teaching to help launch the Massachusetts region of Teach For America in 2009. While doing his doctoral work at the Harvard Graduate School of Education, he was sponsored as an entrepreneur-in-residence at NewSchools Venture Fund, launching an education technology company called the Teaching Genome.

Doannie left his startup to join the Boston Public Schools leadership team as assistant superintendent for academics and professional learning. He led the interdepartmental team that worked with the Boston Teachers' Union to develop the Essentials for Instructional Equity, the district's vision for instruction that would close opportunity gaps, which was recently recognized by the Massachusetts Department of Elementary and Secondary Education as a "bright spot" in the district. In addition to implementing new curriculum and instructional practices, he served on the district's collective bargaining team, working with the union to innovate on their approach to teacher leadership.

Before joining the team at CIE, Doannie served as the assistant superintendent for innovative programs for Fulton County, Georgia. He led the community-driven co-design of two innovative high school models, oversaw innovative school governance systems, and supported the development of the district's professional learning strategy based on the implementation of PLCs at every level from the leadership to classroom teachers.

Since joining CIE, Doannie has helped launch community co-creation projects nationwide, bringing family and community members into deeper collaboration with systems. Doannie supported Kentucky's successful application for a $3 million competitive grant for state assessment from the US Department of Education. Kentucky based its application on co-creating the next generation of assessment and accountability systems with communities, and will pursue the work through 2026. Doannie is also a cofounder of the Georgia Deeper Learning Network, bringing together districts, statewide organizations, and businesses to expand access to deeper learning experiences across the state.

His wife, Holly, is an adolescent medicine physician, and they live in Atlanta, Georgia, with their two children, Elliot and Louise.

INDEX